# The Developing Organization

# O*P*S

## *Organizations, People, Society*

A series edited by
Professor A. B. Cherns

*Already published*

# The Developing Organization

*ernardus*

B. C. J. LIEVEGOED

*Translated by*
J. COLLIS

**CELESTIAL ARTS**
Millbrae, California

Copyright © 1973 by Bernardus Cornelis Johannes Lievegoed

Celestial Arts
231 Adrian Road
Millbrae, California 94030

First Printing, August, 1980

Made in the United States of America

This translation first published by Tavistock Publications Limited, London, in association with Van Gorcum & Comp., B.V.

Originally published in Dutch under the title *Organisaties in ontwikkeling* by Lemniscaat Publishers, Rotterdam, 1969

**Library of Congress Cataloging in Publication Data**

Lievegoed, Bernardus Cornelis Johannes.
     The developing organization.

     Translation of Organisaties in ontwikkeling.
     Includes bibliographies and index.
     1. Industrial organization.     2. Organizational change.     I. Title.
HD37.D8L5313  1980      658.4      80-66227
ISBN 0-89087-271-6 (pbk.)


1   2   3   4   5   6   7 — 86   85   84   83   82   81   80

# Contents

# Foreword

This book has grown out of many hundreds of lectures, and work on it has been stimulated by innumerable questions and conversations over the last twenty years. During these years I have encountered entrepreneurs and civil servants, directors of schools and hospitals, as well as their colleagues at all levels, from department heads and teachers to foremen and workers. There have also been encounters and meetings with students in the economic and technical fields, and with my own colleagues at the Nederlands Pedagogisch Instituut (NPI).

It is for all these people that the book has been written, and I would suggest that those engaged in practical work might do well to begin at Part II and leave Part I until later. Students and former participants of our seminars will recognize familiar material but will also notice that the total concept is still evolving. This book can therefore be no more than the cross-section of a continuing development process.

I owe a debt of gratitude to my colleagues at NPI. We have proceeded in a spirit of true teamwork, supporting one another in the management consultant's difficult task and working together year by year on the concepts. On many points my colleagues have gained more experience, and more specialized knowledge and skill than I have. This book should therefore really be followed by a number of monographs dealing with the various special fields.

The appendix on 'The Use of Quantitative Models' is by Dr A. F. G. Hanken, who has lectured on this subject in America; and the chapter on 'Organizational Development' in Part IV is by C. J. Zwart, M. A. Both are on the senior scientific staff of the Twente Technological University, and my thanks are due to them.

Miss Stolte, also of the Twente Technological University, sacrificed a great deal of her time for the initial typing and has my unqualified admiration for her patience in deciphering my handwriting.

For the rest, may the book speak for itself.

# Introduction and Summary

## CHAPTER ONE

# Management and the Future

The task of management comprises two kinds of activity: stabilizing activities and dynamizing activities.

The first includes all the activities that maintain the existing structure and keep the current activities going. These activities are described in the numerous aspects of business and management science. They are concerned with the management of a group of people whose work is circumscribed by a strictly coordinated network of delegation and control. They include the cultivation of the market, the defence of one's share of the market, the maintenance of quality in production, the maintenance of production equipment, and the preservation of a standard of knowledge in the company. These activities are laid down in sets of procedures and rules which often become as voluminous as a regional telephone directory.

The second kind of activity is dynamic and includes the quest for and selection of new products, new services, new policies, new forms of organization, new strategies. In short, this kind of activity involves the planning of a new future.

The day-to-day maintenance of the existing organization should make only relatively small demands on the time and energy of top management. The level below top management should be responsible for this. However, if top management lacks courage and imagination, if it does not recognize its true task, or if its horizon is too narrow and its foresight too restricted, then it will tend to spend excessive time and energy on all sorts of organizing and controlling activities which are directed towards the current organization.

Thus one of the most important qualities of the top manager is to be concerned with the future.

This involvement with the future should not be onesided or limited. It includes ideas about social, cultural, political, technical, economic, and financial developments, to name only a few. In top management, one-sidedness, and the accompanying bias that influences decision-making, has fatal consequences for the company concerned. Of course this applies to other social structures and organizations as well. But we are concerned here with management and its particular field of operation.

How can those who manage a company in the economic sphere approach the future? They can do so on a basis of rational thinking, emotional considerations, or fundamental choice.

1. Through *rational thinking* the manager can as consciously and accurately as possible conceive a picture of what the situation will be in so many years' time. In order to do this, he will seek to calculate within a deterministic or a stochastic model how certain past trends will create a particular situation in the future.

Within a *deterministic* model all the factors (variables) that the manager considers relevant are accurately known. If the factors that lie outside the model remain constant, then the future can be determined accurately. Within a *stochastic* (probability) model the relevant factors are not accurately known, but with the use of statistics a certain degree of probability with regard to the occurrence of situations can be established.

These two methods, which are part of operational research, would be ideal for discovering the future if there were not a number of necessary conditions on which their proper functioning depends. The model itself is made by people. They decide which factors are relevant (an arbitrary matter!), they apply their own yardstick to the quantification of factors, and what is more, they presume that external factors existing outside the model will not influence it during the period for which the forecast is being made. These external factors can belong to the political, the social, or the technical sphere. Thus the longer the period of time it covers, the more uncertain and even absurd a forecast becomes.

All forecasts about the growth of the population of a country or even of the world are subject to the above-mentioned defects. It is not difficult to calculate the arrival of the point in time when the space available per person on the face of the earth will be one square metre. But this type of logic lacks a sound sense of reality. The future will not follow an exponential curve of the well-known type shown in diagram *a*. At a certain moment a growing counterforce outside the model appears, which reduces the steepness of the increase when it reaches a certain limit (see diagram *b*).

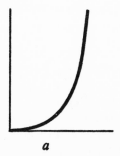

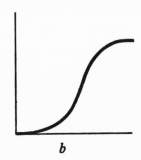

Often the counterforce comes from a sphere which lies quite outside the model. For instance, when work is increasingly circumscribed by efficiency measures, productivity starts to rise. But as a result of a decrease in work motivation this increase gradually begins to slow down and even disappears entirely.

The best results in operational research have been achieved in limited situations and when the questions were simple. In such cases this approach can really be a help to the manager.

Preparing for the future in an entirely different way, the manager studies his situation within a *developmental* model. The questions he asks are concerned not with the prediction of future *quantities* but rather with the forecast of future *structures*. The *structural* change of the model, coming about while quantitative changes take place, is now the object of his research.

At this point we should look in more detail at the developmental model, since it is important not only for the manager but also for the reader to acquire a view of the future. In this context we shall take growth to mean the increase of certain variables (number, length, breadth, weight, etc.) within a framework which remains the same. A crystal can grow; but while its size increases, its crystalline structure remains the same. On the other hand, where organic phenomena are concerned, growth turns into development.

The term development describes the following phenomenon: growth continues within a certain structure (model) until a limit is reached; beyond this limit the existing structure or model can no longer impose order on the larger mass; the consequence is either disintegration or a step up to a higher level of order. This phenomenon can be observed even in the single living cell, which does not grow indefinitely but at a certain moment divides into two new cells, which in turn grow only to their given limits, and so on. The same can be observed in the higher organisms, which pass from one phase of development to the next, both in individual development and in the evolution from species to species.

In plants this development takes place according to a pattern laid down by heredity, which has been termed 'blueprinted growth'.

Similarly in the development of the human being, from babyhood through childhood and adolescence to adulthood, we can observe successive phases when growth within a certain structure is followed by a period of crisis when a step is taken towards the formation of a new structure. This restructuring takes place biologically as well as psychologically. But in the case of psychological restructuring the development is open and not blueprinted.

If we define the developmental model in a highly abstract way, we can discern the following laws:

- development is principally discontinuous
- development occurs in time in a series of stages
- within each stage a system appears which has a structure characteristic of that stage
- within this system variables and subsystems appear, of which one is dominant
- in a following stage the structure differs from the previous one in that it has a higher degree of complexity and differentiation
- the new stage has a new dominant subsystem; this does not lead to a process of addition but to a shifting of all the relationships within the system
- development is not reversible (youth does not return).

Development can be diagrammatically depicted as a flight of steps:

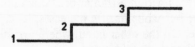

or it can equally well be depicted as a process of spreading, whereby the emphasis shifts from old to new centres:

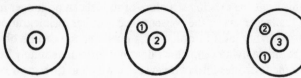

Looking at the picture of development as a flight of steps, we observe that the changeover from one step to the next can be a total metamorphosis in that the earlier step is completely digested by the following one. We also see that the metamorphosis need not be total, in which case some remnants of the earlier step would remain in a recognizable form in the following step. This latter point is important, since social development nearly always takes place in a process of incomplete metamorphosis. In other words, in higher and more complex social structures we always find historical anachronisms, remnants of earlier structures. It is these remnants that lead to social tensions.

The term 'social engineering' denotes the construction of logical, causal, deterministic forms of organization; it also denotes a way of thinking in closed social models; and finally it denotes the introduction of such models into reality.

In contrast, to think and act in developmental models means to set in motion organizational changes in the direction of the next stage of development, of which only the general outline is known. The final concrete form and content of this next stage can thus arise out of the actual potentialities of the people involved; in a flexible process they can adapt, within the overall model, to changing circumstances. Organizational change is unique and momentary, constantly new for the people involved facing the actual situation. Thus development in an open situation takes place, and rapid reaction to external and internal changes becomes possible.

We shall return later to the phenomena of social development, but at this point we should look again at the manager and his efforts to find a way of relating to the future. So far we have dealt with the possibilities involving rational thinking and investigation.

2. Another way of approach involves *emotional judgements*. In this connection we find action programmes based on unsatisfactory situations, or institutionalized programmes based on what is desirable, like political programmes or policy systems. Here the preference for a particular alternative is clearly seen, and in politics is formulated as such.

Emotional preferences are more difficult to discover in many implied suppositions and above all in so-called 'matters of course'. A closer examination of, for instance, the 'relevant' variables for an econometric model will reveal a number of things which are a 'matter of course' only in the eyes of an individual person or according to a current school of thought. The question why a certain variable or factor is relevant and another is not, or why a certain problem is relevant and another is not, cannot be answered with the help of purely rational thought processes. Experience and intuition have to play a part as well. Sometimes there is the simple fact that some factors are quantifiable and some are not.

We therefore accept a choice if it is defined as accurately as possible, but we retain the right to place another beside it. We should not take the liberty of passing sentence on somebody else's choice on the grounds that it is unscientific or based on emotional considerations. Our own 'strictly scientific' choice is also emotional in that it is based on preference, or scientific curiosity, or a personal interest.

3. Lying even deeper in the human personality structure than the springs of emotional preference are the roots of *fundamental choice*, which reveals a definite direction of the will.

Fundamental choices, permeated with wilful purpose, can be of two categories, utopian or ideological. A utopia provides a model for a future in which one believes; an ideology provides a model of a past situation which is to be preserved. The great utopias reigning in our time are Marxism, liberalism, and the Christian, Islamic, Hindu, and Buddhist doctrines of salvation. And among the reigning ideologies (as defined here) we have national ideologies, class ideologies, and even management ideologies.

In general, utopias are revolutionary and ideologies reactionary. But the matter is more complicated than this. Once a utopia is formalized and life begins to take shape accordingly, even involving a development of the utopia itself, then an ideology begins to form within the utopia. This is the explanation of the Marxist-Leninist ideology which has appeared within the Marxist utopia. Conversely, an ideology can assume utopian characteristics when a model of a past situation is set up as an ideal for the future. The French nationalism of Louis XIV, an ideology for many French people, was transformed by de Gaulle into a utopia of *gloire*.

As a man among his fellow-men, the manager has to wrestle with all these problems in establishing his relationship with the future. He proceeds from a certain utopian image of civilization of which he is often only half-aware or which he regards as obvious, an image coloured by anything from the gratification of 'economic man' to the desire to build a better society. He is entangled in many ideologies which he has unwittingly assimilated or which have been imposed on him in his capacity as an employer. He gives priority to certain policies, and his picture of the future is coloured by his political preferences. As a rational thinker he assimilates and judges information as objectively as possible.

However, not only his judgement but also his point of departure for working on the supposedly relevant information and questions is personal and subjective. With deterministic and stochastic planning he builds growth models and arrives at explosive developments or stagnating growth. With this method his thinking has to remain within the existing structures.

He becomes more realistic if he begins to think within a strategic model. In a strategic model a larger and more comprehensive system contains two active subsystems each of which possesses either no information or incomplete information about the criteria governing the other's choice (see diagram). We see here a basic model of all social

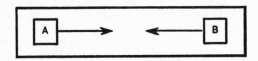

behaviour. We could even describe a happy marriage as a strategic model because, however well the partners are adjusted to one another, they can never completely know each other. They are, fortunately, surprised again and again.

The example of marriage as a strategic model shows, furthermore, that a strategic model can be based either on joint consultation and collaboration or on conflict and strife. Indeed, all strategic models consist of a continuum:

| joint consultation | negotiation | conflict |
|---|---|---|
| collaboration | finding compromises | strife |

Every social situation lies somewhere between collaboration and strife.

Chess is the classic example of a strategic game: in the strategy of conflict the objective of player A precludes the objective of player B.

The 'commercial game' of the manager is also seen as a strategy of conflict. Managers are trained with the help of strategic management games: several groups play at participation in the same market and the winners are those who conquer the largest portion of that market. There is also, however, a 'strategy of collaboration', usually described as joint consultation, cooperation, association, collaboration, and so on. Enterprises which have been fighting each other for years over the same market suddenly grow wise and amalgamate. Together they are stronger in the battle for a larger market.

When this kind of situation is described without any emotional overtones, it becomes clear that people who, prior to the amalgamation, have been used to a strategy of strife now suddenly have to practise a strategy of collaboration. It is not surprising that this presents certain difficulties. There is a very relevant question we should ask ourselves: Would it not be more desirable and more efficient if, in many other relationships in the social field, management were to aim for joint consultation rather than conflict? This would apply to management–government, employer–employee, and producer–consumer relations. A wide field of activity would open up for the manager's social skills, skills which are among the most important he has.

The sphere of negotiation which leads to compromise lies between the two extremes of collaboration and strife. With regard to the future, the manager in a strategic situation always has to compromise between the need for joint consultation and collaboration and the need for strife in which he must either win or lose. Which path he chooses will depend on the extent of his horizon and on the amount of time he dares to allow for the solution of his problems. Most people will come to the conclusion that, in the long run, collaboration is more fruitful, and more economical, than strife.

Within the enterprise itself, too, a high degree of collaboration between the economic, technical, and social subsystems can occur only if the social subsystem is able to evolve with real humanity. Our industrial society will have to become human somewhere. (We shall return to this point later.) One way of approaching this attitude in labour relations would be to search for means whereby the present practice of bilateral negotiation could become more like joint consultation and collaboration.

But the manager will find it particularly difficult in just this social field to arrive at the proper policy decisions unless he learns to take his point of departure from a real developmental model. He will have to acquire two sorts of knowledge:

(a) insight into the development of the human being during the course of life, so that he can include this development in all his plans;

(b) understanding of the development of social structures, and in particular of commercial organizations and of society in general.

The remainder of this introduction focuses on this last point.

As an enterprise develops, its structure changes from an undifferentiated general beginning to successive stages of ever-increasing differentiation and complexity. At each successive stage of development a different subsystem is dominant.

First comes the so-called pioneer phase or pioneer structure. The dominant subsystem ruling all the other factors is the pioneering entrepreneur himself. *He* takes the initiative within the economic subsystem of society. *He* finds the creative pioneering answer to a consumer need which he recognizes in society.

His organization is kept as simple as possible; it is adapted to his personality structure and geared to the consumer need he wants to satisfy. He selects people who appeal to him personally and with whom he can accomplish the work in hand, usually in an improvising style. He thus creates a supple, manoeuvrable, and particularly efficient organization which can operate successfully so long as the dominant factor, the pioneer himself, can bring about the necessary integration.

This phase reaches its limit when the organization has grown so much that the pioneer no longer knows everyone personally, when the technical equipment needed has become so complicated that specialists are required, and when the market has grown so large that the pioneer finds himself working not for known customers but for an anonymous public. At this point the pioneer organization either becomes 'over-ripe' and begins to disintegrate (decrease of profits, increase of customer complaints), or it has to be restructured so that it can start on the next phase of its development.

In this second phase the pioneer with his economic achievement is no longer the dominant factor. The requirements of the technical subsystem in the enterprise become pre-eminent. With the help of scientific management techniques, the structure based on personal relationships is transformed into a structure which provides a logical division of functions involving a hierarchy of delegation and control and providing the prescribed operations required by the technical processes. Gone are the 'good old days' when the 'guvnor' used to 'drop in' whenever he was passing. The man has been replaced by the system, with its forms to be filled in in triplicate and so on.

In this phase the enterprise can again make a leap forward. In addition to the economic subsystem (the enterprise as an active unit in the economic field), the organization and working methods of the technical subsystem are developed, leading to an increase of productivity.

The logical technical framework of an organization in this phase gives the impression that it can be contained in a deterministic or stochastic model in which the human being is reduced to a predictable factor which reacts to economic stimuli.

The limit of this second phase is reached when the neglect of the social subsystem in the enterprise begins to make itself felt. The progress achieved through technical improvements is slowed down by a decrease in the motivation of the people involved. Ten years ago this applied only at shop-floor level (soul-destroying industrial labour), but recently it has begun to show increasingly at middle- and higher-management levels as well.

Feelings of powerlessness against the 'system', of increasing loneliness and alienation, are creeping up the hierarchy. People are beginning to expend a minimum of effort on their work, reserving their creative powers for activities outside working hours. Recent investigations in a large administrative organization revealed that even at department-head level 96 per cent of the daily work required only routine decisions.

So organizations run according to the dictates of scientific management have reached a new limit beyond which they cannot develop unless they step up into a new structure with a new dominant factor.

This third phase can be established successfully only if the social subsystem is integrated with the economic and technical subsystems. This cannot be achieved simply by maintaining the existing structure and adding 'human relations'. What is required is 'rethinking the whole organization'.

The dominant factor is now the community of people working together as the only creative source of innovation and enthusiasm for the achievement of a common goal. The organization must make it possible for every person to work individually and intelligently towards this common goal. This starts with a new style of management which is based not on directives and controls from above but on:

- setting objectives
- creating a margin of discretion within which the best possible way of achieving these objectives can be found
- providing the possibility of self-control.

The last point means that people must be able to judge for themselves whether they have achieved their objectives.

This first step towards the third phase leads to a widening of the range of tasks and to management by exception. Many further steps will have to follow. The whole composition of the organization will have to be revised.

The overall objectives, being the satisfaction of external needs (the typical marketing function), have to be the starting-point (1 in the diagram below). When the objectives have been determined, a study will have to be made of the sequence of activities, the so-called processes, regardless of the present organization, which are necessary to achieve these objectives (2). As a third step, all the resources (3) are organized separately and placed at the service of the processes. Finally, an information centre ensures that all relevant information for planning and control is available wherever needed throughout the company (4). Top management (the board) is brought down from its position of splendid isolation at the top of a pyramid and placed in the midst of all the streams of information, in the centre (5).

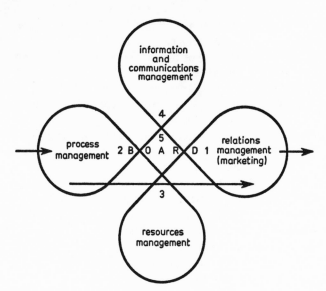

This new 'clover-leaf organization' makes for a maximum of flexibility. It is not to be understood as a new organization chart but as a model of the functions of an organization. The four main functions of an organization, and the fifth leadership function, thus become apparent in their interdependency. The actual structural models that follow from this will depend in practice on the nature of the organization concerned (industrial organizations, service organizations, or professional organizations).

In the following chapters this kind of organization will be discussed fully. At this point it is only necessary to say that old forms will have to be transformed and existing functions realigned if the proper form of organization is to be found for the third phase. Today, industry is facing this internal process of restructuring, which is aimed at creating a flexible, active, participative management, able to lead the operative levels which function independently within certain set limits.

To avoid misunderstandings it should be stressed once again that the primary task of an enterprise as an institution in the economic sphere of society is economic achievement (just as a political party seeks political achievement and a scientific institute seeks scientific achievement). This does not mean that profit-making is the only aim and the rest a pleasing pastime. For an enterprise to produce the best possible results, it is essential that all its subsystems should be able to make the best possible contributions in an integrated fashion. This means that the economic, technical, and social subsystems must all be fully developed, while none of the three is superior or inferior to the others in contributing to the whole.

The need to proceed to this next phase is brought about not only by internal developments but also by external changes. We conclude this section with a closer look at these.

With the advance of Western society into the industrial era, the entrepreneur joined the ranks of those who determine the complexion of a culture. When the transition took place from the old craft establishments to early industrial production, all enterprises were by definition pioneer enterprises or were run in the style of pioneer enterprises. The entrepreneur bore the whole risk, used his own capital and created work possibilities where there would otherwise have been unemployment. Labour was a commodity to be traded on the labour market according to supply and demand. On the commodity market, labour was the last item before the fluctuation of demand.

All problems must be regarded within the context of their own time. The situation that arose in the early days of industrialization led to a need for another power to balance that of the entrepreneur. The exclusively commercial attitude of the pioneering era was only a first step in industrial development. The first aims of the rising labour movement were to achieve material security in the case of illness, old age, and invalidism; adequate housing and reasonable working hours; improved accident prevention and hygiene. If prices were to be kept low, shorter working hours and higher wages could be granted only if productivity could be increased. Frederick Taylor recognized this as early as the eighties of the last century and he developed organizational techniques which made it possible. During the first decades of the present century, the activities of the labour movement, the elaboration of new efficiency techniques, and progress in the technical sphere coincided; it was one of those strange and in this case fortunate historical coincidences which brought success to a social movement.

By about 1930 the foundations for comprehensive social welfare had been laid and accepted. At the same time the transition was taking place from pioneer organizations to the second phase of restructuring according to technical and organizational points of view.

The economic crisis of the thirties and then the Second World War interrupted this process. When it was all over, 'productivity teams' began to go to America and they returned with all the latest notions of scientific management on the basis of which European enterprises and firms were to develop further. Then growing affluence and the accompanying shift from physical to psychological needs, already recognized by the human relations movement, began to become apparent. But managements on the whole were not prepared to take account of these aspects in their policy decisions, and remained sceptical of any picture of the human being that differed from the concept of 'economic' man.

It was not until the working population began to 'come of age' as a result of better education and through the widening of horizons brought about by the mass media that the social subsystems in commercial enterprises began to make their own contributions and to voice their own demands, which could no longer be appeased by good intentions or organized measures such as works councils or shop committees.

Just as the economic and technical subsystems made their adamant demands, though it took us a generation to integrate them both in a theory of business and management, so now the necessity of integrating the social subsystem with the other two is making us ask ourselves what the inner laws of this subsystem look like and how its integration can be brought about.

A new image of man at work will have to emerge. This image will have to encompass man as a being who develops and has purposeful aims; who is able to develop only if he can be creative in his work and can also have responsibility either alone or shared with others; who can then devote himself with others to the achievement of a common goal, thus forming a community based on real humanity, not in a sentimental sense, but in the sense that it is fully accepted that everyone is an independent and aspiring human being.

The organizational requirements for this conception have been briefly outlined above. Humane interrelations should come about and be practised in actual work situations. Meanwhile, in the present phase of development they must be engendered by those who bear the responsibility for the new organizations. It seems, therefore, to be the historical task of management to inaugurate this development. Higher wages can be extorted in a power struggle. But a genuine feeling for one's fellow-men has to be a gift offered again and again until those to whom it is offered feel they can trust the intention behind it.

Furthermore, as affluence increases, the highly industrialized society in which we now live will be replaced by a post-industrial society characterized by 'a *per capita* annual income of 7,500 dollars, four seven-hour working days a week, and enormous sums spent on education and culture'. It is said that the United States, Canada, Japan, and Sweden will have reached this stage in about thirty years' time. Western Europe, the Soviet Union and its satellites, and Australia and New Zealand will then still have their highly industrialized societies with *per capita* incomes of 1,500 to 4,000 dollars. And the rest of the world will still be in the pre-industrial and partially industrialized stages, with incomes of 50 to 600 dollars (which means starvation).

Those who accept such prognoses (which are based on the projection of trends into the future) forget that once industry has brought about a general state of affluence it will lose its significance as a leading system. Just as was the case with agriculture it will become a 'dissatisfier'. That means that it will be blamed if it does not function faultlessly, but conversely will receive no thanks if it works as it should.

New spheres of human life will have become dominant — the intellectual–cultural and political spheres. This is already becoming apparent in the aversion of the younger generation towards preparing themselves for a job in industry, and also in their preference for political engagement and their interest in the structure of our social and cultural life. It could very well happen that the countries which are first to reach the threshold of the post-industrial era will be threatened not by the 75 per cent of the world's population who are starving (underfed people are not revolutionary) but by an internal rebellion against social institutions which are based solely on economic and technological values. The worldwide student movements may still be harmless and they may often peter out (although, as happened in France, they can disrupt a whole country); but they are indicators, seismographs, of an approaching revaluation of our social order.

Recently, students in Delft raised their voices with the slogan: 'Science is the opium of the people!' The student movements have not only turned against the organization of educational institutions with their economic and technocratic bias; they have turned against the very content of science itself. They are opposed to the axioms of an objective, exclusively quantitative, scientific model; they want to redeem man from his position as onlooker and include him as a subject in that model. In the social sphere young people are searching for a genuine commitment to their fellow human beings, and in the scientific sphere they are seeking for the humanization of the scientific model.

We are witnessing the 'writing on the wall'. The manager who is trying to look into the future cannot fail to notice that he is living in a time of turbulent change. He has grown accustomed to including only a few isolated, well-known factors in his policy-making. He will have to learn to integrate new, hitherto external, factors in these policies. There is not much time to lose.

# PART I

# The Importance of Systems Theory for Management

## CHAPTER TWO

# Thinking in Systems and Models as a basis for Modern Management

Everything connected with the management of social entities such as commercial enterprises is at the moment undergoing change and development. J. L. Mey[1] says quite rightly:

> Not only the behavioural sciences such as sociology and psychology, but also economics and even mathematics are becoming more and more occupied with the problems arising out of the organization of human activity tuned to the achievement of set goals.

What is the reason for this interest? For thousands of years the hierarchical 'pyramid' model of leadership was quite satisfactory. Leadership and responsibility for the aims and methods of work were held at the top; by command and by exact delegation of authority these aims and methods were passed down to increasingly wider and lower levels. Direction and control were the task of a higher level on behalf of a lower.

The ancient civilizations and the military organizations that protected them were ruled along these lines. Changes took place so slowly that they became apparent only after generations. Experience and practice guaranteed reliability and were held in high esteem. The older man was the wiser, to be consulted by the young when difficulties arose. Memory was more important than individual creative thinking. Good and evil were clearly defined. Good had to be observed and evil opposed. 'Thou shalt' was the backbone of social continuity. The old ethical values (Neumann[2]) were embedded in the security of society. The reformer was the criminal, the evildoer following his inner voice. Not until he found sufficient followers did his reforms become part of civilization to be included in a new 'thou shalt'.

The sciences of management and military organization are indeed remarkably ancient and have certainly proved their usefulness. Why do we now need something different? Under the influence of the search for value-free explanations in the natural sciences, we have become accustomed to seeking the cause of historical developments in the externally visible conditions of human life.

Of course conditions do influence people; but on the other hand new questions, new interests, and new aims in turn influence social conditions. Really important changes vaguely termed 'signs of the times' come about as a result of a changed and often quite new attitude among people towards the world about them. As a result of this shift of values, human activity is then directed towards different spheres of reality.

The rise of the natural sciences and the resulting development of technology were the cause of one such shift of values. At a time when one's own observations and one's own judgements began to be valued more highly than the authority of traditional thought, the way also became clear for efforts to be directed towards innovation rather than preservation. After a preparatory period in the fifteenth and sixteenth centuries, this urge to determine consciously one's relationship with reality became increasingly strong. All things hitherto taken for granted were now questioned. Research was the force that unhinged the ancient universe. Step by step this intellectual revolution proceeds, in science, in social structures, in world views, and in religion.

In antiquity, cultural life was made manifest by a small group of religious and secular leaders at the peak of the social pyramid (e.g. the pharaoh and his high priests). Then in a later phase we see how members of the next highest level, the military leaders and rulers and the hereditary nobility, began to participate in cultural life. Still later a third class, the free citizens, accepted their share of responsibility. But still there was a social class which did not participate. It was not until the end of the eighteenth century that a fourth class of society began to demand its due. But at the same time a new non-participatory class was developing: the industrial proletariat, which in our century and only in the last few decades has been included in our civilization. This is coming about through the democratization of education, including university education. Furthermore, the revolutionary demand is being voiced for participation in all institutions of society.

It is already a platitude to say that in the twentieth century we are living in an age of rapid changes. In the social sphere the nature of the changes taking place is threefold.

First, there is an *increase in the scale* of all social entities. Villages grow into towns, towns grow into larger towns; small firms grow into medium firms, medium firms grow into large firms, and so on. Since the last third of the nineteenth century all energies have consistently been pointing in the direction of accumulation of value, with the result that a take-off point has been reached, like the take-off point of an aircraft leaving the ground. However, every increase in quantity must reach a limit beyond which structural changes become necessary if the growing organization is to remain alive. An increase of scale in the social sphere means for the individual an increase in loneliness and alienation. Therefore special measures become necessary to cope with this alienation.

The second trend is the *growing complexity* of all social structures. This occurs because growing social entities of necessity become more differentiated. The direct communication understood by everybody has to be replaced by ever more complicated rules and regulations. Growing unease seeks relief in the quest for a scapegoat. 'They' have had another bright idea, 'they' being the management, or even the government. Latent uneasiness in the social sphere breeds an extremely dangerous situation, for sooner or later people will seek a way of escaping their disquiet. The consequences may be seen in various phenomena: for instance, politicians who promise to find 'simple solutions'; or the strong dislike in the West of any form of intellectualism and the accompanying philosophy of 'keep it simple'. Similarly, today's restless younger generation wish to return to a simple, habitable, understandable world and are seeking archaic solutions to their plight.

Third, there is an *acceleration* of all developments. An explosive situation has been reached in many fields: scientific literature, the cost of health services, transport, education, the increase in world population, all these have reached 'critical' points. Phenomena like these create latent fears among people today, fears which in turn could be very dangerous. People escape into the 'golden age' of bygone days, or else they escape into the future: 'If it must come then it might as well come quickly.' Latent fears such as these provide a fertile breeding-ground for nihilism, anarchism, and cultural pessimism.

This increase in scale, this growing complexity, and this acceleration of developments, together with all their consequences, set the scene for the questions facing modern management. An adequate answer will have to be found to the problems created by each of these three 'signs of the times'.

Rapid growth (a merger, for instance, is a form of very rapid growth) is not simply an increase in turnover or in the transfer of shares; it is the creation of an entirely new situation with predictable human and structural problems. By becoming familiar with the laws of development of social structures, the manager can study these problems and make them comprehensible and predictable.

As a first step in this direction it is necessary to free oneself from regarding only the actual situation of one's own organization and to learn to think in concepts of the *development of systems*.

What is a system? System is a word that signifies coherence between several elements.[3] Clocks, plants, schools, and organizations can be regarded as systems whose parts function together in a related way.

A system is a totality of related elements, concepts, or variables selected by man. It has a boundary which is determined arbitrarily by the observer. Whatever lies outside the boundary belongs to the world or the universe outside the system; the unvarying forces that influence the system from out of this universe are 'parameters' for the chosen system.

For instance, one could regard a chromosome as a system and examine it accordingly; the rest of the cell would then constitute the external world or universe. Or one could regard the cell as a system; the chromosome would then be one of the variables (in this case a subsystem of the cell). One could regard a leaf and a plant as a system; or perhaps a plant together with the clump of earth in which it has taken root and the atmosphere which surrounds it; or even the plant between the sun as its source of energy and the middle of the earth as the necessary centre of gravity.

Every system is part of a larger system. In an enterprise the stores can be regarded as a system and examined as such. Or one could regard the totality of purchasing, storage, and production as a system. An enterprise is a system, but the boundary of this system can be drawn according to the task it has to fulfil in the greater system of which it is a subsystem, i.e. the national economy, or a supranational trade area, or the world economy. The boundary line has to be drawn according to the questions and problems to be studied. In addition to the boundary of the system, the relevant internal variables are selected and determined by the observer. He decides which factors are important and which are negligible or irrelevant.

*Every system is a simplification of reality.* One is forced to select in order to maintain a clear view of the infinitely complex relationships present in even the tiniest system. This fact should always be borne in mind. The result of studies carried out according to the systems method does *not* represent reality but only that portion of reality included in the studies in the first place.

At this point we can introduce our second concept: the *model*. The distinction between system and model is not generally agreed upon. It is therefore necessary to explain how these concepts will be used in this book.

The world we perceive around us with our senses is infinitely varied. We may choose one part of it and call it a system. In America the part of reality chosen for study would be termed a real-life system (RLS). The traffic system of London, for instance, or the throughput of the spare-parts store of a garage, could be called real-life systems. A systems analysis is applied to the RLS in the sense that specific questions are asked. The most important point is that the boundary of the system as well as the elements to be examined are selected in relation to the problem in hand.

A model is accordingly constructed in which certain values and a certain behaviour are attached to the chosen factors. This can be done in various kinds of model such as qualitative models, quantitative models, scale models, analogous models, abstract models, etc. (see diagram, p. 34).

From any portion of reality various types of system can be used, and in turn it is possible to make various models out of these systems. One and the same system can give occasion for various models; and one and the same model can serve for the examination of various systems. A model is a further abstraction of a system. Having decided upon the system, one can then proceed to choose a model for the particular problem. Systems analysts are more concerned with qualifying and conceptualizing, and model-builders with concretizing and analysing.

The reader will by now have noticed that thinking in systems and models is really one of our everyday activities. Every experience and every observation is meaningless until we can give it a place somewhere in a model of reality. The phenomenon 'blitz', meaning lightning, was given a place in a model of reality by the Teutonic peoples. The same phenomenon has a place in quite a different model of reality in the Western hemisphere of the twentieth century. In each case, however, the phenomenon has found an entirely satisfactory frame of reference. Which of the two is true cannot be decided by thinking in models.

When I was a student in the twenties a small group of undergraduates were greatly perplexed one day when the physicist Eddington[4] said in a lecture: 'When Rutherford first showed me his model of the atomic nucleus I asked myself: has he discovered the atom or has he created it with this model?' At the time we could not understand what Eddington meant with this story. But if we remember that to create any system we have to *choose* from among many variables and that the model can answer questions only within the framework of the selected variables, then his anecdote makes sense.

Thus every science is a prisoner of the systems and models it has itself created. It is a comfort to realize that in the future other variables will surely be included in our thinking, even though today they may still be regarded as irrelevant. 'Irrelevant' is usually synonymous with 'unscientific' within a given period. In the twenties in Amsterdam, when the first thesis on experiments in colour psychology carried out in Wundt's laboratory was being defended, a professor of neurology exclaimed: 'Gentlemen, if we accept this, it will mean the end of science.' It would have been more exact if he had said: 'This does not fit in with my scientific model.'

Discussions on scientific theory have once again got under way; now there is a discussion between students and professors about empiricism and values in science, a controversy waged, at least on the part of the students, with the vehemence of a crusade.

Without being aware of it, we all work with systems and models every day. We all distinguish, judge, and make plans according to the conceptual framework taught us at home and at school, which we have since individually added to and modified. The encounter with other cultures is enriching because it gives us the opportunity of perceiving and valuing the same totality in a new way.

However, conscious methods of working with systems and models have come into being only during the last few decades. Will the different disciplines still be able to understand each other while each has its own basis in its chosen model? Or are we heading for a specific deafness to the language spoken by those outside our own discipline or system? If we could conceive a general systems theory maybe we could also find a universal language understood by everyone, even though each discipline would continue to create its own models.

A study of the literature on systems shows that many authors make their own classifications of kinds of system. In the following a selection is made, together with a suggestion for a system of systems. Systems are composed of *elements*, *concepts*, or *variables*. Various kinds of system can be formed from these:

1. *Static closed systems:* In these systems the relationship of the selected factors to one another does not change. Factors outside the boundary have no influence on factors within the boundary. For example: within a defined span of time a piece of stone, or a bridge, or a ship can be regarded as a static closed system.

2. *Dynamic closed systems:* The time factor is included in this type of system. Within such a system the factors change in a certain way. All clockwork systems are therefore internally dynamic closed systems. Clocks, many types of machine, a vibrating tuning-fork, or our planetary system can be seen in this way.

3. *Static open systems:* Static open systems have an input and an output. Factors come in from outside and react with the system. Then they leave the system, more or less changed by their passage through it. The system itself is *not* changed. Recently the headmaster of a grammar school unwittingly gave an unfortunate example of a static open system. On the occasion of an anniversary celebration he said: 'Children have come and young people have gone; a succession of teachers and head-masters have come and gone; *but the school has remained the same....*' (What an admission in this age of stormy educational development!)

4. *Dynamic open systems:* This type of system differs from the previous type in that it undergoes changes while working on the throughput between input and output. Every living organism is a dynamic open system. The human being is such a system spiritually as well as physically. By digesting information he changes himself, he *learns.* Every system that includes human beings is by definition a *dynamic* open system.

5. *Dynamic open systems in changing environments:*[5] These are systems as described in (4) above, and in addition the environment is changing, so input as well as other parameters also change. New structures have to be formed continuously so that the totality can continue to exist.

The ability to continue to exist regardless of necessary adaptations to a changing environment is called the *identity* of a system. A system can have a strong or a weak identity. Through many changes it can either preserve or lose its identity. In the first case the 'relevant' variables are able to control the system. In the second case these variables either disappear or are relegated to positions of secondary importance. Total loss of identity leads to the disintegration of the system.

We speak not only of the identity but also of the *potential* of a system. The systems of living organisms bear within them a potential which enables them to make manifest the identity of their kind throughout many metamorphoses, for instance a plant proceeding from seed to blossom. If the potential is too weak, the process will peter out halfway.

Social entities such as societies or firms can also have stronger or weaker identities and greater or lesser potential for further development.

An industrial organization is an example of a system of the fifth kind. It is a dynamic open system (if only because it includes people) within a changing environment. Changes in the economic, technical, and social environment affect it. Control and innovation are therefore basic essentials for the life of an industrial organization.

The above division of systems into five categories can be seen as a suggested outline for a general systems theory. Burns and Stalker[6] speak of mechanistic and organic systems; Bennis, Benne, and Chin[7] speak of system models and developmental models. We would class the mechanistic systems and the system models as closed systems, and the organic systems and the developmental models as open systems.

Kenneth Boulding[8] has provided us with the most thorough basis for a general systems theory elaborated so far. He distinguishes between nine levels of organization. In this hierarchy each level contains all the levels below it and adds a new dimension which was not included in the lower levels. Therefore the higher the level, the greater the degree of differentiation and complexity. Boulding's nine levels are:

9. The level of transcendental systems
8. The level of social organizations
7. The human level
6. The animal level
5. The genetic–societal level (plant life, organ formation)
4. The level of open systems or self-maintaining structures (the cell)
3. The level of cybernetic systems (built-in control)
2. The level of clockworks
1. The level of frameworks.

Let us begin at the bottom:

1. Frameworks are spatial, static structures such as the geography and anatomy of the universe, atomic models, chemical formulas, the organization chart of a company, etc.

2. Clockworks are simple dynamic systems with predetermined fixed movements. The added factor is time. Examples are: simple machines, clocks, our solar system; also simple equilibrium systems, and even a calculation of compound interest.

3. In cybernetic or thermostat systems one of several variables is fixed by means of feedback of information. This has been used in many technical instruments.

4. The mystery of self-maintenance in a changing environment makes its appearance with open systems or self-maintaining structures. This is the level of the cell and also of self-reproduction and the passing on of the total information of the (living) system.

5. The genetic–societal level is higher than the level of cell life because on this level (in the plant) the system causes *groups* of cells to form organs whose pattern is *predetermined* (blueprinted growth).

6. The added dimension of the animal level is the ability to digest and store information within the system. Animals have specialized information receptors (eyes, ears, etc.). They also have awareness, an image or knowledge structure, and a view of the environment as a whole. The information received from outside by an animal is transformed into something essentially different from what it was originally.

7. With regard to the human level, the individual human being is considered as a system. In addition to all the previously mentioned capacities, man possesses self-awareness, a self-reflexive capacity. He not only knows, but he knows that he knows. This property is connected with the capacity for speech and symbolism. Man is the only creature who is aware of time. He can thus consciously anticipate future events.

8. As for the level of social organizations, man only becomes 'human' in social situations. Man is dependent on education. He plays different roles in different social organizations. And these social organizations have their own variables in the form of values, norms, aims, and expectations as well as their own social relationships. Culture, with all its wealth of science, art, and religion, emerges within social systems.

9. At the transcendental level, systems comprise such non-material matters as logic, axioms, and faith. Concluding his discussion of this highest level, Boulding says: 'It will be a sad day for man when

nobody is allowed to ask questions that do not have any answers.'*

The advantage of Boulding's scheme is that it shows us where we stand in our scientific development. 'Modern' science began with the exact description of framework systems. Geography, anatomy, biology, physics, and chemistry are examples. The next step is the study of the system level comprising phenomena which repeat themselves in time, for example the laws of oscillation, free fall, or mechanics. Many machines can be constructed with a knowledge of these two levels alone. Next, and relatively late, the cybernetic systems were discovered, for example the float in the WC cistern or the centrifugal governor which opened and closed the steam valves in early steam engines.

Natural science today is still confined solely to the three lowest levels. In biochemistry great efforts are being made to proceed to the fourth level. But in spite of much optimism the 'life' we are attempting to copy still needs support from outside (third level) and lacks the essential characteristic of the fourth level. At present we are able to study and copy only the framework, clockwork, and cybernetic aspects of life, but not yet self-preservation and self-reproduction.

At the opposite end of the scale, philosophy has been elaborating, rejecting, and reviving transcendental systems for over two thousand years.

If we consider that a science of management, being a social science, should correspond to the eighth level, it is humiliating to realize that we have so far learnt to use only the primitive concepts of the three lowest levels. Thus we can treat structures as framework systems (organization charts), flow processes, balancing phenomena, or cybernetic systems, but we cannot treat them as living organisms. On the other hand, since the social sciences belong to the eighth level they are very close to the transcendental level from which they often borrow their values, principles of selection, priorities, and aims (for example, prosperity of the economy, or self-realization in education).

Having gained an overall view of general systems theory, let us now

---

* It may be noted that there are two ways of regarding this hierarchy of levels. If you start at the bottom and work your way up, each level develops out of the one below through increased complexity. If you start at the top, then each level comes about through a process of reduction and subtraction from the one above. The first approach depicts the use of materialistic nominalism, while the second is an example of intelligent creation, of spiritual realism. The battle between nominalism and realism has been going on for centuries and has never been resolved. Some scientists prefer one and some the other, but the battle continues to appear in conceptual differences and in scientific methodology.[9]

return to the importance of thinking in systems with regard to a science of management. There are a number of further points which should be considered.

It is possible to describe an organization as though it were an economic system, a technical system, or a social system.

Those who think in terms of large economic systems such as national economies, financial budgets, or national production targets will regard firms as economic subsystems. If management exclusively considers economic variables, then other subsystems will be neglected.

The engineering staff, on the other hand, may place more importance on the perfection of the technical system, thus neglecting the economic and social aspects.

Not until recent decades did it become obvious that every firm is also a social system. Only a group of people working together can set itself targets and organize the means of achieving them. For far too long the opinion has prevailed that human beings are economic variables behaving in a predictable and rational way and reacting to economic stimuli. It is the task of management to integrate the economic, technical, and social subsystems within the organization. This theme will be the thread running through this book.

If this task of integration is to be accomplished adequately, thinking in terms of general systems structures will have to be condensed into a series of *models* which provide the framework for tangible and rational action. For this purpose, within one and the same geographical area a choice will have to be made between different functions which provide the concepts, elements, or variables for the composition of systems which are differentiated functionally and not geographically.

Just as an organization can be regarded as a functional integration of an economic, a technical, and a social subsystem, so a national community can be regarded as an integration of a number of functional subsystems, in this case a cultural–moral, a political–civil, and an economic subsystem. Different laws govern each of these subsystems. But every citizen moves in all three, with the emphasis on one of them depending on whether he is a scientist, artist, or politician, or is involved in commerce and industry.

These larger social systems will be dealt with in Part V of this book. It will be seen that a commercial or industrial organization is one of many subsystems in this context.

REFERENCES

1  MEY, J. L. *Management aspecten van de automatisering*. Utrecht, 1965.
2  NEUMANN, E. *Depth psychology and a new ethic*. Trans. London, 1969.
3  BEER, STAFFORD. *Cybernetics and management*. London, 1959.
4  EDDINGTON, SIR ARTHUR. *Philosophy of physical science*. Ann Arbor, Mich., 1958.
5  EMERY, F. E. & TRIST, E. L. The causal texture of organizational environments. *Human Relations* 18(1), 1965, pp. 21-32.
6  BURNS, T. & STALKER, G. M. *The management of innovation*. London, 1961; second edition, 1966.
7  BENNIS, W. G., BENNE, K. D. & CHIN, R. (eds.) *The planning of change*. New York, 1961: revised edition, 1969.
8  BOULDING, K. General systems theory: the skeleton of science. *Management Science* 2(3), 1956, pp. 197-208.
9  WINDELBAND, W. *Geschichte der Philosophie*. Tübingen, 1928.

## CHAPTER THREE

# Transforming Systems into Models

In condensing systems into models we can distinguish between qualitative and quantitative models, and these can be further subdivided into descriptive and normative models (see diagram overleaf).

## QUALITATIVE MODELS

### 1. *Descriptive*

(a) Conceptual models. These can be:

— *empirical generalizations* in the form of hypotheses. Van Leent[1] refers in this case to the dimension of breadth, the observation of a wide spectrum of phenomena and the establishment of a tentative hypothetical order which leads to an atomistic model.
— *theory constructions.* Here we have the dimension of height. One proceeds by way of logical thinking, from time to time casting a glance at reality in order to verify the theory. Connections arrived at by deduction are formalized.
— *valuations,* examinations in depth. We now have the dimension of depth, the dimension in which phenomena and models appear in perspective, so that if one fact or model is more relevant than others it is, as it were, seen in the foreground.

In Van Leent's terminology, real-life systems usually require a 'three-dimensional approach' if all possibilities are to be dealt with exhaustively. *The model of development is a mixed model like this.*

(b) Type models. These can be:

— *classification types.* They contain a clear generalization of phenomena and have a predictive value in the sense that, once the type is indicated, a number of specific characteristics can be comprehended. *The phases of development of organizations, to be discussed later,*

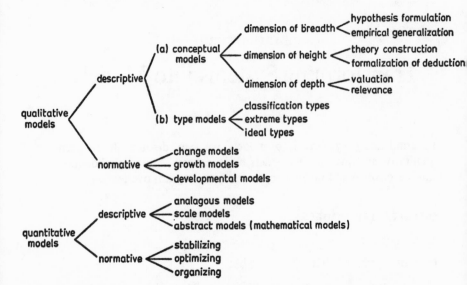

*belong to the classification type of model.* Hempel defines these models as 'a cluster of concomitant characteristics'.

— *extreme types*, also called pure types. All the classifications between two polar extremes (pure types) belong to this group, as do also series of comparisons with regard to particular characteristics.

— *ideal types*, as described by Max Weber. According to Weber, descriptions of ideal types should be able to give explanations of the unity of phenomena (e.g. Western capitalism). The interactions within ideal-type models also have a 'significance' which must 'give satisfaction' to the observer (dimension of depth). Ideal types are created through imagination and they can be intuitive or theoretical. They are intuitive if they contains *a priori* truths.

## 2. *Normative*

Normative qualitative models are models that are designed not for explaining or ordering something, but for the purpose of *action*. They are the systematic basis for the control of operations.

— *change models* are used, *inter alia*, for controlling reorganizations;
— *growth models* are used, *inter alia*, in planning departments, for the prediction of quantitative changes;
— *developmental models* are used in controlling structural meta-

morphoses in cases of quantitative growth and increasing differentiation.

## QUANTITATIVE MODELS

There is a wide variety of quantitative models. The requirements according to which a conceived model can be quantitatively worked out are dealt with in the appendix.

There is a tendency for people in the technological sphere to look upon systems and models as being exclusively quantitative, but such a view overlooks the fact that quantification is always preceded by qualitative and conceptual activity for which, in turn, all the dimensions of conceptual models are used. Accordingly, the Case Institute of Technology (Cleveland, Ohio) defines its introductory course on systems theory as the 'theory of abstract *mathematical* models of real or conceptual systems'.

Further difficulties arise concerning quantification if a problem is approached from an interdisciplinary standpoint. Mey[2] says:

It is justifiable to doubt whether the related factors which are important for decision-making, even if they are quantifiable, can be united within a single model. Thus one cannot just bring together data of an economic nature with social and psychological data and give them all a common denominator.

In addition to the division of models according to *content* into economic, technical, or social; or according to *method* into qualitative or quantitative; there is a third way of classifying them, based on the *objective* for which they are to be used:

- deterministic models (explanatory models, of which stochastic models are a subdivision)
- finalistic normative models (of which strategic models are a subdivision).

*Deterministic models* are used for the description of closed systems in which the behaviour of the variables is definitely predictable. They are also called causal models. All machines are built according to deterministic models. Even wear and tear can be included in the model.

The success achieved with deterministic models in the technical field has led to their application in other fields as well. They are used in a variety of ways in economics, and they are even applied in the biological and social sciences as though Boulding had not described any system levels higher than his three lowest. In these cases it is, however, essential to correct the concrete but alarmingly simple results with 'plain common sense' in order to avoid the pitfall of mistaking the partial truth for the whole truth. In the nineteenth century the tendency was to strive for a deterministic picture of the world as a whole. Everything that could not be explained in causal mechanistic models was therefore considered unscientific. Fortunately this point of view has now been overcome.

*Stochastic models* cannot be used for the exact prediction of events, but they do make it possible to calculate to a certain degree of probability what may occur. In physics, many of the old deterministic models have been replaced by probability models, and as a result the use of stochastic models has increased enormously in other scientific fields. Operational research, for example, deals for the most part with probabilities and risks.

*Finalistic normative models* describe reality not as it is but as it should become. In particular, with regard to social systems, finalistic normative models create the future. Objectives, preferences, action programmes, political party programmes, and utopian models such as Marxism belong to this category.

*Strategic models* are a subdivision of finalistic normative models. They are used to describe two or more intelligent subsystems which enter into a reciprocal relationship without being fully informed about each other. Practically all social systems can be described as strategic models, ranging from marriage (in which, however hard one tries, one can never reach a complete understanding of the other human being) to relationships between nations which have to live together on one planet.

Chess is a strategic game *par excellence*. Within the game, which is the strategic system, subsystem A takes certain initiatives in the expectation that subsystem B will undertake certain countermeasures. In a strategic situation one always takes one's opposite number into account when selecting a path to follow to a certain aim.

The most ancient strategic model is the battle situation. As with chess, battle calls for a strategy of opposition. In other words, A's aim precludes B's aim; they cannot both win. Either A or B must win, or the battle remains undecided.

For industry, the important fact is that commercial activity takes place within a strategic model. Except in the case of a monopoly we share a market. Therefore, in addition to pursuing one's own target one must constantly take the actions of one's competitors into account. One can, of course, apply the theory of probabilities (stochastic model) in order to determine what the other will be likely to do. But the whole point of participating in such a strategic model is that one does not do what seems most likely.

A strategy of collaboration or 'with each other' can be placed beside a strategy of competition or 'against each other'. The former could be cooperation or in other cases joint consultation. We thus see that there is a continuum from joint consultation to conflict:

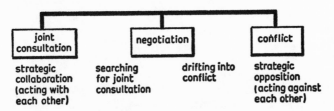

| joint consultation | negotiation | | conflict |
|---|---|---|---|
| strategic collaboration (acting with each other) | searching for joint consultation | drifting into conflict | strategic opposition (acting against each other) |

Negotiation becomes joint consultation if there is a common aim, and information is openly shared. Negotiation becomes conflict if the aims preclude each other and information is withheld (succeed or perish).

So the choice between collaboration and opposition calls for a decision, either voluntary or enforced, to choose between two models of action.[3] In a later chapter we deal with the techniques of consultation, negotiation, and conflict.

Many managers, through being tied up in a commercial situation, have acquired a kind of professional deformity which causes them to negotiate or fight where they could obtain better results with joint consultation. Not many people have mastered the technique of joint consultation, and when they use this term they usually mean no more than clever negotiation.

Finally, a word about the importance of a conscious selection of systems and models. When one faces the reality of a social situation, one experiences it as concrete and unique. With the help of experience and imagination one tries to operate within a certain system of values. This can be compared with an arithmetical calculation involving only concrete figures. The jump from arithmetic to algebra can be compared with the transition from a unique concrete situation to a model which remains correct even if different magnitudes are inserted: $(a + b)^2 =$

$a^2 + 2ab + b^2$. In this way, clarity is brought to complex situations which would otherwise require a new 'calculation' each time.

An ageing pioneer entrepreneur, feeling his growing firm slipping away from his grasp, experiences this as a unique situation and seeks to discover the mistakes he has made. But if he had come across the model of a growing pioneer organization, he would have known well in advance that this moment had to come. And he would have been able to take action in good time to transform his model of a pioneer organization into a new model with a different structure.

Thinking in systems and models of organizations is the algebra of organization theory.

REFERENCES

1 VAN LEENT, J. A. A. *De sociale psychologie in drie dimensies.* Utrecht, 1961.
2 MEY, J. L. *Management aspecten van de automatisering.* Utrecht, 1965.
3 VAN BEUGEN, M. *Sociale technologie en het instrumentele aspect van agogische actie.* Assen, 1968.

## CHAPTER FOUR

# The Concept of Development

We have already referred to this conceptual model and its importance for management. In the following chapters the concept of development[1] plays a large part, particularly the development of forms of organization, of management systems, and of styles of leadership. It is therefore necessary to define this concept more clearly. To do so we have to distinguish between three concepts: change, growth, and development.

*Change*

'We are living in a changing world' is a phrase that appears almost daily in newspapers and journals. As a generalization, however, it is fairly meaningless. It is given a content only if we define and describe where and what changes are taking place. Then it becomes evident that the concept of change can have almost any content and that the same phenomenon is described differently by different people. The term 'change' simply tells us that nothing is static and that everything is moving in the stream of time. Thus it becomes necessary to investigate whether change takes place haphazardly and by chance, or whether there are fields where one can find a system in the change. The latter could be a manifestation of natural laws.

For instance in physics we know the law of entropy: unequally distributed energy tends towards equal distribution and levelling out. This tendency towards the levelling-out of differences appears also outside physics in 'higher' biological and social systems. In biology we study a force of differentiation and a force of equalization. The former typifies life, and the latter typifies dying. Riesman,[2] among others, has described these two tendencies in the social field: 'inner-directed' people create tensions through their personal behaviour, and 'other-directed' people seek an increased social entropy through conformism.

These indications will suffice at this point. The behaviourists have produced a wealth of literature based on the many aspects of emphasis on the individual or conformity to the community (fight and flight).

## Growth

We shall reserve the term growth to describe the kind of change that brings about a quantitative increase in size or weight within one and the same system. Thus growth depicts a quantitative increase within the same basic structure. In other words, growth describes a change not of the model as such but only of one of the variables (quantity). This kind of 'genuine' growth takes place only in the inorganic world. A crystal grows in size and weight but its basic structure remains the same.

Once we enter the sphere of life we find that growth at critical points leads to a *change in the whole structure of the system.*

## Development

We shall use the term development to describe this last form of change only. Dale Harris[1] says: 'Development is fundamentally biological.' When an organism (system) grows quantitatively, it reaches a point at which its increased size can no longer be held together by its original structure. Further growth will then lead either to a disintegration of the organism (biological death) and a return to the physical laws of entropy, or to a restructuring of the organism so that this new structure can continue to control the increased mass. This restructuring always leads to increased differentiation and a more complex structure.

Kenneth Boulding defines development as 'structural growth'. This already expresses a first law of development.

*Development is a discontinuous process.* Development 'grows' from structural crisis to structural crisis, passing through the following phases:

— *growth of the whole system* or parts of it (quantitative increase)
— *differentiation and organ formation* (subsystem formation), whereby functions initially carried out by the system as a whole are now concentrated in subsystems and thus made more effective
— *hierarchization:* differentiated organs are governed by others; this is also termed 'hierarchical integration'
— *integration:* this involves the formation of a new system of greater complexity and containing specialized subsystems.

The biologist Schneirla[1] describes the process of development as *growth* (increase in tissue), *differentiation* (changes in structure as the organism grows older), and *development* (progressive changes during the course of a lifetime).

Weisz[1] points to the antagonism between growth and differentiation. After a period of rapid growth and tissue increase comes a period when growth slows down and an intensive inner differentiation of tissues into new tissues and organs takes place. Then comes a further period of growth, and so on.

The *biological* concept of development includes the principle of finality, which is inherent from the beginning and achieves its goal through a series of stages of development (blueprinted development).

Heinz Werner (again in Dale Harris's book[1]) points out that biological development follows the same basic rules as those described in the orthogenetic law of perception and learning. First comes perception, an overall generalized taking-in of the physiognomy of an object. Then follows a process of analysing the specific nature of the parts (differentiation). And, finally, in a process of synthesis the parts are integrated again into the whole.

Seen biologically, development is a number of steps in levels of organization, with hierarchization, and with direction towards a specific objective. A remarkable trait of the concept of hierarchization is that the control of the lower levels by the higher ones does not take place by means of commands but through *selective permission to function specifically*. In other words, the higher levels in the hierarchy govern the lower subsystems by sometimes *selectively restraining* and sometimes *selectively permitting* their activity.

The question now arises as to whether it is permissible to apply the biological concept of development (Boulding's fifth level) to the growth and development of social organisms (Boulding's eighth level). In our opinion it is permissible, provided the following differences are not forgotten.

First, the biological organism develops from the smallest complete unit (the single cell) until it achieves its predetermined goal, the adult form of its species, *which in the form of information has been present from the start* (an unfolding process).

A social entity can develop towards a predetermined goal only if this goal is consciously set by the people who are the bearers of initiative and power. These force the rest of the group towards the preformed objective.

It is also possible to imagine an 'adult' form of social organization in which all the members strive out of their own insight and conviction towards a *jointly agreed objective*. This does not mean that there is no hierarchization of subsystems. A conventional hierarchy functions from the top downwards, but a new form of hierarchization can be developed at Boulding's eighth level, the level of social systems: this is a hierarchy that functions from below upwards. This comes about when a higher level of insight, organizational talent, and expert knowledge is freely recognized by lower levels which therefore voluntarily subordinate themselves in certain fields because they know their own place in the organizational model. It is then no longer a question of power but rather a question of influence within a hierarchical order of subsystems.

An adult form of social organization at Boulding's eighth level is an entity that can bring to fruition the new and intrinsic qualities of this level because its foundations are built upon adult human beings who have already brought to fruition the intrinsic quality of the seventh level, namely the development of the self as an individual.

'Immature' forms are those that are based on lower levels of system, as in the plant kingdom with its predetermined blueprinted information, or in the animal kingdom with its rigid insect colonies or the instinct of submission to the bell-wether. In immature forms of organization the hierarchy is headed by those who most clearly perceive the target, are most strongly committed, and therefore master the necessary instruments for its attainment. In extreme cases the other members of the group are regarded likewise as little more than instruments directed towards the achievement of the target.

A natural biological *organism* can be regarded as a model for a social *organization* provided one very great difference is not forgotten: the members of a social organization are independent human beings and not cells in a biological structure. For independent human beings who work together in a social organization, a jointly accepted objective must exist to which they are prepared to subject themselves out of their own conviction.

Wherever people rise above their merely biological level they will strive to form social organizations as described here.

It is what we call modern mature forms of organization that are at stake in the present social and political conflict within human organizations. The path towards these mature organizations is the path of organizational development, which is described in Chapter 12.

A second difference lies in the kind of objective. In a biological organism the target of development is the adult form of the species.

In a social organization the adult form is a *means* of achieving an aim which lies outside the system. A social organization is an organization with an objective. The objective permeates the organization as it passes through the several phases of structural development. At the beginning, all functions are implicit and not yet differentiated; later, specialized subsystems such as departments are created through *differentiation*; and finally, through *integration*, everybody is oriented towards the common goal, while each individual fulfils his specialized task knowing that the others are fulfilling theirs and that the objective can be achieved only if there is a concerted effort.

With Harris[1] we can describe the development of social organizations as a process of *progressive change in organization structure taking place throughout the life-history of the organization.*

As a reaction to nineteenth-century views of evolution, the concept of development was for a long time regarded as suspect in social science. The objections to those theories of evolution were mainly that they were too generalized and could not be verified empirically, and that often in practice they did not appear to be correct.

In recent years, however, problems of development have once again been receiving attention. This became possible when a start was made on the elaboration of a systems theory which replaced vague terms like 'totality' and 'image' with defined systems and models. Unfortunately these attempts have not yet led to a uniform usage of terminology. The terms most commonly used are therefore defined below:

— *growth:* quantitative increase without any essential change in quality
— *maturation:* ripening or unfolding; existing predispositions are caused to mature (blueprinted development)
— *change:* change in the value of related factors; this term is therefore always used in connection with structures and systems
— *development:* this term is used for non-fixed change processes (that is to say, processes brought about by people) which are accompanied by qualitative transformation. The old pattern usually remains in existence in a more or less changed form in the background, as an undercurrent, or in a subordinated or repressed form, or as a historical relic, etc. These could also be called 'historical anachronisms'.

So at the biological level we speak of growth and maturation, and at the human level of change and development.

In summing up we can say:

— development is a discontinuous process, is irreversible, and takes place in time
— the time process follows the sequence of: general initial model, differentiation, integration in a model of greater complexity
— it is a process which takes place step by step, whereby earlier steps or levels may remain as subsystems in a dormant state
— thus development leads to the formation of a *layered* structure:

According to the concept of social development described here, a social organization is always 'on the way' from a given past to its own future. The given past consists of a series of decisions which have been made and have resulted in entities with concepts, values, and motives which must be accepted as given. In the future lies the sector of freedom, which means a new choice of objectives and principles.

The development of a social organization always takes place within a wider field. Every social organization is a subsystem of a larger system. Internal development is always influenced from outside by concepts, values, and motives which are parameters affecting the system. Therefore every social organization must be regarded in the light of its cultural environment. Social change as a process thus has an internal and an external side. Not only is a social organization influenced by its cultural environment, but it in turn exerts an influence on this environment. An example will make this clear: the manner in which a firm conducts its personnel policy will have an influence on the extent to which aggressive or non-aggressive tensions emerge in a part of the community outside the firm.

Development can be described from various points of view. In conclusion, the following may be mentioned:

1. In looking at the *direction* of development we can speak of 'evolution' and 'involution'. Biological and social evolution leads from simple to more complex structures in which differentiated substructures (organs) emerge. This process is irreversible. Involution leads to increasing entropy, the dissolution of structures, indeed to chaos. In the social field, involution in development (decline of a civilization or

of a firm) can run parallel with the evolution of a new structure (rise of a new civilization).

2. In looking at the *process* of development we can ask: How does differentiation from simple to complex structures take place, and what laws can be discerned? This aspect will be dealt with in detail in the chapters that follow, because it constitutes the basis for planned development.

3. Development can also be described as a *situation* in which structures of varying degrees of complexity find themselves living together. In this case we can speak of structures which are developed to a greater or a lesser degree, and we can also mention international development aid. The degree of development varies in different countries and in different cultures. The same applies to the different departments with their varying functions within a firm. A highly differentiated production department can run side by side with a fairly primitive sales department, and so on. The existence side by side of social structures of different degrees of development leads to tensions (for instance the Negro problem in the United States and in South Africa).

4. Finally, we can look upon development as an *activity*: planned change, guided innovation, and organizational development. It is obvious that, for an activity to be carried out, the *direction* as well as the *process* of development must be known. Development as an activity calls for:

— goal-setting (the direction of the development)
— policy-making (the strategy of the development process)
— planning (the concretization of practicable steps).

Policy-making is here the most important because a clear policy in connection with development as an activity can provide an action model. Policies, however, work only when they are converted into action, when they are *accepted* by the people concerned. The policies of separate social units can come into conflict with one another; this is termed a conflict of policy systems.

The concept of development is focused in this book on the development of organizations within the economic sphere, namely enterprises, whereby enterprises are seen as organizations directed towards an objective and encompassing an economic, a technical, and a social subsystem. A number of typical stages in the development of enterprises will be described.

REFERENCES

1  HARRIS, DALE B. (ed.) *The concept of development*. Minneapolis, 1968.
2  RIESMAN, D., with N. GLAZER and R. DENNEY. *The lonely crowd*. New York, 1950.

# Recommended Reading

*Chapters 2-4*

LEHRS, ERNST. *Man or matter*. London, 1950.

CARTWRIGHT, D. & ZANDER, A. *Group dynamics*. New York, 1953; London, 1954; second edition, 1960; third edition, 1968.

MILLER, D. W. & STARR, M. K. *Executive decisions and operations research*. Englewood-Cliffs, New Jersey, 1960.

PARSONS, T. *The social system*. Glencoe, Ill., 1951; London, 1952.

JOHNSON, R. *et al. The theory and management of systems*. New York, 1963.

# PART II

# The Use of Type Models

## CHAPTER FIVE

# Phases in the Development of Enterprises

In this chapter we describe a number of typical phases in the development of enterprises and organizations in the economic sphere. The reader will thus become acquainted with models described on the basis of obvious factors, attitudes, and organizational methods. This will enable him to compare typical situations with his own experience and thus make a 'developmental diagnosis' of his own firm, in this way determining which phase of development it has reached, which problems are the most important, and which ones are likely to appear during the transition to the next phase.

Alister Hardy, the English biologist, made the following distinction between natural history and science: 'Natural history is the qualitative description of nature whereas science is the quantitative and experimental analysis of its interactions.' He then added: 'Discoveries by observation may be just as fundamental as those made by experiment; *both are important.*'

As Hardy says, natural history is concerned with describing as exactly as possible various type models. Mammals, insects, amphibia are types which have been specified after exact observation of typical specimens which possess as completely as possible all the specific characteristics of the type model. With these typical manifestations, these classification types, clearly defined, one can then go on to discover where the transition to other types takes place.

The whole system of the plant and animal kingdoms is thus given many subdivisions, right down to species and sub-species, as a basis for more detailed research and experiment by the natural scientist.

Here we follow the same method with reference to the development of organization models of social structures in the economic sphere. This method of establishing a system of type models has hitherto not been sufficiently described and systematized. After giving a general description of 'organization history' (this being analogous to 'natural history') we shall turn to the problem of further analysing parts of the models described.

In quantitative systems analysis, what matters is not so much the technique of quantitative analysis as such (this can be learnt) as the ability to ask meaningful questions within meaningful subsystems. A description of types can provide a basis for the latter.

## THE PIONEER PHASE

In its pure form, a pioneer enterprise is an enterprise that is still being run by its founder. It comes into being as the result of a creative act by a human being. This person is an entrepreneur; his personality structure is such that his perception and imagination are directed towards actual needs in economic life. He has a 'realistic imagination'.

At some point in his life, the pioneer noticed a *consumer need* and, instead of saying 'someone ought to do something about this', decided to set about it himself, *providing a creative answer to the need at a price the consumer was willing to pay*. With a few helpers and probably very little capital he set to work and founded a small manufacturing firm, or a small transportation business, or some other service. Twenty years later we find that through diligence and thrift he is now at the head of a flourishing little business with about a hundred employees.

### Characteristics of Pioneer Enterprises

What does the organization of his firm look like at this moment? The pioneer is primarily interested in economic and technical performance (i.e. answering a need at a price the consumer is willing to pay). His thoughts are occupied with the product he makes and the market he creates. He has a concept of a real objective and his organization is therefore the simplest form of an organization geared to an objective.

1. *Leadership is autocratic:* The pioneer runs his enterprise with an autocratic style of leadership which is based on the prestige he enjoys in the eyes of 'his' men. At the present time, autocratic leadership of this kind is not very popular, but in the case in point it is socially acceptable and indeed accepted because the pioneer's autocratic behaviour is balanced by the fact that he has the respect and trust of his employees at all levels.

If there is trouble, the 'guvnor' will always find a way out of it, and his success in doing so proves that 'he's done it again'. The pioneer has a special charisma, he works 'under a good star'. His absolute authority is also connected with the following factors:

- He knows all his employees and their family circumstances personally. He has engaged them himself and they are 'his' chaps.
- He knows all the jobs, having performed most of them himself at one time or another. If he finds someone making a mess of things, off comes his coat for an impromptu demonstration.
- He is successful in business, and in this situation success gives him prestige.

2. *Communication is direct:* The pioneer communicates straightforwardly and directly with all his employees. He gives direct orders to his foremen and his workers, in the latter case quite naturally bypassing the foremen who owe their position to him. Since everybody knows everybody, no difficulties worth mentioning arise out of this kind of behaviour. Nobody knows better than the boss, and the method works efficiently. These direct contacts are also useful because they make many secondary communications possible and the order is given a personal touch. Long discussions become unnecessary when an incident referred to is remembered by all. (Pioneer: 'Those bikes are to have pedals like the ones we sent to Middletown last year. You know, that black-haired chap you had a bit of a row with.' Employee: 'Oh, you mean *those* pedals! I noticed there were a few left in the store the other day.') The pioneer speaks the language of his employees. In many cases his roots are in the same milieu as theirs, and at least in the early years he has worked in very close contact with them. Close psychological proximity between the pioneer and his workers makes communication flexible and effective. There is as yet no need to formalize communication and set up information channels. There are no job descriptions to regulate each person's duties and rights. Neither are there such things as procedures, task descriptions, code numbers, stock transfer notes, specified regulations, etc.

3. *The style of organization is person-oriented:* During the course of his career, the pioneer has always passed on the tasks that do not appeal to him personally. The others have done just the same. Similarly, each person has sought to keep for himself the jobs that interest him and that he is good at. Thus gradually a kind of flexible division of tasks comes about, whereby each person creates for himself a job which fits him like a glove. In consequence, work motivation is particularly high

in a healthy pioneer enterprise. The pioneer strengthens this tendency systematically by employing people who 'appeal to him personally' or whom 'he considers promising' rather than functionaries who are to carry out specific tasks. When a man is taken on he is told: 'Have a go at this or that, and if you are any good you'll go a long way with me.'

Unconsciously the pioneer collects around him a group of co-pioneers. This can also have negative effects if the enterprise grows too large. In one case a pioneer enterprise had grown until it had six geographically separate production plants and one large head office. There was no official division of tasks within the company and everybody had at least five superiors who frequently gave contradictory orders. When it was gently suggested by a management consultant that perhaps the demarcation of tasks below top management should be examined, the seventy-two-year-old pioneer director replied resolutely: 'Certainly not, I like seeing the strongest come out on top!'

This pioneering style leads to a sort of patchwork pattern with little bits of purchasing and selling going on here and there, carefully hoarded little 'individual' stores, and small pockets of administration all over the place. If you try to make a chart of the organization as it stands, the result is a jumble of lines. By any healthy organizational standards an enterprise like this ought to be seriously sick. And yet it functions excellently and shows good economic results.

4. *The working style is improvisational:* In a pioneer enterprise all problems are solved by improvisation. This ability to improvise is its real strength; it creates a high degree of flexibility. Because the employees of the company are skilled and can be called upon to do more than one kind of task, production can be rapidly adapted to demand, and the special requests of customers can be met.

5. *The work force: 'one big family':* In pioneer enterprises at the end of the last century, labour was the closing item on the budget. The labour market was open, and when work was slack workers were dismissed, while if work was plentiful more were hired. Those times are passed. The twentieth-century pioneer is economical with his workers. Those who feel at home in the firm make progress, those who do not usually disappear quietly and look for work elsewhere.

The labour factor is not an object of conscious policy, although the patriarchal efforts of the pioneer often touch even the very personal affairs of his people. In many cases the wife of the pioneer is a kind of welfare worker for her husband's men and their families. 'We're all one big happy family' is a favourite phrase of many a pioneer (until the first strike gives him a moral shock from which he usually never quite recovers).

6. *The pioneer's market: known customers:* The pioneer does not know what it is to operate in an anonymous market. He works in a limited geographical area and knows all his customers. His most important concern is keeping these customers through personal contact.

The pioneer works *from one order to the next,* so that he produces only what is already sold. He does not restrict himself to certain set products, and keeping a stock of what he produces seems superfluous to him. He has a good, often intuitive, knowledge of his customers, and it is his relationship with them that is important. His great strength is his ability to *keep his customers.* He makes whatever they order, and he will often delay other work to oblige a long-established customer. The production method of the pioneer is really like an enlarged version of what goes on in a craftsman's workshop, with all the same advantages and disadvantages. As a result of improvisation, the pioneer does not know how much certain jobs and services cost him. He is concerned with the total profit, which, however, he cannot determine until he has finished an order. He relies on his intuition and experience.

7. *The long-established growing pioneer company:* The true pioneer stands 'head and shoulders' above his employees. This situation is unconsciously furthered by the pioneer who cannot tolerate any other true leaders either beside or beneath him. If he does choose a director, usually from among his employees, to work beside him, the man nevertheless remains his subordinate.

If any of his sons join him in the firm they fare no better. Many pioneers realize this and are sensible enough to have their sons trained elsewhere. But even after many years the younger men are unable to build up their own authority as long as 'the old boy' is still actively concerned with the running of the firm. *The pioneer wants to lead without allowing any management to develop under him.* Thus when he finally drops out, the company invariably faces a crisis.

The financing of a pioneer company is usually weak. There was too little capital at its inception and since then thrift and internal financing have provisionally supplied immediate necessities.

So far we have described the strong, successful, healthy pioneer enterprise with its great advantages of *flexibility, readiness for service,* and *strong internal motivation.* In a healthy pioneer company everybody is concerned with the company's objectives. They are simple and clear: success or failure (complaints from customers) can be witnessed by all. A pioneer organization is healthy so long as:

— the pioneer himself knows all his people
— the pioneer himself knows all his customers
— the production processes or services rendered remain relatively simple
— the accumulation of experience is an asset because technology and the market show stability.

From the picture we have given we can conclude the following. The pioneer regards his organization as a closed dynamic system of which his customers and his employees are a part. The pioneer is primarily interested in his economic and technical achievement. He thinks in terms of the product he makes and the market he has conquered. For the pioneer, profit is personal income as well as the measure of his success as an entrepreneur. Within the social subsystem he operates intuitively in accordance with the model of a craftsman's workshop. Differentiation into economic, technical, and also social subsystems is confined to a minimum. Improvising as he goes along, the pioneer finds his way within a world known to him personally. He rejects any interference in this world. His self-esteem is linked to his success. If the balance-sheet is positive 'God has been good to him'; if it is negative 'God has humiliated him'.

The closed nature of a pioneer enterprise is at once its strength and its weakness. So long as influences from outside do not disturb the system, a pioneer enterprise can grow and even be taken over by the next generation without much difficulty. But if the 'external' world starts to move, if technology develops so that quite new products become available to satisfy needs, if market conditions start to change and competitors break into the pioneer's field with brand-new sales techniques, if the market grows so that personal contacts with customers are no longer possible, if extensive shifts take place in the social structure so that a patriarchal style of leadership is no longer acceptable, then the pioneer phase has reached its limits. If the company continues to be run in accordance with the model of the pioneer phase, in spite of external circumstances, it can be said that this phase of development becomes 'over-ripe'.

The first thing that happens when a pioneer company becomes over-ripe is that the employees begin to entertain doubts about 'the boss'. At the same time, his prestige begins to decrease and his patriarchal, autocratic manner becomes intolerable. Then a few mistakes begin to creep in. For instance, a crisis in the market is met in the same way as forty years ago 'when we also had bad times'. The pioneer who has hitherto rejected any attempt at interference by the government now suddenly asks for protection for his 'honest endeavours'.

Once the influence of these external factors becomes so great that it can no longer be seen as an isolated incident but as something affecting the very structure, the pioneer enterprise has reached the threshold of a new development. The symptoms of such a crisis situation can be:

— decreasing profits
— leadership conflicts
— increasing customer complaints
— decreasing manoeuvrability
— communication blocks
— decreasing motivation.

*Summary*

Just as the unicellular organism can accomplish all the functions that are essential for its life, so a pioneer company in its embryonic form can fulfil all the necessary entrepreneurial functions. The strength of a pioneer enterprise lies in its *potentiality* and in its strong *identity*, both of which are concentrated in the person of the pioneer or a successor carrying on in the same style.

The *objectives* of the company are visible down to the lowest level. Each person knows what he contributes to the achievement of the objectives and how successful he is in doing so. The *policy* is not defined or discussed, and yet everybody knows what it is because it is the style in which the boss likes things to be done. Long-term *planning* is non-existent. People improvise as they go along, fulfilling the wishes of the customers unless they are interrupted by one of the pioneer's new ideas. The *organization* is 'shallow'; there is usually only one level of management, or at most two, between the company director and the shop floor. The demarcation of tasks comes about historically on the basis of personal preference and ability and it therefore changes if there is a change of personnel.

*Innovation* comes from the top or in the technical field from motivated workers who usually put their own ideas into practice immediately.

*Control* is exercised on the one hand through the direct contact with the customer and on the other by the annual results. The total performance of a pioneer enterprise is directly related to the total ability of all those working for it. If a particular man with a special skill drops out, then the firm can no longer fulfil certain tasks. The know-how is at shop-floor level and the level directly leading it.

The pioneer style described here can be found in the history of nearly all medium-sized companies. Today it is still present in garages, small construction firms, small transportation firms and building contractors, and it is also a permanent feature of many trading organizations as well as of the agricultural sector and the hotel trade.

A healthy pioneer enterprise has a particularly efficient way of working: it has small overheads and great flexibility. The employees of a pioneer company are still people who have a wide range of skills and are very inventive. Their motivation in serving the customer is high, and they are not averse to lending a helping hand outside working hours as well.

The limitations of the pioneer model are obvious: the number of employees, the nearness of the objective, the vitality of the pioneer himself, the complexity of technical and market requirements — all these determine where this model can operate successfully and in a healthy way.

Many pioneer companies exist today only because the large concerns are not flexible enough to include the production of special series of parts or some semi-finished products or even some finished products in their production programmes, and prefer to save money by passing this work on to smaller companies. General Motors have about 30,000 suppliers of this kind, Renault 6,000, and Daimler Benz 17,000. Some examples of the articles and services supplied by these small firms are: punched cards, printed labels, screws, nuts and bolts, gudgeon pins, ornamental parts, metal parts, wooden boxes, ship repairs, scrap-processing, etc.

If a pioneer enterprise becomes too dependent on one or a few large firms in this way, its range of products or services becomes too small. And if the large firms concerned stipulate a high standard of quality, higher investment in capital goods becomes inevitable and the advantages of low overheads and greater flexibility disappear. Then if a period of economic stagnation or decline should occur, forcing the large firms to limit production, the small suppliers will suddenly lack work and quite possibly face bankruptcy.

The prevalence of small and medium-sized firms is shown in statistics from the 1968 yearbook of the Dutch Central Office of Statistics (see table below). If these enterprises are grouped into categories of

*Persons working in industry, distributed by size of enterprise*
*(at 31 December 1966)*

| Size of enterprise (no. of employees) | No. of enterprises | No. of persons |
|---|---|---|
| 10- 24 | 4 381 | 65 500 |
| 25- 49 | 2 681 | 92 900 |
| 50- 99 | 1 661 | 114 700 |
| 100-199 | 852 | 117 900 |
| 200-499 | 534 | 161 300 |
| 500-999 | 178 | 121 500 |
| 1 000 and over | 131 | 465 400 |

*small* (under 100 employees), *medium* (100-1,000 employees), and *large* (over 1,000 employees), the following picture emerges:

| Size of enterprise | No. of enterprises | No. of persons |
|---|---|---|
| Small | 8 723 | 273 100 |
| Medium | 1 564 | 400 700 |
| Large | 131 | 465 400 |

It is clear from these figures that considerably more people work in small and medium-sized enterprises than in large ones; moreover, the small and medium-sized firms still represent a larger turnover in money.

*Further Growth and Significance of Pioneer and Family Enterprises*

In practice in some cases the further growth of pioneer enterprises is coped with in the following ways:

*The conglomerate:* The original enterprise is split up into a number of smaller units, each of which is run in the pioneer style. The central unit becomes a kind of financing body. Young employees with a pioneering mentality are engaged or taken from the parent enterprise; they are given an initial capital sum and told to build a new subsidiary company or a special branch. All these 'pioneers' are personally responsible only to the pioneer in the central unit. The whole operation could be described as an investment with risk. This conglomerate form, of which there are a number of examples, makes it possible to implement very successful and often aggressive market policies. The pioneer style can be maintained on a much larger scale and with a greater degree of diversification.

*The family business:* Although a family business need not be identical with the pioneer model, it invariably started as a pioneer company and bears some characteristics of this model for a long time, especially in the style of leadership.

We speak of a family business:

— when the management has been in the hands of a particular family for more than one generation
— when the wives and sons of former directors are members of the board of directors
— when the style of the company is identified with the style of the family concerned
— when the activities of members of the family concerned can help or damage the firm even if they are not employed by it
— when the family finances the firm even when losses occur
— when the careers of employees are a matter of discussion in the family council
— when a person's position in the firm determines his standing in his relationship with the family.

Since the family business is still the most frequent form of medium-sized enterprise, and since the medium-sized enterprise is still the backbone of our whole industrial society, we must examine the advantages and disadvantages of this form of organization a little more closely. In doing so we shall in part follow Robert Donnelley's[1] analysis of the family business.

The weak points of the family business (which should be avoided) are:

— conflicts within the family and between different family interests, which have an effect on the business
— lack of knowledge about real production costs; continued production of 'image' products on which the firm was originally founded; prestige actions of competing members of the family

— immobility of market position: new markets are not covered quickly enough; insufficient development of new products
— nepotism: some members of the family have to have a position in the firm even if they are incompetent
— rejection of external financing on the capital markets and concealment of the actual financial situation.

The strong points of the family business are:

— the family is prepared to advance capital, even in difficult times, and also temporarily to forgo dividends; as a rule the family is prepared not only to share the profits but also to make sacrifices
— the respected family name opens the door to good business relations
— the staff of the firm is loyal and is dedicated to making every effort for the firm
— the body of shareholders is united and is interested in the continuity of the firm
— there is an acceptance of social responsibility (the reason for the firm's good name)
— continuity and integrity of management.

In some families, extensive enterprises are managed with success. Strong principles are often the foundation:

— family members are allowed to participate actively in the running of the firm only if they can achieve at least a comparable position in the outside world (it is cheaper to send 'nephew Harry' to the Riviera with quite a large annual compensation than to let him earn even a small salary causing confusion in the firm and undermining the authority of the family)
— family members and sons-in-law judged to be suitable are carefully trained elsewhere and prepared for their future tasks
— good specialists are given important positions and take a valid part in decision-making.

Family enterprises that recognize these principles can function in a healthy way.

### THE PHASE OF DIFFERENTIATION

The historical answer to the problems of the over-ripe pioneer enterprise came in the form of *scientific management*. This form of management is already looked upon as 'classical management' and we can therefore be brief in our description of it.

In the second half of the nineteenth century, as a result of rapid changes in the technical and economic spheres, firms and enterprises — particularly in America — were confronted for the first time with industrial production on a large scale. These new conditions, which became manifest in the appearance of *large-scale enterprises*, called for a reorientation and reorganization of management. For the first time the organization problem was systematically examined in the search for new and effective methods.

Two people laid the foundations for a new philosophy of management, Taylor in America, and Fayol in France. Both were already engineers of some calibre when they were quite young, and they complemented each other. In the years following the First World War their two methods of organization, which had already proved themselves in practice, were combined to form what we now call 'scientific management'. No doubt the term 'scientific' was deemed necessary as a means of distinguishing the method from the 'unscientific' personal style of organization during the pioneer era.

Taylor (1856-1915) came from a wealthy home. At the age of eighteen an eye ailment forced him to abandon his medical studies at Harvard University and he decided to undergo an apprenticeship as a pattern-maker in a pump factory and later to work as a labourer in a machine factory. And there, as a young intellectual on the shop floor, he experienced all the inefficiency of what was later called in Germany the *Meisterwirtschaft*.

The directors reigned supreme and were interested purely in the commercial side. The engineers were regarded as simple technicians for whom the office milieu was inappropriate. The master-craftsmen were the ones with the real know-how, based on well-tried skills specialized over decades of experience.

In this situation Taylor began to think about two things: on the one hand, the lot of the workers who had low wages and long working hours coupled with a high accident risk; and, on the other hand, the possibility of rationalizing production so that it could be increased. If the latter could be achieved, the workers would be able to earn higher wages with less effort and in more dignified conditions, and the entrepreneurs could make higher profits which would in turn pay for technical improvements.

This attitude had tragic consequences for Taylor himself. A number of organizational principles elaborated in his scientific management were taken up, but his social ideas were rejected as those of a clever but impractical idealist. Against his doctor's advice, Taylor spent his evenings studying to become an engineer. After passing his exams he soon patented a number of important inventions and quickly became financially independent. Thus at the age of thirty-seven he was able to become the first independent management consultant devoting all his time to publicizing his ideas. When in 1912 the American Federation of Labor finally pronounced him workers' enemy number one, his life's work collapsed and he died in hospital three years later, lonely and embittered.

Taylor was a brilliant personality, exceptionally gifted technically and also socially inspired. And yet a study of his life reveals a trait of character which also found its way into his theories. Today one would say Taylor was an obsessional neurotic, and this showed itself even in his youth in numerous almost compulsive actions. A similar compulsive kind of thinking appears in his system: whatever *can* be distinguished *must* be separated. All his principles were absolute. The system was more important than the people, for whom nevertheless he wanted to do so much. Taylor thought that he could grasp a social organization in a deterministic system in which all variables were known and could be stipulated.

The best way to rediscover Taylor's greatness is to read the report of his hearing before Congress. His answers are those of a brave and clear-thinking man in a highly awkward situation. Patiently he explains his system, answering all the unpleasant questions and leaving us in no doubt as to who is really leading the discussion.

His system was one-sidedly worked out by his successors who saw in it nothing but a striving for efficiency. In this form it came to Europe after the First World War, where far-sighted entrepreneurs founded such institutions as the Dutch Institute for Efficiency (1925).

Fayol (1841-1925) was another highly gifted personality. At the age of nineteen he became the youngest mining engineer in France. At first it seemed that he would devote himself to science as a geologist, and his book on geology was a standard work in this field for a long time. But then he was asked to take over the running of an ill-functioning, almost bankrupt, mining company.

With the same systematic thinking he plunged straight into his new task, was able to transform the whole organization in a short time, and was thereafter called to ever-higher positions. During the First World

War he held a high position in connection with the economic organization of the war effort in France. He attained a ripe old age and was a celebrated man until he died.

Fayol built up his administrative organization according to a number of definitions, elements, and principles. The following fourteen principles have become the best known:

1 Division of labour
2 Authority and responsibility
3 Discipline
4 Unity of command
5 Unity of direction (objectives)
6 Subordination of personal interests to company interests
7 Good remuneration of personnel

8 Centralization
9 Hierarchical structure
10 Order
11 Justice
12 Stability in the position of personnel
13 Initiative
14 *Esprit de corps*

Having studied the first twelve principles in this list — centralization, discipline, order, subordination, unity of command, and so on — one wonders where there is any room left for initiative. Indeed, Fayol's principles of organization could have been formulated by the Sun King himself!

With these two personalities, Taylor and Fayol, we have two biographies, two characters, and two entirely different attempts to save the over-ripe pioneer enterprise.

Taylor begins from below, with a rational organization of the workshop, with improvements of resources and machines, and with a systematic division of labour and specialization of performance. Not until decades after his death did his principles penetrate to other spheres beyond production; and they never reached top management.

Fayol, as a good Frenchman, starts from the top with a centralized organization and works downwards. His principles hardly reached the shop floor. Rational management for him was called 'administration' and his question was: 'How can I control the whole company from the top by means of a logically constructed hierarchical order of authority and responsibility?' He made the first large organization charts of the well-known 'christmas-tree' type (the star at the top, and below at every level small parcels with the names of interrelated functions and tasks).

Before his death, Fayol was himself able to end the argument between the Taylorites and the Fayolites by declaring that the two systems were not contradictory but complementary. Since then, through the merging and further refinement of the two systems, scientific management has continued to grow.

The efficiency of production methods was developed on the basis of engineering science as a whole (Taylor's successors), and the corresponding efficiency of economic administration grew out of a theory of internal control and management developed by economists (Fayol's successors). We shall discuss the *principles* of the resulting organization theory, which are essential for an understanding of company structure in the second phase.

Seen historically, scientific management has led to a form of enterprise whose main characteristic is *differentiation*, which has arisen out of the initial homogeneous structure of the pioneer enterprise. That is why, as a classification, the *second stage of development* of a system or organization geared to an objective has been called the *phase of differentiation*.

Scientific management is based on a logical ordering of functions, tasks, things, and processes. It assumes that the productivity of an organization increases the more the people concerned succeed in behaving according to the formal organizational plan. The norms for human behaviour in the work situation comply first and foremost with the demands made by the technical process.

## Some Characteristics of the Phase of Differentiation

Taylor and Fayol and their successors were not primarily concerned with providing a scientific explanation of what occurs in the actual running of an enterprise. They gave practical organizational procedures whose application was intended to guarantee maximum efficiency.

The main organizational principles of the phase of differentiation are: mechanization, standardization, specialization, coordination.

1. *The principle of mechanization* implies that technical resources must be used wherever possible. *Human labour* must be replaced by *machine labour* as far as possible. Mechanization is not concerned exclusively with machines, but covers the whole production process and also the information processes.

2. *The principle of standardization* is concerned with interchangeability and uniformity. Standardization means that every thing, every process,

every working method can be whittled down to an exactly described standard. From a number of alternatives one possibility is chosen and is declared to represent the norm for reasons of expediency.

The mechanization of production processes would not be profitable if standardization had not made serial and mass production possible. The principle of standardization, however, affects human beings as well as things. In addition to interchangeable standard parts and standard quality norms, we find standard function descriptions, uniform performance requirements, standardized assessment techniques, standard instructions, interchangeable functionaries, and so on.

It is impossible to stipulate production norms without carefully analysing the cause and effect of relevant phenomena. When this is done, the complicated interplay that goes on in an enterprise becomes *controllable* and *predictable* and can be *planned*. As development continues in the second phase, however, this controllability threatens to become an end in itself. As norms and standards become more and more refined, the controllability of the production process increases, though this is usually at the expense of the necessary *flexibility*. For the departments directly or indirectly involved in the production process, the actual objective becomes: meeting planning requirements. The real objective of the firm, namely to satisfy a need of the market, disappears more and more into the background.

While methods and techniques for controlling and developing the internal organization become increasingly scientific, the sales department continues to function anachronistically in the pioneer style. It still works from one order to the next, relying on personal contact with customers. On the one hand the elaboration of norms and standards has led to a thorough knowledge of production costs and production output, but on the other hand much less is known about sales costs and the benefits obtainable from possible alternative sales techniques. This development leads to an *aggressive sales mentality*: the firm's products are 'forced' onto the market.

3. *The principle of specialization* means that the restriction of effort to a small field leads to improved performance in *quality* and *quantity*. Mechanization and standardization lead as a matter of course to specialization. Mechanization requires an ever-increasing perfection of equipment as well as concentrated knowledge and experience with regard to every part and every technical aspect. Standards can be met only if all the causes and effects that could influence the object

to be standardized are minutely controlled in every detail. This can best be achieved through specialization.

Threè modes of specializing appear in the phase of differentiation:

– *Functional specialization:* Similar activities are concentrated in a single department under one specialized department head, who in turn engages further specialists. Purchasing, selling, production, administration, research, etc. become separate departments. According to need, further departments are divided off. Thus, for instance, departments for production planning, maintenance, and storage are divided off from the production department.

– *Specialization of management levels:* This leads to a vertical management structure. The top is concerned only with policy-making: *constitutional management*; in the middle these policies are translated into organizational measures: *organizational management*; and at the bottom of the hierarchy immediate direction and control are exercised over the shop-floor level: *supervisory management*. The relationship between superiors and their subordinates is one of *direction* and *control*. Management is interpreted on the one hand as the right to give orders, and on the other hand as the duty to see that these orders have been correctly carried out. This form of management is *formal* and *autocratic*. It is *formal* because the exercise of authority (as seen in Max Weber's model of an ideal bureaucracy) is to a great extent based on a person's powers resulting from his position in the hierarchy; and it is *autocratic* because the traditional style of management behaviour of the pioneer entrepreneur is usually copied.

– *Specialization by phasing the work process:* The application of the principle that everything that can be distinguished must be separated is applied, so that the three essentially interrelated phases of human work, *planning*, *execution*, and *control*, are recognized as being distinguishable and are duly separated. Departments are organized for the sole purpose of planning and preparing (general planning offices, production planning, drawing offices, and so on). Other departments appear with exclusively controlling functions (quality control, cost control, auditing, etc.). What remains in between is 'pure' operating labour. With the help of *work analyses* and *time and motion studies* the entire work process is broken down into basic elements with corresponding standard times. On the basis of the requirements of the production process with regard to layout, the supply and dispatch of materials and parts, the speed of the production flow, etc., tasks for human beings emerge which consist of basic elements rationally joined together. These tasks are attuned to one another according to technical norms and have to be performed by a prescribed method (one-best-way principle). The resulting unskilled work is void of content and calls almost exclusively for *manual dexterity*. Human labour is reduced to an *automatic activity*. The phasing of the work process in this way is not restricted to the factory. For white-collar workers, research workers, and even in the domain of the expert, increasing specialization leads to much routine work.

4. *The principle of coordination* serves to counterbalance the centrifugal force of differentiation which becomes increasingly prevalent in the second phase. The numerous and varied activities which come into being have to be held together.

Coordination comes about directly and indirectly in the following ways:

— *Unity of command:* In order to avoid the issuing of contradictory instructions, each person has only one superior. In principle, horizontal communication between two employees should take place via their superior.
— *Span of control:* Since the relationship of a superior to his subordinates is one of direction and control, he must have a detailed knowledge of all his subordinates' activities in order to have his department well under control. This is possible only if the number of his subordinates is not too large.
— *Staff–line construction:* As the number of specialists increases, it becomes more difficult to maintain the principle of unity of command. Staff–line construction is a solution to this problem. Specialists are placed in staff departments outside the line of command. They act in an exclusively advisory capacity while the line of command keeps its full authority.
— *Performance remuneration:* The assumption is that good pay is the only thing that motivates people. Man acts rationally and tries to reap the maximum benefit from the bargain, in this way safeguarding his own interests (the concept of economic man). In an enterprise, this bargain situation means the execution of work for a return in the form of good remuneration. By roundabout means, self-interest is used to direct the activities of the employees towards

the interests of the firm. Put briefly, organization is, therefore, directing resources and people towards an objective.

— *Communication techniques:* A complicated network of information distribution must ensure that management remains informed about the activities of its personnel and that they in turn are informed about the plans decided on by management. Internal post systems and mailing-lists are methods applied.

— *Introductory courses and training programmes:* Systematic transmission of knowledge and skills ensures that people will do their work in the way prescribed by the formal plan. It is typical of this kind of coordination that it takes place outside the work situation to which it pertains. The higher level coordinates the lower level.

With regard to the task of top management, the above development shows *that its attention in the phase of differentiation is directed mainly inwards.* In the pioneer phase, the external marketing function was the most important. The internal set-up had to give the least possible trouble and had, as it were, to translate the smallest hint into action. In the following phase it becomes more and more necessary to give attention to the internal organization. *Administering and controlling the internal structure of the company becomes the most important task of management.*

In the triangular relationship of management, work, and people, the pioneer directs his attention primarily to the people and motivates them to do the work. In the phase of differentiation, management concentrates in the first instance on an analysis of the work (processes), which it then passes on to the people divided up into portions.

Through the technical and organizational structuring of the company, scientific management has achieved an enormous increase in productivity. The method of analysis and differentiation has made it

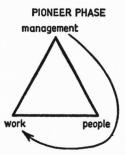

**PIONEER PHASE**

**PHASE OF DIFFERENTIATION**

possible to investigate in detail, and learn to control, every activity in the firm. Mechanization and stardardization have led to new methods of production aimed at the mass markets, which have considerably increased the living standard of sizeable groups of the population in the Western hemisphere.

In the pioneer phase it was a matter of *piece production*. Each product was manufactured by itself as a whole. This form of production is still found in capital goods industries, e.g. ships, diesel engines, electrical installations, telecommunications systems, and so on. Items are produced individually or in small lots. The work is completed in consecutive homogeneous segments, and the division of work is already present to a considerably greater degree than in craft production. Where piece production is still undertaken, the *acquiring of orders*, i.e. the external marketing function, is in the foreground. The *cost price is relatively high.*

In the phase of differentiation, old-style mass production, new-style mass production, and process production appear side by side and sometimes also successively.

*Old-style mass production* usually involves standardized interchangeable components and standard manufacturing methods, and the end-product is also fixed. There is only one variety (cf. Henry Ford's remark that 'people can have whatever colour car they like, so long as it's black'). Old-style mass production means that the end-product and the production process are rigid. The customer has to learn to be satisfied with the available range. Individual customer relations are less important than an effective sales organization and the penetrating and covering of a wide market. Long production runs make the cost price relatively low.

*New-style mass production* combines the advantages of low cost prices with those of a relatively flexible production process and a very varied end-product (e.g. automobile production). The problems here lie in high investment, inventory costs, working to capacity, running the organization, marketing. Although the introduction of operational research, network planning, etc. technically creates the conditions for entering a third phase of development, the organization and management style of the phase of differentiation prevent a company from doing so.

*Process production* makes the end-product strictly dependent on the technical installations. Production calls for high capital investment and the production-line installation can really only do the task for which it was designed. A new product requires an entirely new or considerably altered installation. Basically, production is secondary; the main concern is selling, finding and cultivating markets which are prepared to accept the end-product in one or only a few of its variations in large numbers at low prices.

Thanks to these new forms of production, Taylor's social ideas, namely that scientific management should bring about low cost prices, good wages, less need for physical effort, and a high degree of social security, have been more than realized.

Thanks to scientific management, an entrepreneur can now cope with a wider 'area': a larger enterprise, a more varied assortment of products, a larger market; in short, a greater complexity.

Of course, the organization itself now claims a large part of management's attention, which is focused upon the profitability and productivity of the production process. In a certain sense, contact with the market is lost as a result. Management is faced with marketing problems for the large series it has produced, while at the same time competition increases. Decreasing profit margins strengthen the need to give attention to internal efficiency and rationalization. Selling tends to become aggressive, and production pressures arise.

This also explains why the organized aspect of a company's internal structure, its formal organization, becomes so important. *The rational ordering of tasks, things, and processes becomes the organizational principle of the phase of differentiation. The integration of human activities is based on a formal hierarchy of authority and subordination.*

The phase of differentiation is in many ways the *antithesis* of the pioneer phase. It is rational instead of intuitive, mechanistic instead of organic, impersonal instead of personal, and based on organizational instead of situational principles.

### The Limits of the Second Phase

The differentiation that takes place in the second phase is an *essential condition* for a company if it is to function on a long-term basis on a larger scale and with greater complexity. Specific 'organs' have to be developed. Differentiation leads of necessity to a diversity of parts which have to be bound together and oriented towards the company's objective.

*In the second phase this is done through formalizing relationships and interconnections.* The informal and personal pioneer style, which continues for some time in the second phase, for instance in the style of management, ensures that the negative sides of the formalizing process do not become apparent immediately. *In a certain sense the informal organization makes it possible for the formal organization to exist.*

In some cases management realizes this and in policy-making gives particular emphasis to personal relationships within the organization. This kind of policy often grows out of a nostalgia for the earlier pioneering days. However, it is impossible for anachronistic elements of this kind to compensate sufficiently in the long run for the bureaucratic tendencies of the organization. People cannot, on the whole, be expected to solve the problems of the second phase by 'knowing each other personally'. *The relationship of company structure and company behaviour is then dysfunctional.*

Although at first scientific management brings clarity and order into the over-ripe pioneer situation, as growth continues, crisis phenomena begin to appear again, indicating a need for restructuring and orientation towards the next phase of development.

Some symptoms are:

*Rigidity:* The flexibility of the organization is drastically reduced through formalization and bureaucratization. This can become fatal if the dynamics of social and market conditions increase. The possibility of a rapidly adjustable policy is reduced.

*Coordination problems:* Through specialization and sub-specialization the departments draw further and further apart; they lose their understanding of each other's tasks and can no longer communicate because they no longer speak the same language. Small functional kingdoms with their own objectives and their own standards arise, and this makes coordination even more difficult. Personal assistants begin to act as 'liaison officers'; coordination committees are set up, but are little more than stopgaps. Finally, in an effort to solve the coordination problem, stronger managers are called for, which is a step back to the days of the pioneer. In addition, fewer and fewer top managers are produced by the system. The 'promotion ladders' up the various functional 'pillars' are so long that, by the time they have reached the right age, managers have become unsuitable for general management tasks as a result of their ingrained one-sidedness.

*Vertical communication problems:* Communication is disturbed not only between departments, but also vertically. It has already been pointed out that mangement in the second phase is autocratic and formal (lower levels are derived from higher levels; tasks are created through the downward delegation of authority). This style of direction and control, together with the organizational measures of unity of command and span of control, leads to an ever-increasing number of levels in the hierarchy. At the top, less and less is known about what is going on at the foot of the pyramid, and vice versa. The need for official distribution of information increases, and signalling data systems are established. In consequence, the number of indirect workers increases disproportionately, administration grows, and overhead costs rise. Because lower down in the organization people lose sight of the totality, they find it very difficult to bear responsibility for decisions of which the consequences lie outside their vision, and therefore problems are unloaded upwards. *Accumulation of responsibilities and overloading at the top emerge.*

*Staff–line problems:* The staff–line structure, which is built on the difference between advice and command, is found to be untenable in the long run. The expertise of the specialist staff means that their advice takes on the characteristics of command, while within their departments superior staff members acquire line authority. In addition, the line manager will often find himself giving advice to his colleagues. So the difference between staff and line becomes blurred because there seems to be no way out of this cul-de-sac. These problems will continue as long as the difference is formally maintained.

*Motivation:* One of the most serious problems is the decrease in motivation and individual productivity. The reasons for this are manifold: people feel that the work is void of intelligent content and therefore experience a kind of qualitative under-employment; they feel reduced to a number, a mere extension of the system; they no longer perceive the overall coherence and therefore find it very difficult to see any sense in their work. To identify with the objectives of the company becomes well-nigh impossible. The place of the motivating objective has been taken by a closely prescribed task which leaves little room for personal identification. Tasks are fixed and adjusted to technical requirements, and change insufficiently with the growing ability of the worker. He is forced to use an ever-decreasing proportion of his capacities the more his task is sharply defined on a long-term basis. He is taxed only with regard to speed and manual skill.

*Management by drives:* The more complicated the structure becomes in the second phase, the more top management attempts to solve its problems by initiating special drives such as efficiency drives, cost-cutting drives, productivity drives, etc. Without fundamental structural changes, these drives become less and less effective. The law of diminishing returns is in operation here: the result of management drives, expressed in the difference between expenditure and returns, becomes increasingly disproportionate until finally it becomes negative.

We have described the *second phase* as a causal deterministic model in the form of a 'pyramid' command organization, oriented mainly towards the expansion of the *technical system* as regards both production technology and organization techniques. As a result, top management devotes a large proportion of its time and attention to running the internal organization.

At first, the economic system did not grow in proportion to the development of the production process. The managers chosen by the shareholders behaved in the style of the owner–entrepreneur and found it very difficult to accustom themselves to the new specialists who were expected to 'manage through organization'. In production organizations the technical mentality of the engineer was dominant, and in commercial and service organizations the old merchant mentality remained in the foreground.

The specialists became advisers, left in a siding and having to sell their advice to the line organization which had developed as the line of command in the late stages of the pioneer phase. In the whole logically constructed model, with its network of minutely coordinated tasks and competencies, there was no room for co-pioneering and individual initiative.

Because of the depth of the organization (almost always more than five levels of management between top and foreman), the objectives of the company as a whole were no longer visible and recognizable below the third level. Instead, the subsystems had their own objectives, e.g. purchasing, production, administration, selling.

At shop- or office-manager level, people's horizons did not extend beyond their own workplace or office. In the model of the second phase a wider horizon was unnecessary. The relationship with people was instrumental; they were regarded as tools serving the achievement of objectives. Organization meant directing resources and people towards an objective.

For this to be achieved, human beings had to be reduced to organizational variables behaving in a predictable and rational way and reacting to financial stimuli. The peculiarity of this kind of financial motivation was that work satisfaction was achieved not through the actual work but through being able to spend one's wages away from one's place of work. There was no genuine satisfaction to be gained from the work in office or factory, since it was devoid of real content and meaning.

Whereas in the pioneer phase the emphasis was on objectives and direct control of these objectives, we now find that planning and organization come to the fore, though entirely within the technical system of the company.

The company's *external relations* also undergo an important change in the second phase. In the pioneer phase, external relations meant promoting customer ties and producing what had already been ordered. The customer was part of the system; he was a known factor who always wanted things done in a certain way. In the second phase the customer is no longer a known factor. The rationalization of the production process, brought about by an analysis of production techniques, has led to an enormous increase in productivity. Machines have to be used to a certain capacity and the production flow must not be interrupted. Mass-produced articles flow out of the factory and *have to* be sold to an *anonymous* market. This anonymous market is no longer included in the system of the company.

Instead of satisfying needs, the moment comes when it is essential to push products onto the market. The customer becomes an antagonist. Formerly the customer was given what he asked for. Now selling becomes aggressive and the customer is expected to adapt his wishes to what is offered.

In keeping with the second-phase attitude, this problem is also approached in a causal, analytical way, and a new specialization of sales promotion arises. Advertising and persuasion techniques place the consumer under pressure. *He is seen just as much as an instrument as is the internal work force*: he must not think or judge or choose for himself; he must just reach for the branded product at the command of his influenced subconscious. A new commandment appears: in the sweat of thy brow thou shalt consume!

The internal work force, oppressed by the impersonal organization model, increases the counter-pressure by organizing its power *against* the employer. The workers still cherish the old image of the entrepreneur pocketing all the profits as his personal property. And the consumer, bombarded with an avalanche of advertising and temptation, is today also beginning to found consumer organizations as a counter-force. Tension builds up on both fronts with the result that the 'image' of the employer becomes worse and worse, although he is himself no more thaṅ the recipient of an annual salary who works for objectives controlled by others.

The development from the first to the second phase can be summa-

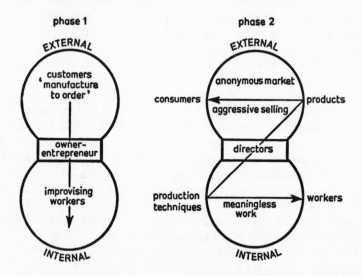

rized in the diagrams above. Workers and consumers stand at the end of an impersonal process of rational analysis and construction. Both are under the same kind of pressure. The strange thing is that it is the *same people* who feel oppressed by the same model both in and outside the work situation. Henry Ford was the first to see this connection, when in the twenties he decided to pay his workers a wage high enough to enable them to buy his cars.

The second phase was a historical answer to the over-ripe pioneer phase. The pioneer–entrepreneur consciously gives pre-eminence to economic achievement and wants as little trouble as possible from his organization. In the second phase, managing and running the organization become pre-eminent. The economic achievement gradually comes under pressure from the swelling stream of production or the demand for continuity of services.

In the second phase the economic system works against an ever-growing resistance coming from within and from outside in the form of decreasing motivation on the part of the worker and increasing mistrust on the part of the consumer: a kind of social law of diminishing returns.

In order to escape from the dilemma of the over-ripe second phase in which most companies find themselves today, the time seems to have arrived for a complete revision of the model. The new model would be a third phase in the development of enterprises in a society which is still an industrial one.

In Part V of this book an attempt is made to describe a post-industrial society involving quite different conditions.

## THE PHASE OF INTEGRATION

When one considers the phase of integration, the important thing is the development of the social subsystem and its integration with the already developed economic and technical subsystems. This leads to an entirely new concept of organization, which seeks to make it possible for every employee within the organization *to be able and willing to act intelligently* in the interest of the whole. This aim can be achieved only a step at a time.

### Requirements of the Third Phase

The third phase will have to give answers to the following problems of the second phase.

*Communications:* With regard to *internal* communications, the line of command is too long. The company objective becomes vague and is replaced by sub-objectives. Reporting upwards breaks down at every level; hardly any information is available at the top about what is really going on a few levels lower down. Horizontal interdepartmental communication is hampered by a specific deafness to the language and basic mentality of others. With regard to *external* communications, live contact with the customer or consumer is lost. The manufactured product or standardized packaged services, rather than the solution of problems for others, are in the foreground. Contact with the authorities and the trade unions has become antagonistic.

A model of the third phase will have to reveal new possibilities for internal and external relations.

*Process management:* The process of accumulating value between input and output runs falteringly through a number of departments. In each one a series of activities is concluded, and then the throughput is taken up again elsewhere and dealt with once more. The control of a process in time is satisfactory only where there is a static situation; as soon as varying or unrepeated activities are required, the throughput takes too long.

A model of the third phase will have to create the possibility of surveying, steering, and controlling all the different process flows as one great flexible, adaptable network.

*Rigidity and qualitative under-employment of personnel:* By the end of the second phase, integrated co-pioneership has been lost. Nevertheless, people still like to be master of their own house, i.e. subsystem, and to fight their own little battles. Changes are met with deep-seated resistance and are covertly or overtly sabotaged (the reorganization of a large administrative department was once nicknamed by the staff 'Operation fasten your seat-belt'). There is qualitative under-employment at almost every level; this means that people have far greater potential than they are permitted to use in their prescribed work. The resulting latent dissatisfaction is expressed in aggression or apathy. People have learnt to use their creativity *outside* their work, while they do their work for the most part 'with more brawn than brain'.

A model of the third phase will have to ensure that co-entrepreneuring, integrated with the total objective of the company, is extended right down to the level of the foreman and the worker. This means that:

— Alertness to change, intelligent participation in and thinking ahead about innovation, must become an inherent attitude in the whole of the social system. The organization itself will become a supporting function changing according to need.
— The superior-oriented vertical line system will have to be replaced by horizontal orientation towards those who come before and those who come next in the sequence of activities. This means that each person will be oriented towards the output of the processes and that there will be joint interest in maintaining an optimal throughput within the boundaries of policy and network planning.
— Management development and task enrichment must be able to raise the personnel resources of the company to ever-higher levels.
— Continual innovation becomes normal; its consequence is continual education.

— Finally, after the economic and technical subsystems have evolved, the *social subsystem must also be brought to maturity* and integrated into a totality consisting of all three subsystems. Only then will the enterprise have reached full maturity.

Having set out the requirements of a new, more highly differentiated model, we must show how the transition from the second to the third phase can be achieved.

If we start with the entrepreneurial initiative of the pioneer as our thesis, then scientific management is in a certain sense the antithesis, and a third step will have to be the synthesis: a synthesis of the positive elements of the first and second phases with the addition of a new element that makes this synthesis possible — the mature social subsystem.

For lack of a more suitable name, we term the third phase the *phase of integration*.

### An Overall Picture of the Third Phase

The phase of integration is based on a conception of the human being which rests on the conviction that every person can and wants to develop, and that real work satisfaction is connected with the question of whether any personal fulfilment can be achieved in the work situation.

Such a situation is approached when the organization allows individuals as well as groups to *act intelligently in accordance with the objectives of the totality*. For this the *objectives* must be known, and the resulting individual sub-objectives must be visible. Furthermore, there must be a *policy* known to everybody which depicts the style and the standards according to which the objectives are realized in the company concerned ('This is the way we do things here'). Finally, a continual training activity is required, to ensure that people can carry their new responsibilities.

With regard to the execution of tasks, efforts should be made to leave some of the planning (micro-planning) to groups and individuals. (No one-best-way regulations, but objectives with a margin for initiative and self-control.)

All this becomes possible if there is a change of attitude in management. As mechanization increases and islands of automation begin to form towards the end of the second phase, it becomes increasingly difficult for those at the top to cut Gordian knots by power of command. Complex problems are already increasingly solved by joint consultation among experts. These consultation structures, which were originally rather rigid both in their composition and in the time pattern of their meetings, have of necessity begun to take on a more flexible character in the form of task forces and problem-oriented consultation groups. The permanent committees have thus been relieved to a considerable extent.

Through all this the social system begins to unfold. But in order to achieve the integration of the economic, technical, and social subsystems, a form of organization is necessary which is significantly different from those of the previous phases.

The pioneer phase had a shallow, broad form of organization; the phase of differentiation had a deep, pyramid form, with the directing and controlling board of directors at the top (christmas-tree organization). And now, for reasons that will be dealt with in detail, the phase of integration demands a form of organization which we introduce here as the *clover-leaf organization*.

REFERENCE

1   DONNELLEY, R. G. The family business. *Harvard Business Review*, July/August, 1964.

## CHAPTER SIX

# The Clover-leaf Organization

In the clover-leaf organization the board no longer stands at the apex of a pyramid which it has to direct and control. It is now situated at the centre of the organization at the crossing-point of all the channels of information and communication, and surrounded by four subsystems which it guides by objectives and policies:

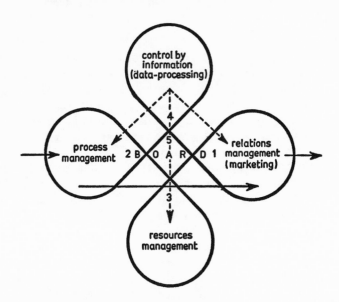

The clover-leaf organization is a special version of the input-output model already discussed:

Between input and output the *process* of accumulation of value takes place. This process is divided up into a network of consecutive activities which are interdependent as to their timing. The processes run 'horizontally' through a number of 'vertical' departments (see the columns in the diagram below), which provide the material basis (resources) for the process flow. These resources are primarily buildings, machinery, and people who are ready to carry out tasks.

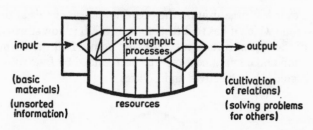

The *raison d'être* and the objective of a company as a structure within economic life as a whole is *economic achievement*: to answer a recognized need at a price the consumer is willing to pay. Working backwards from here we come to the question of what *processes* of value accumulation are necessary if this need is to be answered. And then we must ask ourselves what *resources* are required so that the processes can take place and be managed.

The extent and complexity of market exploration, process management, and resources management make it necessary to provide a separate place for controlling and adjusting by *information-processing*, as a service to the above three spheres of activity.

It is the task of the *board with its management team* to determine the objectives for the whole system as well as to integrate the processes with the necessary resources, assisted by a swift information system. The board's style of leadership with regard to its team of managers is no longer a matter of directing and controlling. It is rather to stimulate, to ask questions, to form judgements, and where necessary to take initiatives which can then be passed on to management.

Therefore the board must concern itself systematically with the above-mentioned functional spheres. It is supported in this by its own staff who go more closely into the questions raised and translate them into a language that can be understood in the functional area concerned. These areas, although not geographically separated, are *functionally* divided into relations management (including marketing), process management, resources management, and control by information management. These four functions are described below.

### 1. *Relations Management*

The management and cultivation of relations refers to both external and internal relations.

(a) *External relations:* The most important external relations are those involved in marketing. In marketing the true task of the entrepreneur reappears: the discovery of a consumer need and the answering of this need by *solving problems for others.* Marketing is the starting-point of entrepreneurial activity in the third phase. Everything else is derived from this primary task, and *is for the exclusive purpose of realizing it.*

Other external relations are associations with the authorities, with trade unions, and with other social systems. And, finally, there are the relations of a company with its shareholders and with the public in general (annual report).

(b) *Internal relations:* These are of a different character. With internal relations the important thing is the attitude towards and relationships between the employees. This is determined by the style of leadership. In the third phase, this style is characterized by the provision of objectives which people are helped to achieve while being left a margin (exception) for individual initiative and self-control.

Other aspects of internal relations will be discussed in connection with information-processing and distribution.

In addition to the preparation and formulation of policy, the sphere of internal relations includes the presentation of policy. It also includes the stimulation of internal innovation as a continual activity of all employees. This last aspect means that the cultivation of internal relations must be counted among the tasks with which the board itself is concerned.

### 2. *Process Management*

This function is directly linked with the cultivation of external relations. Between the input and the output of a company there are many activities of a material nature (production flows) and of a non-material nature (information flows) which follow one another in time. Both are accompanied by the costing processes of the internal economic system. With the help of network analysis, subsystems of these process flows can be contained in quantitative models (at least within the technical subsystem). Then subsystems can be joined together and through automation grow into larger units with flow production.

In all these material flow processes, and particularly in information flow processes, human beings are used (or become superfluous), and therefore process management becomes the crucial test for the genuine integration of the social system. Already in the draft stage of a production process, one can take account of the situations that will face those involved in the process.

In the resources organization of the second phase, people were organized *vertically* in a structure that was *superior-oriented*. Now emphasis is placed on the organization of people who are *work-oriented horizontally within the process flow*. In these horizontal consultation groups, people are oriented towards those who precede them and therefore influence their work, and towards those who are next in the process flow and whose work is influenced in turn.

In process control there is close interaction between the technical and the social system; one speaks in this connection (using the language of information-processing) of the 'hardware' of technical and the 'software' of social requirements and possibilities. Only the two together guarantee a truly functional process flow.

## 3. *Resources Management*

Resources of many kinds are necessary in order to make possible the process flow, which is determined in turn by external relations and directed towards the output. The procurement, management, and disposal of these resources at the right place, in the right amounts, and also at the right time, comprise a third, quite differently focused subsystem in a firm.

Resources management (this brief expression covers all the above-mentioned functions in the whole company) is a *service* function. (Marketing and process management are primary functions; resources management and information-processing are service functions.)

In the terminology of the old second-phase organization, resources management can be described as including the departments of finance, administration, organization, personnel, research and development, management development, and material supplies. Looked at like this, as an *inventory* of differentiated functions, it is indeed a motley collection!

However, the whole function can also be described as follows: *the provision of resources for a goal-directed organization, and the creation*

*of efficient and lasting collaboration among people working towards a
common goal.*

Therefore the organization of resources will differ in a number of
important points from the old departmental organization of the second
phase (in which resources management and process control all came
under the same management). Now 'resources' still comprises material
resources, such as capital, buildings, machinery, and so on, but it also
includes non-material resources, i.e. people and the total know-how
of a company.

This know-how consists partly of the knowledge and skills of *all* the
people in a company, and partly of the possession of inherent knowledge, patents, etc., which are fixed. The two together constitute the
*non-material resources* of the company. In the third phase, these
resources are more important than money or capital goods. Given
aware and potential non-material resources, money and goods can be
acquired, whereas the opposite is possible only in part.

It is an important task of the board to keep watch over the three
functional areas discussed so far, so that they can develop in a balanced
way. In this the board's first care must be for *marketing and for the
development of the company's non-material resources.* For practical
reasons it will often be necessary within the resources management
function to deal with the non-human and the human resources under
separate managements. This will certainly be the case for the early
period of the third phase.

### 4. *Information Management*

Control by means of information-processing has grown quantitatively
and qualitatively to such a degree in the third phase that it warrants a
completely separate subsystem. It is therefore given a place as one of
the leaflets of the clover-leaf organization.

Like a nervous system which permeates the whole organism but has
its own centre, it receives its policy direct from the board. The task of
this organ is to send every piece of information to the place where it is
required so that those concerned can act intelligently in the interest of
the whole company. This service function is manifested in the question:
Who needs what information in what form and at what moment in
order to be able to carry on with his work undisturbed?

Its job is to *distribute information* in a form which is useful for
everybody as regards content, frequency, and intelligibility. There are
many temptations, for those who possess information have power over

others. A central information-processing apparatus could lead, in the style of the second phase, to a stricter manipulation of people by making them entirely dependent on short-term orders whose range of influence they cannot oversee.

An information-processing centre can lead either to an Orwellian nightmare and thus the death of the non-material resources, or to a greater capacity for responsibility among employees by giving them the information necessary to control the achievement of objectives. In order to bring about the latter, as many people as possible must participate in *preparing* the external objectives (*what* is to be achieved?) and the internal policies (*how* is it to be achieved?). It is the responsibility of the board to define the chosen objectives and the chosen policies in such a form that at all levels *standards* can emerge for the process flows and resources management. And it is the task of the information centre to use the assembling, processing, and distribution of information to enable people individually and in groups to adjust and control, independently, within the framework of the defined standards. In this way it becomes possible for everyone to act intelligently within the context of the overall objectives.

The information-processing organ in the narrow sense is a service of such objectivity that its function could be carried out by an outside organization. In other words, the computer need not be within the company at all; often it would be sufficient (and cheaper) to buy computer time elsewhere. However, the software, the actual information programs, can be compiled only within the company itself. They are the result of the relevant requirements and of the policies of information distribution. Their elaboration requires the completely open collaboration of every employee.

The information-processing centre will have a department concerned with *external functions*, primarily *marketing research*, and it will have an *internal department* serving the *administrative*, financial, and management functions. The part of the internal department serving *process management* will have to collaborate with the engineers.

Collaboration, mutual consultation, and an attitude of service, these are the characteristics of the information-processing system.

When a clover-leaf organization is created, one and the same activity will take place in separate geographical areas. This will be the case in the first place in the execution of production and economic control, but also in connection with sales, research, etc. In a group working together in a specific geographical area, part of the process management and

The design and introduction of an information system for a machine factory (Koninklijke Machinefabriek Stork) by G. Akos (from the journal *Informatie*, February 1969)

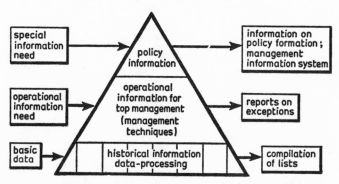

System philosophy:

The first step was to formulate a philosophy, a system philosophy, on which to base the design. In order to evolve this philosophy, reference was made to the well-known information triangle (see diagram above).

There are three distinct phases in the development of computer use in the administrative sphere, or rather in the management sphere.

In the first phase (processing of parts) the isolated parts of the administration are automated. There is hardly any hint of an integration of these parts. The information obtained refers to the past, to the fixing of historical data.

In the second phase more emphasis is given to the management aspect. Information obtained in this phase must enable management to influence events in the company and take corrective action in good time in cases of deviation from the set standards (management by exception). This is made possible through the use of modern management techniques.

The third phase is known as the management information system. It is characterized by a high degree of integration in which not only the operations (short-term decisions) but also the policies (long-term decisions) of management are supported by the information system.

resources management will take place, and part of the controlling information will be available. These constitute the operational units which are tuned to one another through the objectives and the joint policies.

Management of more sizeable units in a company will in future have to be carried out by a small management team consisting of:

— the manager of the material resources of the unit (previously a superior in the hierarchy)
— the process manager (previously staff department organization)

— the manager of human resources development (previously the personnel manager).

In such an organization, each of these three functionaries is linked with the appropriate directors in charge of resources, processes, and relations, and if necessary each is supported by an office staff of his own.

The information-processing centre has its own more mobile collectors of information who as 'task forces' collaborate with these teams.

If it becomes necessary to find a *primus inter pares* the choice should fall on the man in charge of processes.

## The Board

The board is situated at the centre, in the heart of the clover leaf. Instead of being at the top of a pyramid in splendid isolation, it is now placed at the point where all the channels of communication cross, where it can selectively guide, encourage, stimulate, ask questions, and give support. Such a board must function as a team whereby it is understood that its members must have *sufficient proficiency and interest in* the four main subsystems to ensure that they can form balanced judgements and take corrective action as well as initiate and innovate.

A team of this kind is always person-oriented in its composition. If for various reasons one of the functions is weakly represented on the board, a more specialized deputy director can give support. In the picture of the third phase there is no longer room for a director of production, a director of finance or sales, or any other director who is exclusively concerned with a single function.

The *board as a team* determines the external objectives of the company and also the internal policies (the way in which the objectives are to be achieved). This requires *long-term strategic thinking*, which takes into account possible developments in the economic, technical, and social fields.

If a company is more like a group, with several parent and subsidiary companies, then there are a number of further tasks for the group board, namely the cultivation and safeguarding of aspects of policy within the functional areas.

Though the group board will function as a team, each of its members will have to take responsibility for a certain aspect of policy. This member will then provide for the rest of the team an entrance to that aspect. If these aspects are distributed so as to give each member of the team tasks relating to more than one functional area, this will mean that each member will always have to consult another in connection with his own policy considerations. Policy-making comes about by posing activating questions to parts of the group and by assessing the proposals that come from the boards of the individual companies and from the group's staff departments.

At the level below, unit or company boards are established like the boards of independent companies, with the understanding that their policy-making will be derived from that of the group board. However, they do in fact participate in policy-making at group level through submitting proposals.

The creation of production organizations with exclusively supervisory management impoverishes the group, because in units concerned only with production the human resources are not developed.

In all cases the primary task of a board is *to manage innovation and development*.

## CHAPTER SEVEN

# From the Second Phase
# of Development to the Third

Having given an overall picture of the model of a third phase, which for the moment is the final objective of change, we can now proceed to discuss how a company which has reached the limits of the second phase can grow towards this model. Numerous *ad hoc* measures, designed to solve problems of a particular area or part, already point in a fragmentary way to the new model, *but without the totality of this model they remain disconnected emergency measures.*

Thus the social system has been under scrutiny ever since the beginning of the human relations movement. First came the Hawthorne inquiry (1924-33). This resulted in a crumbling of the belief in *homo economicus.* Man does not live by bread alone; he also has psychological needs associated with recognition, attention, and friendship.

The discovery of satisfiers and dissatisfiers was another step. Many of the measures introduced to meet psychological needs turned out to be dissatisfiers, i.e. if they were *absent* there was dissatisfaction and aggressiveness, but if they were introduced the mere fact of their existence did not lead to any lasting satisfaction either. For instance, if there are no decent toilets or canteens, or if manners in general are bad or holiday arrangements are poor, the result is dissatisfaction. But any improvements introduced in these matters soon come to be taken for granted and do not lead to better work motivation.

True satisfiers, bringing long-lasting motivation, are to be found in the sphere of psychological needs, the most important being self-realization, development, and responsibility in one's work. The *work situation* itself becomes the new development area of the social system.

Peter Drucker[1] gave great impetus to this in the fifties with his 'management by objectives', which goes hand in hand with training and assistance. Drucker was the first to make the courageous statement: 'Self-control is always more efficient than control from outside.'

However, for self-control or evaluation of one's own work a number of conditions are necessary, both of a material kind (feedback of information, clearly stated standards, the possibility of improving performance) and of a kind involving characterological and situational variables. Motivation for self-control, and thus for improvement and innovation, functions if the environment as it is manifested both in the style of leadership and in the organizational model challenges the inherent capacities as well as the latent faculties which can be developed in people. In other words, satisfiers will not develop within the social system unless the company aims at maximum cultivation of existing and latent psychological resources.

Here we may introduce a side issue. The increased availability of modern management techniques and tools, such as process control through network planning, information-processing through linear programming, optimization of stock control, minimization of waiting-periods, marketing mix, research, and so on, means that there could be a *renaissance of the second phase* in which the social system would be excluded as far as possible. This tendency is increased by many mergers, which often mean that independent medium-sized companies with their own totality of management problems are downgraded to mere production or service units, producing only one group of articles or giving only one kind of service and left with partial management. They are directed from the outside by remote control, and the unit has no insight into or say on what is happening. If, in addition, all processes, standards, and margins of tolerance are dictated from outside, then this means killing the goose that laid the golden eggs. The goose that lays the golden eggs is the creative potential of the whole of the social system. In cases like this it will be seen that those who have a development potential will leave the company because their work is increasingly without meaning or content. At most they will be able to improvise a little to counteract the faults of the system and keep it going.

If inherent human potential is not given an important place elsewhere in the company, a trend like the above will mean:

— that the opportunity to develop managerial abilities in practice will disappear
— that those who can provide intelligent information will disappear from the working processes.

The alternative to this trend is to create a central service organ for information distribution, making data available everywhere, and in addition to set up localized control of the process flow within certain standards.

The above-mentioned trend must not be confused with a healthy shrinkage of departments in which information-processing tasks that are automatic anyway can quite justifiably be taken over by computers. The computer can do very beneficial work. Even in decentralized parts of the total organization it creates new possibilities of bringing relevant information to the right place at the very moment when it is required by individuals or groups for the evaluation of their achievements. Thus the question that must then be asked constantly throughout the whole organization is: How far can I go with my programming when I give people tasks? How much freedom can I give them for self-control?

Rigid norms make people dependent and turn them into automata. Moreover, they increase the vulnerability of the process flow to stoppages, which can only be corrected centrally with great losses in the total operation. In contrast, norms setting certain standards call upon the special skills and the initiative of the individual to make adjustments *himself*, to prevent stoppages before they occur and keep the process going.

Elliott Jaques[2] has pointed out the important distinction between 'prescribed' and 'discretionary' work. In doing prescribed work a man is treated as a part of a machine. But as a means of production man is too valuable for this, so as soon as possible machines should take over all prescribed work. Man is in his proper place doing discretionary work — work that gives him freedom of action and attaches a value to his task. In the discretionary part of the work an opportunity is created for the motivation to solve problems.

The more machines take over the prescribed work, the more it will become necessary to develop the latent human resources of the company at all levels. Experience has shown that we can always assume that there is *much more to be developed in a man than his superior would have believed.*

But lack of knowledge about the possibilities and methods of developing people — so that they can become 'founts of wisdom', able to react far more flexibly than any programme — will tend to promote the renaissance of the second phase. Talking to people who have a rather rigid approach and who think quantitatively, one is aware of their fear of including that elusive product 'man' in their plans; and where they cannot do without him he must be given as little freedom as possible. So it will be necessary for top management to balance these tendencies. It can do this if it regards marketing and the creation of non-material capital as its primary function. Having touched upon this problem of a renaissance of the second phase, we can now return to the main theme.

We have pointed out that towards the end of the second phase a number of third-phase problems already become apparent and that *ad hoc* measures to cope with them also begin to appear, though without an all-embracing conceptual model. This applies to the human being as a psychological subject, and to some parts of process control, information-processing, and marketing techniques; resources management also receives new possibilities of optimization. As we have seen, there is a danger of applying these fragmentary new techniques within the organizational model of the second phase; when this happens, certain negative aspects of the model are increased even though there are short-term economic advantages.

We shall now describe a way of realizing the third phase without falling into such traps.

The most important step is to *prepare the social system for its new tasks well in advance,* and to let *the social system itself take part* in this planned innovation so that through this activity it can *develop the skills* necessary for functioning in the new situation.

If this strategy of 'planned change' is carried through properly, it constitutes a challenge for the best and a learning experience for the others. New managers come to the fore during the process of change. They notice that effort is rewarded with greater responsibility. Others will doubtless fall behind at first, but experience has shown that they can be useful in other positions where they can grow further at their own speed. And when 'the group' is established as a source of innovation, many people, who if working alone would offer resistance to change, are given the opportunity of developing new capacities within the group.

Part IV discusses in more detail the techniques of planned change, also called organizational development. The tasks and roles of external advisers in such a process are examined as well.

The path from the second to the third phase, which is outlined now, is not absolute, though the step described first will probably always have to be the first taken; the following ones can be taken in a different order, depending on the situation. It is important to leave much of the initiative to the working groups appointed for the planned change. In practice one's own plan usually works better than any ideal plan imposed from outside.

## THE TOP MANAGEMENT TEAM

The *first step* in going from the second phase of development to the third is the formation of the *top management team*. We shall go later into the division of tasks within the board itself. At present we are concerned with the first 'ring', comprising the board and the top management level; in some cases this level will consist of assistant directors, and in others of heads of functional 'columns' (purchasing, production, etc.).

It is most important that the *third phase should begin at the top* and not on the shop floor at the foot of the pyramid, or anywhere in the middle, because this top management team must set an example by using the new style of joint consultation. This is where life must be given to the new policies and the new form of organization, first in ideas and then in concrete plans.

The board must commit itself to discussing important problems with the top management team. Before taking decisions, the board must give the members of the team an opportunity to collect facts and figures about a problem and to form their own opinion; and the opinions expressed by the team must be taken into account when decisions are made. In this way the members of the top management team participate in problems that lie outside their own 'column'; they are thus educated towards general entrepreneurial activity and learn to assess and compare factors relevant to different subsystems.

Not until an open and alert top management team has arisen can this process of management by participation in decision-making be introduced lower down.

For this, the system of what Likert has called 'linking pins' comes into being (see diagram below). Down to three and sometimes even four levels of management below the board, every person is included in one ring consisting of his colleagues and his manager, and in another consisting of his subordinates with himself as head.

In this chain of interlocking rings, the information line from the top

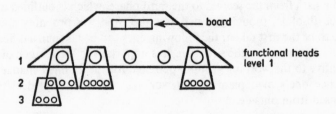

downwards can function in an entirely new way. The problems discussed by top management at Level 1 in their own ring are given the form of departmental tasks with a view of the place of each task within the totality of the whole organization. At the next management level the tasks of each sub-department are seen in their relationship to the work of the whole department. And this must be continued downwards.

A person at a certain management level is always *involved* in the considerations and problems of his *superior*. This widening of horizons is a part of management development. It shows that a new style of management is beginning to work its way downwards from the top. If a development of this kind were to be started in the middle of the hierarchy instead of at the top, it would be noticed that those who had been 'converted' would find themselves up against a brick wall with regard to their immediate superiors.

In the second phase, the flow of information from the bottom upwards served the control of results. It may generally be assumed, however, that this flow of information functioned even less well than that from the top downward.

But with the interlocking rings this flow is given a new impetus. In a discussion within a certain ring a task is given to a department (in the light of the chosen objectives of the whole company) in the form of a problem. How can we solve this problem? Who must do what, and in what sequence and within what time-limit?

Let us suppose that a department has three sub-departments, A, B, and C, each of which will have to do a part of the work consecutively, for example: A, development; B, trial manufacture; C, manufacture. Thus the tasks are set, and at the next meeting the questions asked are whether A can accomplish the necessary development in four months, whether B can complete the trial manufacture in six months, and whether C can be ready in ten months to start production (space, machines, people). At this second meeting an attempt is made to achieve the result, if possible, that A, B, and C accept their tasks as subcontractors.

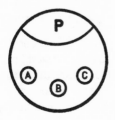

In the following weekly meetings the only question is: Is there anything special to report? If there is nothing, then the item concerned has been dealt with. *Difficulties* only are reported upwards, i.e. if the target has *not* been reached. If the target is reached, this is a matter only for the level of management concerned; only trouble is reported upwards.

Now the question is whether P, in his position and with his budget, can solve the problem. If the answer is yes, then the problem can and must be solved at that level. If the answer is no, then P must raise the matter with the top management team, because now the whole project is threatened and an alternative decision or a change in timing must be made.

This form of reporting is called management by exception. Normal matters are the responsibility of the person concerned. He reports only *disturbances* to his superiors, not in order to receive 'punishment', but so that he can be given *help and support* by a higher level of management in a situation which cannot be mastered at his own level with the available resources. Thus management by exception belongs to a system which includes a top management team and interlocking rings. A new rule of thumb is formulated: if a matter can be attended to at a certain level, the boss *may not* look into it unless he is asked to do so.

It is clear that this step is made still within the organization model of the second phase. But already a number of future crucial areas are beginning their embryonic development. Because emphasis is given to dependence on one another in time sequences, one becomes aware of the *first beginnings of a process organization.*

A *new style of management,* based on teamwork and real delegation of tasks accompanied by a willingness to give help and assistance when asked, sets in motion the development of independence and an entrepreneurial attitude at every level. To go through these experiences is essential if at a later stage the complete third phase is to be accomplished.

## ORGANIZATION AT SHOP-FLOOR LEVEL

While the system of interlocking rings is still in its initial stages, a beginning can also be made at the lowest level. A. H. Bos summarized this process as 'knitting' the organization together.

The second-phase organization does not include teams at lower levels in its philosophy. It is concerned only with the tasks of individuals. If these become too large, they are divided into sub-tasks to be carried out at the next level down. The link between these sub-tasks lies at the level above and is laid down either by a staff department or by outside consultants. The classic example is the assembly belt. This requires not a team of workers but a series of individuals, and the relationship between these individuals (the so-called coordination) is laid down by the work-study engineer. There is nothing to talk about in relation to the work itself, so the need for conversation is usually diverted to negative comments about the management.

The full responsibility for coordination at worker level rests with the supervisors, who as a result tend to direct their attention primarily 'downwards'. The same applies to those on the next level of management, whose task it is to coordinate the supervisors. As a result, the second phase acquires an autocratic and top-heavy style. An organization of this kind literally has 'frayed edges'. At the lowest level there is really no cohesion to speak of, because nobody is responsible for this cohesion. Therefore people have the feeling of not belonging. The resulting symptoms have already been described in connection with the sickening of the second phase.

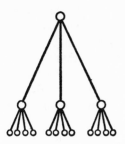

This 'unravelling' process tends to continue within. The foremen, too, begin to feel alienated and start organizing themselves in unions in order to determine their position *vis-à-vis* higher management, and so on. The same process can be observed in offices and laboratories.

In the third phase, therefore, one of the prime concerns is to 'knit up' the unravelled organization at the lowest level. This means the formation of horizontal groups which can be given responsibility for a number of coordinating functions relating to the division of tasks within the group as such: elements of micro-planning and self-control, trouble-shooting, adjustment activities, regulating information, rotation of jobs and mutual instruction, cleaning the department, innovation, etc.

It is interesting that this 'knitting' process also continues inwardly. When at the shop-floor level a certain horizontal responsibility (for the relationship between tasks) emerges, the foremen no longer have to turn all their attention 'downwards'. They have more time to concentrate on coordination between departments. This leads to new possibilities of integrating staff departments. These were originally offshoots of the supervisory level which they constantly threatened to undermine. When the company is restructured from the bottom upwards in this way, it is found that in the long run fewer management levels are required, so that the staff departments acquire a new role of giving answers to questions from below rather than handing out instructions from above.

What has been said shows that what matters is to achieve job enlargement (elsewhere called work-structuring) at the lowest level, with the aim of finding complete jobs for individuals, or better still for teams, which have an obvious relevance for the whole work task. Such jobs are created when they include a certain amount of planning as well as execution and control. Depending on the nature of the work process, attempts must be made to find elements of planning which can be given back to the group, as well as possibilities of self-control with regard to quality and time-keeping.

Furthermore, it is important that the work of each group should be a coherent whole. In administration or production, where can we find the natural units which are clearly visible steps in the process? With a small amount of training, a group can often be given responsibility for such a section of activities instead of having to do disconnected pieces of work after the manner of the assembly line.

Although, in the second phase, increases in productivity are achieved through improvements in work techniques by separating planning, execution, and control, it is found that in the third phase, when these are brought together again, the increased motivation of the people involved leads to a new increase in productivity.

In the fifties the mistake was often made of regarding job enlargement at the shop-floor and foreman level as the only change necessary. But when the initial success had become considerably diluted within two years, it became obvious that at higher levels nothing much had changed. Therefore job enlargement is always a second or third step on the path to an integrated organization model.

ESTABLISHING THE PROCESS ORGANIZATION

One of the next steps, which must come about as a result of thorough study by groups of management, is the separation of the process organization from the resources organization.

The organization and maintenance of resources calls for a mentality that cares for things that are lasting. This permanence is manifest in buildings and machines, but also in people and in a certain style of procedures and regulations. We hope we will not be misunderstood if we call this the 'female' caring aspect of the company. It requires constant attention, steadiness, and thrift, which could of course also turn into rigid conservatism.

The procuring, maintenance, and organization of resources constitute a category of functions quite different from that of managing the processes which flow through the resources organization. Organizing the process streams calls for a definitely dynamic category of functions. It requires the supervision of the streams which flow through all the subsystems between input and output. Furthermore, the activities of the subsystems must be held in balance both quantitatively and qualitatively. Finally, it demands the regulation and mastery of the time element. For the latter it is appropriate to think in clockwork and cybernetic systems; the totality can be made visible with the help of network analysis. More is said about this in the appendix. Here it is important to obtain a clear picture of the cooperation required between those who *provide and take care of* the resources and those who *use* them.

The central function of process management is to study and chart all processes and procedures (network techniques are better than staff diagrams for making more complex processes visible). The second function is to ascertain whether the existing process flows are logical and efficient. For instance, administrative files, which often make the most astonishing journeys for the sake of collecting 'prestige' signatures, can be redirected along more logical routes. But in production departments, too, one comes across quite remarkable irrelevancies which have usually arisen in exceptional situations and subsequently become sacrosanct. It is obvious that the moment must come when the central organ of process management is given authority to find and introduce completely new paths and methods.

If several activities pass through one and the same geographical spot, it becomes obvious that priorities have to be established on the basis of central knowledge of the effects of intervals in the processes. It is now a matter of fair play between the resources manager, who is in charge of buildings, machines, and people, and the processes manager, who works alongside him and knows what consequences the sequence of processes etc. will have going through a number of such geographical subsystems. The railway system can illustrate this point: the time-table operator has to collaborate with a number of station masters who have the necessary resources for receiving and dispatching trains.

The principle of this form of cooperation lies in the fact that in addition to a fixed schedule, with sufficient tolerance to allow for minor corrections to be carried out at lower levels, there must be a point from which larger breakdowns can be seen in their wider context and rapidly corrected.

Something of Taylor's old ideas about a speed boss and a maintenance boss has appeared once more, but this time in a more sensible form because it is not possible to view the situation in its totality from a higher position. The resources organization can be allowed by and large to keep the old organizational structure of the second phase, though with a consultation system of interlocking rings; the process organization will also have to be given a structure with levels; both will have opposite-number colleagues at every level, to ensure that through their cooperation optimal performance will be achieved. This means that on all important levels two functional bosses will collaborate in achieving the best possible utilization of resources and an understanding of the optimal throughput of the whole system.

The strategic task of the central process organization is the general planning of throughput processes whereby it has to determine the decision margins granted to lower levels. Its second, tactical task is the supervision of the decision margins and their correction if they are exceeded owing to unforeseen circumstances.

Particularly at the very lowest levels there must be sufficient scope to allow workers and foremen to make their own judgements, to find their own compromises, and to seek the best combinations within the set margins. If lower management loses control of processes at the worker and foreman level, the process manager of the department can take matters in hand within his own discretion margin, or even consult the central process organization. It will usually be possible to keep detailed information concerning the various possibilities of process regulation within the department concerned, as long as block achievements are known to the process organization centre. This avoids overloading the centre with too many variables.

The central organization will also have to take action if one of the subsystems falls below its standards, since the following subsystems will have to be warned so that they can revise their process planning.

In contrast to this, the second phase thought in terms of fixed tasks with as little leeway as possible. The top-to-bottom line of command in the second phase, with its management by task assignment, is too narrow. In such a situation all *initiatives* have to come from the top, and all *stoppages* are reported back to the top. As a result, top management is overloaded with two kinds of task at the same time, while those lower down are not really occupied.

A healthy process organization will have to find the happy medium between margins which are too narrow (economically efficient as long as there are no stoppages) and margins which are too wide (interim storage too great and corrections too difficult).

This form of organization means for the social system a further step on the road towards the ability to act intelligently in the context of common objectives.

## FEDERAL DECENTRALIZATION

It is necessary to deal with a further important step in the transition from the second to the third phase. This is the *federal structuring* of the organization, which could also be called federal decentralization.

Through the establishment of interlocking rings, an open consultation structure has come into being; at the same time, events within the organization have become transparent as a result of process analysis and organized process management. Now it is possible and indeed desirable to give certain parts of the organization greater independence. The criterion for making a unit autonomous is its *objective*, which must be a more or less self-contained and meaningful totality, experienced and recognized as such by those who work in the unit.

There is a difference between *functional* and *federal* units.

In the second phase, the company is divided into functional units such as sales, production, administration, production planning, etc. The objectives of these functional units are derived from the objectives of the company as a whole. Some units, such as sales and production, are close to the overall objectives of the company, but others move further and further away. The further they move from the original primary objectives through the splitting-off of sub-tasks, the less inspiring these objectives become. They are then tempted to make their own objectives to give themselves status and influence. These objectives are reached by making artificial bottlenecks in the process flow, or being difficult in consultations.

Federal units, on the other hand, have primary objectives, for instance their own product and/or their own share of the profits. A federal unit can function properly only if it is in possession of the main management functions. This implies the *decentralization* of functional departments such as administration, planning, personnel, etc.

The first need for federal decentralization arises when medium-sized companies grow larger. The increasing depth of the line hierarchy makes it impossible for the overall objectives of the company to be experienced below the third level from the top. Communication upwards also becomes increasingly blocked. The top no longer knows what is really going on at the lower levels.

It is known from experience that the maximum workable depth for an organization, *even* one with a system of interlocking rings, is three levels of management below the top level; so it is obvious that the time must come when the company has to be split into a number of federal autonomous units of a size that *can be run with a maximum of three levels of management* (see diagram).

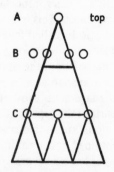

Below the top (A) a number of functional central organs remain (B), which are directly connected with the board or with the level of deputy directors. These could be, for example: central purchasing, central production planning, central administration, central personnel department, central sales promotion.

The production department can then be split into three units. Each unit will have a clear, rounded-off objective, its own budget, and the obligation to supply the following unit on the basis of internal price agreements. The objective of one of these units could be one complete step in the production process, for instance casting, machining, or assembly. Or the objective could be to cater for one complete section of the market, for example producing domestic furniture, or hospital furnishings. Or certain groups of products could be combined and separated from other groups (so-called departmentalization).

The *criterion* is that the unit must not again be allowed to grow so large that it would need more than the three levels of management. In the event of its becoming too broad or too deep, the unit could be split into two parallel units. However, if the interlocking-ring system functions and the job enlargement and enrichment measures have been successful, then far larger units can in fact be managed with fewer management levels.

The managers at level C, who are the new heads of the units, will have a number of assistants under them who are linked to their own central offices. In the organization chart they can be shown underneath the unit manager; but functionally they come under their central department. Thus the administration of the unit will have to fit into the general administration system, receiving its policy from the centre. So the unit administrator has two superiors, one hierarchical and one functional. If the organization is healthy and if it has an open consultation system, this should not give rise to any difficulties.

Other possibilities would be the creation of an autonomous machine factory, or a sales office, or a training centre, and so on. The company then gradually takes on the characteristics of a group. Intercommercialization usually develops between the parent company and the federal units: supplies change hands internally at true market prices and no longer at special internal prices. The units are authorized to buy from or sell to third parties if this can be done more favourably outside the group than within it. Though it does not usually happen on a large scale, internal commercialization is an important stimulus to cost consciousness and a challenge to be really enterprising.

Federal decentralization opens the door for greater freedom and independence. It requires a greater degree of *maturity* in those concerned and presupposes that they possess a fair degree of *social skill*. The central top management will still be responsible for a certain number of policy decisions. It can further the working of this organization form by systematically promoting and transferring promising managers throughout the organization.

DEVELOPING THE COMMERCIAL FUNCTION

Another activity to be fully developed is the *commercial function*.

In the pioneer phase, this primary function was still person-oriented. One knew the customer's face, his moods, his wishes. The primary commercial objective of the company was achieved by means of personal customer relations and service. This lasted longest in the capital goods industry.

In the second phase, with its emphasis on rational production techniques and large series, the product flows off the assembly belt with relentless regularity. To *sell* this product now becomes the great problem, and *price competitiveness* the weapon. The typical salesman thinks in terms of 'his' product. Sitting in a train, the salesman of electric kettles will glance at every village flashing by, estimating how many kettles he could sell there. *Thinking in terms of the manufactured product and of price competition* is characteristic of the second phase. *Sales promotion* and action plans for the market are the watchword.

In the third phase, attention hitherto glued to the product must now turn primarily to the environment, the 'universe' of the system.

Once again 'enterprise' means *solving the problems of others*. For this purpose, products are only incidental. If they do happen to be required, it is still not essential to produce them oneself. In order to distinguish it from sales promotion with its emphasis on the product, we use the term *marketing* for this new attitude, which is primarily concerned with providing a service for others. Since the word marketing has many meanings in recent literature, it is important at this point to define what we mean by it in this book.

With marketing, one's train of thought starts with the purchaser or consumer. In the second phase, the housewife wishing to prepare a meal was expected to do her shopping at the *ends of various production lines*: butcher, baker, grocer, greengrocer.

But now the modern *supermarket* thinks from the point of view of the customer. It unites the end-points of various production lines in one place. It asks what amounts, what packaging, what method of payment, what place, and what time will be helpful to the customer. Service competition comes into the foreground, and different people require and receive different kinds of service. A discount store has as much right to exist as a specialist shop with good service.

'All-in' service is becoming more and more important, provided by an organization which quite possibly accounts for only a part of this service with its own products. Like the supermarket with its self-service for the housewife, the engineering company has come into being to serve those who require investment goods. For instance, a developing country might require 'turn-key' projects such as a complete harbour installation with dredgers, docks, buildings, cranes, and even a telephone switchboard together with training for the necessary staff. A dredger company or a machine factory could equally well undertake the whole project, carrying out what it could not do itself in association with others.

*Marketing* calls for branch despecialization where consumer goods are concerned, and cooperation in the field of capital goods. *Marketing means solving problems for others.* This is the mentality that permeates the whole enterprise.

Where, in the second phase, profits decrease because of ever-increasing price competition, real service leads once more to a rising profit margin. *In the third phase the emphasis moves from low production costs to low distribution costs,* combined with service to the consumer. The development of the internal social system in the phase of integration is accompanied by increased awareness of changes in the social field outside the company.

Not only employees but also consumers have come of age. They no longer want to be treated like simpletons to be hoodwinked with slick slogans and advertising tricks. They have become price conscious, not only with regard to the lowness of prices but also with regard to the relation between price, quality, and service. They wish to make their own choice. The mature consumer has the right to:

— determine his own needs
— choose freely the product he wants
— be informed about the quality and properties of the product.

The second phase sought to deprive the consumer of just these three rights or to conceal information by means of advertising campaigns. The true marketing of the third phase starts with honest information about the quality and properties of the product, avoiding monopoly situations and 'hidden persuasion'. Where possible, marketing will strive for joint consultation with the consumer. This means that a representative consumer organization would be of advantage to management. *The future lies in joint consultation wherever possible, and not in coercing people to purchase articles or services which they do not really require.*

Just as it was difficult for the pioneer to make the transition from customers to an anonymous market, so that he often fell behind with his sales techniques, so it is now difficult for the second phase to take the step from price competition to service competition. The same is true of other aspects of the third phase: long-term thinking is constantly being inhibited by short-term decisions and advantages: 'the present is gobbling up the future'.

The phase of integration requires a management which can think strategically in terms of marketing, technical development, and the application of science. Within this strategy it can be confronted with difficult policy decisions, for instance if a new technique has been devised. The product of the moment, an answer to a definite consumer need, could then become superfluous. The question requiring decision would be: Shall we be loyal to the product or to the new technique?

For example, in the precision industries, watchmakers have been confronted for several years now with the advent of the electronic wrist watch. This has already appeared on the market, but it is as yet too expensive to compete with mechanical watches. However, in a few years' time these watches will be available for less than £10. They need no winding and run for a year very accurately on a cheap battery. What should the manufacturers of mechanical watches do? Some have decided to collaborate with the electronics industries; others have started to apply their precision know-how to other mechanical precision products.

Strategic decisions of this kind determine the lot of many employees. An accurate analysis of the many variables affecting the decision can be helpful. Joint consultation can also clarify certain aspects of the decision. The final decision can only be made by a small group, *who then do all they can to implement it*, supported by the confidence of a number of management levels who fully participate in the implementation of the decision.

## SIX TASKS OF MANAGEMENT AND THEIR INTEGRATION

In the transition from the second to the third phase, the measures described above have gradually led to the creation of a number of management tasks.

For the pioneer phase the economic *choice of objectives* was the basis of all activities, and the *control* of these objectives was effected by the way in which the environment reacted to the activities of the pioneer company.

In the phase during which scientific management developed, the setting of objectives and their control continued to take place, but were no longer directly perceived by the majority of workers. New in the second phase is the development of systematic *planning* and carefully thought-out, logical, though static, *organization*.

Not until the third phase is the actual *policy* task systematically developed. Clear policies make it possible to give a certain margin of discretion for solving problems in accordance with the policies of the company as a whole. Finally, *innovation* as an ongoing activity becomes the basis for the development of management.

These six tasks of management can be arranged in the following order:

```
goal-setting
policy-making
planning
organization
innovation
control (evaluation)
```

*Goal-setting* is the task of the central board. In larger companies, the board will probably receive proposals of possible objectives from the lower levels. It is still the board's task to ratify these proposals; or, if none is forthcoming, it must take the initiative itself or encourage others.

As a next step the central board will have to be mindful of its own *policies* and make conscious choices. The formulation of policies and specifically their communication means that they can permeate the whole company system as a structuring force. It must be remembered that there are two kinds of policy statement. The one means that a number of brief points are formulated by the company as a declaration of principles. The other involves a 'policy manual' as thick as a regional telephone directory explaining the exact method required for every task. What we mean by policy lies between the two. On the one hand it is more than the 'Ten Principles of Johnson and Johnson' framed in gold and displayed in the reception area; but on the other hand it is far less than a policy manual which has become a set of regulations and procedures.

Policies are required concerning the most important tasks within the third-phase functional areas described. General policy is subdivided into a marketing policy, a process policy, a resources policy (financing etc.), and a communications and information policy.

The formulation of policy is particularly difficult and is part of the management techniques of the third phase. It has to be learnt and requires practice. A good policy is like the magnet under a paper containing iron filings. The scattered particles come together in an ordered manner and form a pattern. If there is a good policy, the organization can be far less strict, and leeway can be given for initiatives which fit in with the totality of operations.

Once objectives and policies are known, *planning* should be no more than a question of technical implementation. However, the matter is not so simple, since unforeseen problems begin to appear when actual planning starts (particularly with regard to flow processes). Thus, in the course of planning, some *ad hoc* policy-making takes place for the solution of problems. Since this *ad hoc* policy-making (really a contradiction in terms) often comes about at middle-management level unnoticed by others, it is necessary for the board to be particularly watchful in this respect. *Ad hoc* policies can also arise in the processing of quantitative information, and are not recognized in the final results (see the appendix).

*Organization* becomes a supporting service function in the third phase. It has a certain structure only as long as this is useful for certain forms of cooperation. When the pattern of cooperation changes, the structure must be able to change easily with it. One of the possibilities for this is provided by the separation of the resources management and the process organization in the way already described. What is important is that in the third phase the tasks must be able to grow with the increasing abilities of the employees. Otherwise their work does not provide them with a challenge. A *flexible organization* such as this is conceivable only where there is a system of group tasks within the interlocking rings, together with management by exception.

*Innovation* as a policy and as an attitude of mind among all employees has to be striven for and won in the third phase. There are embryonic forms, such as the suggestion-box system, but these are very imperfect. Attempts to link the degree of innovation with remuneration, as in productivity premium systems, are no more than first experiments.

The Scanlon Plan described by McGregor[3] goes the furthest so far. McGregor remarks quite rightly that this plan is successful only if there is already a good spirit of cooperation and involvement with the objectives of the company.

So these conditions are necessary! In Chapter 12 we discuss ways of providing these conditions.

*Control* in the pioneer phase was obvious to everybody. The satisfaction of the customer was the criterion for assessing the suitability of the objective. A second control was provided by the annual balance-sheet, though this was known only to the entrepreneur himself, since the money was his.

In the second phase, control became a technique which permeated the whole company. Directing and controlling were the tasks of every manager. Control from outside the line was a principle of every job.

In the third phase, control becomes *evaluation*: assessing the value of achievements against the background of the general policy and the specified margins of discretion included in the task. Evaluation carried out by the person who has done the job makes it possible for him to learn by experience and thus improve his performance. Evaluation of group tasks is a particularly effective means of increasing the interest of each person in the work he is doing. (At shop-floor level this evaluation could take the form of a weekly discussion, during which the group could review its own work, ask questions, and make suggestions to the management.)

In viewing these six functions of management, which Schlenzka[4] describes elsewhere in a slightly different form as the 'pillars of management', we see that for the centre there remains a seventh important task: the *integration* of these six functions. This means an unfailing watchfulness to see that none of them falls behind, and to ensure that all six come to life equally for every employee.

It is the conscious integration of the six tasks of management of an organization that brings the organization to maturity. As mature social entities, companies will then be able to fulfil their tasks in a developing post-industrial society, in which problems of a cultural, moral, and political nature will become central.

REFERENCES

1  DRUCKER, P. F. *The practice of management.* New York, 1954; London, 1955.
2  JAQUES, E. *Measurement of responsibility.* London, 1956.
3  MCGREGOR, D. *The human side of enterprise.* New York, 1960.
4  SCHLENZKA, P. H. *Unternehmer, Direktoren, Manager: Krise der Betriebsführung?* Dusseldorf, 1959.

## CHAPTER EIGHT

# A Model of the Phase of Integration

## A Concept for Meaningful Structuring

In the previous chapter we discussed a number of measures and developments which *can* be a part of a new overall concept, the clover-leaf organization.

It has been asserted by some practitioners working in the field that the complete model of the third phase could be incorporated in the functional organization of the second phase. The central organization would then be the resources organization. The other three would be staff departments more or less directly linked with the board. With staff offices for process planning, market research, and information-processing, the same result could be achieved.

This opinion shows clearly how difficult it is to move away from a model with which one has grown up. If one attempted to introduce the third phase within the present staff–line concept, its essential element would be lost. However, this attitude among those who have grown up in the second phase is understandable. At the beginning of the second phase, production was a real and visible activity, though usually fairly static technically. Here was the tangible reality of the company. All the other non-material functions were side-issues on which one spent as little as possible. After all, 'a good product sells itself'.

This model was realistic in the early days of industrial society, when needs were greater than production capacity. But in a fully developed industrial society there is a surplus of goods, and consumers have a margin of choice for their expenditure. In addition, the once simple production process has become so much more complicated that information has become an economic factor to be reckoned with. For the value increase between input and output and for determining the nature of the output (the marketing function), the non-material aspect (information) has become more important than the material.

The model of the phase of integration honours this situation by giving the four main functions an equal validity within the basic structure. The profit of the company depends on the ability of these four functions to work together while aiming at an optimal value increase.

The *first conclusion* we may draw is that the *intelligent action* of every individual, *together with others* and directed towards the common goal, determines the efficiency of the company.

The ever-increasing speed of change in the technical, social, and hence also economic, fields has led to a number of problems. The organization of the second phase is by definition a static organization, with the result that every change meets with resistance to change. A third-phase organization should be able to change and adapt rapidly in order to survive in a changing environment. An important characteristic of the new model will have to be a capacity for internal innovation and adaptation, not only as a reaction to external events but also in anticipation of coming events. *Only the social system* can innovate, foresee, and initiate.

As long as these activities remain localized exclusively at the top, this is where the total burden of dragging along an inert organization will have to be borne. An alert organization should be able of itself to suggest and implement innovations. In the third phase, the central board is no longer the tractor dragging the whole company along behind it. Its job now is to stimulate and assess initiatives which come to it from all sides. *Central management has the function of selectively slowing down or supporting initiatives* which come from all four functional areas.

Initiatives taken by the centre tend to be in the form of questions and suggestions rather than in the form of directives to be implemented. Encouraging the study of new problems takes the place of directing. In the organization itself, social skill becomes as important as technical skill. The question of who is *above* whom no longer matters so much. What is important is who has to *work together with* whom in order to carry out a common task.

In the development towards the phase of integration the social system constitutes the bottleneck. What is needed now is an alert, open management, ready to suggest innovation and accept responsibility for the resulting decisions; looking more to the future than to the past; and regarding the present as a momentary snapshot on the path of development towards an objective still to be discovered. It is essential, therefore, to have a clear picture of the possibilities offered by the new organization.

Having given a general description of the functional areas and the place of top management among them, we shall now describe the organization of the four functional areas separately. Here again only a general outline can be given, since even more than in the second phase the third phase is a process of continuous change and adjustment.

### THE ORGANIZATION OF FUNCTIONS WITHIN THE CLOVER LEAF

#### 1. *Relations Management*

With regard to external relations, in addition to the existing apparatus for selling, services, and acquisition, a department for *market policy* is established in close contact with top management.

This department will be primarily concerned with discovering and researching existing and possible new markets. In this field, questions asked by the board will be answered, and suggestions will be made to the board which are as far as possible already based on quantitative information. The questions to be answered here are:

— What will our present market look like in five to ten years' time?
— Where are the potential new markets?
— What must be done to bring these within the radius of the company's activities?

The department will be concerned, in the second place, with *product policy*. The central question here is: Do we make good products? Do we provide good services? In other words:

— Is the answer the company has hitherto given to recognized needs still the correct or best one?
— In what respects is the taste of the public changing? Where are political or technical changes taking place which will lead to a change in the public's preferences?
— Where are entirely new answers possible, either through technical progress or as a result of mergers?

When it becomes necessary for a company to become active in this sphere, medium-sized companies can be given outside help: through the branches of organized research institutes, or through good consultants, or through cooperation with companies which have similar markets.

In many cases it could be fruitful to ask whether a company, instead of embarking on a merger with all its consequences, might not enter into cooperation or make an associative agreement with another company in the field of *market policy* or *product policy*. *Through joint consultation,* companies forming an *association* of this kind could turn to *different facets of production and together produce a more valuable product or a greater variety of products.*

Such an arrangement would make it possible for them to achieve greater impact on the market and greater diversity of products. Furthermore, companies of a manageable size, with a complete management structure and objectives visible right down the line, could be preserved. In our opinion this alternative to total mergers has not been sufficiently examined.

It will be clear that to arrive at a flexible *market policy* the help of the information-processing group will be needed, just as the help of production engineers and research will be needed in finding an optimal *product policy*. (Many researchers complain that they are not given enough information about and contact with problems of market policy.)

Companies with worldwide markets should include in their external relations team an expert on *international finance,* not only so that they can be warned in time about economically attractive but financially dubious areas, but above all so that they can make rapid use of changing credit advantages from development banks, quotas, and so on. The services of this specialist are also required in the negotiation of contracts.

Internal relations are dealt with below (see p. 117).

## 2. *Process Management*

Process management has a *central organ* which has a clear view of all the process flows, material, financial, and informative, *like a great network*. It is the task of this central organ to lay down the path of all the throughput flows and also the approximate throughput times. It may work with so-called black boxes, i.e. blocks within which the detailed throughput planning is left to a lower organ, while the central organ retains responsibility for overall standards and margins.

For each important unit within the other functional areas, this central organ has its decentralized organ which, in close collaboration with the management of the unit, elaborates the network of its 'black box' and remains responsible for it.

This could be called the *constitutive part* of the process management's task. In addition there is an *operational part*: the continuous correction of disturbances. This is usually the responsibility of the level below and is reported to the central organ only in exceptional cases when the disturbance is of such a degree that it requires an adjustment of the whole network.

The collaboration of the process managers with the managers of resources for the operational units is discussed with the organization of the appropriate functional area.

The overall organization of a clover-leaf process management could be depicted as in the diagram below, where P stands for process functionaries and R for resources functionaries. The process manager

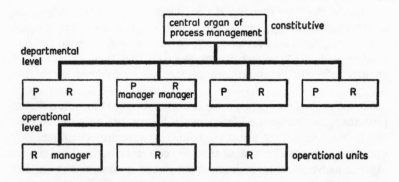

at departmental level has a limited constitutive task (elaboration of the 'black box' of his own department within the overall network) and a corrective task with regard to the work done within his department. The departmental manager for resources must collaborate with the process manager in providing the minimal resources needed for achieving optimal throughput conditions.

The resources manager at operational unit level (shop floor, offices, etc.) receives for his operational unit a throughput plan with priorities and time-margins. With his people he has to elaborate group tasks which do not overstep the time-margins. Whether he can do this himself or whether he needs the help of a process man for his operational unit will depend on the kind of work within his unit.

## 3. *Resources Management*

Depending on the nature of the company, the emphasis will be either on technical production resources or on human resources. In information-processing companies such as banks, insurance companies, and commercial companies, and also in professional 'know-how' concerns such as consultant, planning, or research firms, human resources and thus management development are the most important. Technical production resources play an important part in manufacturing companies, haulage companies, and so on.

In comparison with his tasks in the second phase, the resources manager of a unit is now concerned less with some aspects of the work and more with others. With regard to equipment, maintenance, and personnel matters in his department, his cares are the same. But he is now less concerned with work planning, on which he is consulted by his process colleague but for which he is no longer primarily responsible. In its place he has the far more important task of developing people in and through their work. By creating groups which as far as possible carry out complete and meaningful tasks, and with whom he discusses and regulates the work in hand in consultation with his process colleague, he involves people as much as possible in achieving an optimal throughput.

Within these task groups there must be a degree of discretion with regard to the distribution of the work and also the possibility of self-control with regard to the agreed standards. A file will have to be kept on each member of the department recording his development and his development potential. There must be a development plan for each person, which is known to him and which is reviewed and revised with him from time to time.

The second-phase fear of having 'too many skilled people for unskilled jobs' is no longer valid in view of increasing mechanization and automation in the third phase. On the contrary, there will be a shortage of people for tasks requiring individual intelligence and responsibility in order to achieve optimal throughput.

In general, departments will have fewer hierarchical levels of management and more operational units working side by side and having their own micro-planning and their own self-control. In the new organization, the *resources manager* will become a *manager of people* who achieves his aim by delegating responsibility to people.

## 4. *Information-processing Services*

The manner in which these services are organized will depend, among other things, on the size and complexity of the company. In general, the service group will have an external and an internal department, and a section for top management information.

(a) The processing of external information will in the main involve collaboration with the market policy and product policy sectors. Market research, optimal product planning, and participation in market combinations will be among the matters for investigation and elaboration. Policy-making will be supported by calculations (or responsible estimates) of the results of alternative choices.

(b) Internal information-processing involves:

— supporting process management with the 'tools' for making calculations; here the main requirement is that there should be feedback of data concerning quantity and quality for the work groups themselves and in another form for the heads of departments;
— feedback of administrative data for internal budgeting, personnel administration, etc.

In these fields the computer has already been introduced.

(c) Information is essential for policy-making at higher levels. Hitherto the content of information has been assembled 'lower down' the company, compiled in detail, and then summarized in larger figures and further generalizations to form an overall picture higher up the hierarchy. But the usefulness of these figures at the higher level was often disappointing for the giver and frustrating for the receiver of the information.

It is obvious that information for middle and top management must be of an altogether different nature from that required at lower levels.

*At the lowest level* information must be concrete; it serves the control of flow processes in a limited area. Simple feedback and supervision of processes are needed. In administration, for instance, management is done by procedures. Deviations from these have to follow the process flows and must at the same time be made available to the operational groups in a suitable form.

*At middle-management level* one is concerned with the *operational management of complex projects*. Here again constitutive work is necessary for the planning of non-repeated operations with the help of network planning (for instance the introduction of a new product) or to optimize information flows and the alternation of products. One is concerned here not only with feedback and supervision but above all with the *designing* of new models to implement policy decisions given in general terms.

Finally, *at the highest level* we are concerned with genuine policy information as a basis for drafting long-term strategies. In order to be able to provide policy information, the heads of the information-processing centre will have to share the thoughts of the board on policy matters. In general, the management of this centre will have to be an interdisciplinary team consisting of, for instance, an economist, an engineer, a social psychologist, and a mathematician. Precisely because work on policies requires a team like this, we have already indicated the possibility of several companies forming an association and together maintaining an information-processing centre of this kind.

So much for the main part of information-processing. There is also a decentralized part, namely roving programmers who collect the necessary information everywhere and store it in systems and programs. In addition to their technical knowledge about certain parts of the company, they must possess highly developed social skills in order to be able to collect reliable information. In future no doubt every largish department will have its own programmers who will then count as 'regular' colleagues.

## THE CENTRAL POSITION OF THE BOARD

The task of the board has already been generally described as selectively guiding, encouraging, stimulating, and questioning. This is the style in which it internally steers the subsystems. The managers of the functional areas must be capable and creative enough to be able to operate independently in their own area.

What is still missing is the *integration* of these activities through making short- and long-term *objectives* explicit, and through formulating *policy* which gives direction to problem-solving and indicates the style in which it is to be undertaken. This matter of style is very important, for it fashions activities throughout the organization. Companies with clear internal policies need far fewer rules and procedures and can thus retain a flexible mode of collaboration.

*Internal relations* (referred to on p. 113 above) are the instrument for the integrating function of the central board. There is a conscious striving for open relationships. In the third phase the style of communication, of leadership, of defining tasks, and of vertical and horizontal collaboration changes to a significant degree. The fact that in the 'interlocking ring' each person is involved with the problems of his superior(s) and can see his own task in perspective against this background; the fact that, in addition, information about his own achievements is fed back to the person concerned, so that he can manage himself: these things place the actual content of communication in a different atmosphere. The creation of a communicative atmosphere is essential for the functioning of internal relations.

It has already been said that the board functions as a team. This does not mean that all important points of contact with the functional areas must not be cared for and watched over. No point of contact must be left unattended for any length of time. Furthermore, the members of the next management level must know to whom they can turn in the first instance with questions and proposals. The following functions must therefore be taken care of:

— Market policy: in which markets do we intend to operate?
— Product policy: are we making the correct products?
— Production policy: where and how are we making them?
— Financial policy: what investments should we make and how should we finance them?
— Social policy: where should we undertake management development?
— Information policy: should we centralize or decentralize?
— Research policy: what research should we undertake? Should we take out licences?
— Various smaller matters, depending on the nature of the company.

It is a good idea to put each director in charge of one main function and one other function from another field. For instance: market policy and research policy; product policy and investment; production policy and management development; financial policy and international contacts; social policy and internal information policy.

When distributing tasks in this way one must take into account the interests and abilities of the individuals concerned, and also the emphasis placed by the company on the functions in question. But no important function should remain 'fatherless'. If a board has no member with the necessary specialized knowledge for a certain function, then one director must take on this function and have an experienced deputy director at his disposal. Together with him he can form his opinions which, in joint consultation with his colleagues, can contribute to the board's policy-making. (See also Chapter 15, 'Mergers and the Clover-leaf Organization'.)

Some typical aspects of third-phase organization are:

(a) Policy-making through mutual agreement at the top.
(b) Marketing, which means thinking from the point of view of the external relations function.
(c) Striving to solve problems for others.
(d) The whole company is a means for achieving objectives.
(e) For this to be possible in the future requires:
— the development of human resources
— long-term investment in know-how
— flexible organization.
(f) Striving for association with other companies:
— as suppliers
— as market partners
— as joint users of information-processing.
(g) Striving for healthy relationships with:
— consumers
— the authorities
— trade unions
— shareholders
— the public.
(h) Striving to integrate work with human development.

# Recommended Reading

*Chapters 5-8*

IJDO, M. G. *Taylor: over het karakter van chefs en ondergeschikten.* Alphen a/d Rijn, 1955.

DALE, E. *The great organizers.* New York, 1960.

MERRILL, H. F. *Classics in management.* New York, 1960.

THIERRY, H. *Organisatie en leiding.* Leiden, 1960.

HORRINGA, D. *Leiderschap en organisatie in de Nederlandse onderneming.* Assen, 1961.

LUYK, H. *De organisatie en werkwijze van de topleiding.* Alphen a/d Rijn, 1968.

V. D. SCHROEF, H. J. *Leiding en organisatie van het bedrijf.* Amsterdam, 1962.

SIMON, H. A. *Administrative behavior.* New York, 1957.

ARGYRIS, C. *Personality and organization.* New York, 1957.

— *Integrating the individual and the organization.* New York, 1964.

LIKERT, R. *New patterns of management.* New York, 1961.

LEAVITT, H. J. *Managerial psychology.* Chicago, 1964.

BROWN, W. *Exploration in management.* London, 1960.

HAIRE, M. (ed.) *Modern organization theory.* New York, 1959.

JAQUES, E. *The changing culture of a factory.* London, 1951.

— *Equitable payment.* London, 1961.

DRUCKER, P. F. *The effective executive.* London, 1967.

MAYNTZ, R. *Soziologie der Organisation.* Hamburg, 1963.

— The study of organizations: a trend report and bibliography. *Current Sociology* 13(3), 1965, pp. 95-119.

BOSBOOM, P. H. Wat kan de organisatiekunde bijdragen? *De Ingenieur*, No. 37, 1966.

HERZBERG, F., MAUSNER, B. & SNYDERMAN, B. *The motivation to work.* New York, 1958.

GROSS, B. M. What are your organization's objectives? A general-systems approach to planning. *Human Relations* 18(3), 1965, pp. 195-126.

FRIEDMANN, G. *Où va le travail humain?* Paris, 1953.

— *Le travail en miettes: spécialisations et loisirs.* Paris, 1964.

MECHLER, H. *1000 Arbeiter - 1000 Unternehmer.* Stuttgart, 1956.

KEPNER, C. H. & TREGOE, B. B. *The rational manager.* New York, 1965.

HARDY, A. *The living stream.* London, 1965.

# The Need for Conceptual Models

## CHAPTER NINE

# Some Conceptual Approaches

In an interesting article Bertram Gross[1] says that most work suffers from the lack of a conceptual framework into which information may be fitted. There is, he says, a 'need for new concepts to describe and analyse new phenomena'. These words express what we are dealing with in Part III of this volume. Managers need numerous *useful concepts* as a basis for their understanding of the bewildering developments taking place inside and outside their organizations. We now consider some such concepts.

So far in this book we have followed a certain path. We have taken a longitudinal view of organizational development, looking at the developments which take place in an organization during the course of its history and become manifest as a kind of inner law. The disadvantage is that to do this one has to look at the company as an autarkic system which develops in accordance with archetypal laws governing levels of increasing maturity. But a company is not an autarky; it is situated in a wider field where not only the market but also other social developments affect it.

If one wants not only to understand social developments after the event but also to anticipate the effects of external developments on one's own development, one needs a number of concepts which can help one to understand the possibilities inherent in one's own situation. We have described one approach in the longitudinal developmental models already discussed. We now look at two further viewpoints.

First, we shall consider organizations according to the types of aims they have. If one compares professional, service, and industrial organizations, one sees that the answers they provide to needs take the form, respectively, of a plan or project, a series of actions, or a tangible product. Each of these organization types has its own laws and limitations. Concepts gained in looking at organizations in this way make it possible to understand the roots of many conflicts which can then be rationally solved. One's attention is turned from conflicting human beings to conflicting organization systems. This could be called a *transverse* way of looking at things.

Second, we shall examine various ways of dealing with the future, depending on whether one's model of the future is based more on *rational thinking*, or on *judgements of feeling and emotion*, or on a *willed choice of direction*.

### TRANSVERSE MODELS

Let us now turn to the transverse view and describe the three main types of organization, examining their various development characteristics. The three types are:

(a) professional organizations
(b) service organizations
(c) industrial organizations.

Hitherto we have described only the third of these. The difference between them is that their 'output' really constitutes different phases of work. Work done by people and ending in a tangible product has three phases:

— the plan or design: mental work
— a number of actions: a process during which a value increase takes place
— the final product: this leads its own life outside the organization.

### (a) *Professional Organizations*

Every responsible member of a professional organization has a high standard of knowledge and ability and is often highly specialized. He places his knowledge and ability directly at the service of his clients. The 'product' of his work is, in a way, the first stage of any ordered action, namely a *plan* or project. It is the fruit of his specialized knowledge and ability, it is an intellectual output, whether it takes the form of advice, a design, a plan, a method, or information.

Some examples of professional organizations are: a firm of architects, a firm of solicitors, an engineering firm, a group of specialists in a hospital, a research group, a firm of management consultants, a university faculty, a teaching or educational institution, a notary's office, a merchant banking firm.

The characteristics of these organizations are:

— Each member of the professional group has his own clients or patients for whom he is personally responsible.

— The services rendered by each member of the group are personal, of a high standard, and often unique (the client wishes to consult Mr A and not Mr B).

— The auxiliary staff is limited and consists of assistants, typists, clerks, analysts, technical draughtsmen, etc. The hierarchy is shallow, and communication is direct and couched in the technical jargon of the specialist field.

— Professional people tend to work on their own and act only according to their own conscience. The responsibilities of these 'loners' towards society are usually codified in a set of professional ethics, and most professions have their own tribunal and penal code.

— Each professional member of the staff carries out his own projects, maintains his own contacts, and does his own consulting. His work can thus unfold in an individual way and his motivation and work satisfaction are very high. Professional work always has a high status, and a certain amount oft his importance and status also falls upon those who act in auxiliary capacities. Irregular hours of work are accepted as a matter of course and there is always an interest in the content of the work.

— The different specialists in this kind of organization interrelate as colleagues and work as teams when they collaborate.

The legal forms of these professional organizations vary from country to country. The form of the organization has much in common with that of pioneer organizations:

— autocratic personal leadership with a high status
— shallow hierarchy with direct communication
— improvisation in the work, because every task is new
— the organization of the specialist and the auxiliary staff is person-oriented.

An efficient professional organization should not be too large. It must remain possible for people to meet in a group of manageable size for a direct exchange of ideas and experiences. Success is therefore a problem for this kind of organization, for success brings increasing demands from the outside world. Some consultant firms or trust companies tackle this problem by scattering small offices over a wide geographical area. These are then virtually independent and perhaps share only a pool of auxiliaries, or an information pool, or their specialist training.

The senior members of professional organizations often have a charisma in the eyes of the public: the great surgeon, the wealthy banker, the famous architect, the successful lawyer, the most brilliant member of the faculty, etc. In many cases the remaining colleagues and the auxiliary teams are merely appendages of the great man.

## (b) *Service Organizations*

The service or 'product' offered by a professional organization is unique and tailored to individual requirements. A service organization is quite different in this respect. Here the service is a routine matter; it is the same for everybody and is part of an organized process. The service organization offers not a mental product but a process of action. Some such processes are:

— transportation of goods
— information-processing (administration, automated data-processing)
— establishing contacts (wholesale trade)
— distribution (retail trade)
— bringing together knowledge (insurance companies, banks)
— caring for the sick (hospitals)
— administration (authorities)
— teaching and educating (schools and universities).

Once a process has been evolved, it is this very process that is offered as the 'product'. The work of a service organization is not exclusive. Many people could learn to do it.

Competition takes the form of establishing a certain image which differs from that of other organizations offering the same service: respectability, politeness, accuracy, speed, humaneness of attitude, and so on. In order to maintain this image, all employees have to undergo strict training to standardize their behaviour, just as the processes also have to be strictly standardized. As a result, service organizations pass quickly from the pioneer phase to a kind of bureaucratic second phase. Max Weber saw this in the bureaucratic authorities of his day and described it as the 'bureaucratic organization form'.

A service organization can grow quite large, and once it is well established it is very difficult to bring about any change in it. It is in this kind of organization that the phenomenon of resistance to change has been mainly studied. The extensive standardization of work, behaviour, and procedures selectively attracts people who seek for security in their work and dread anything adventurous.

There are three kinds of service organization:

(i) First there are the public services with their centuries of history and the ancient traditions of hierarchy, formalism, strict control, lack of compulsion to achieve anything, and poor measurement of results; in short, bureaucracy as such, an endless source of jokes. In these organizations, whose task it is to represent the public interest, it is a matter of honour to preserve a mode of treating everybody the same. And a condition for the promotion of the civil servant is his avoidance of creating precedents.

(ii) Second, we have modern commercial service organizations. These see the service they provide as a product on the market and as of direct assistance to the customer whose problem has to be solved and who is happy to pay for its solution. Since competition in this field is usually great, poor or slow or impolite service usually leads to a rapid loss of customers. People working in commercial service organizations usually find themselves between the devil and the deep blue sea. On the one hand, the provision of a service is profitable only if the process is organized and standardized extremely efficiently; and, on the other hand, direct contact with the customer or patient makes one want to give a personal, less standardized service or treatment. The problem is the same for a counter-clerk in a bank coping with a long queue of people and for a nurse in an overcrowded ward.

To offer a service means that one has to wait until that service is required. Using statistical methods (see the appendix) one can reduce waiting-time by having the right minimum of personnel.

On the whole, the profit possibilities of commercial service organizations are limited. This applies to aviation, shipping, dockyards, and haulage firms, and also to the commercial side of banking and insurance (which offers services rather than specialized advice from a few highly qualified individuals, as is characteristic of the merchant side of banking).

(iii) Third, there are the internal service departments within industrial organizations, and here the work of most of the people involved is not directly productive.

There is a considerable tendency for these departments to become bureaucratic and this can be countered only by giving them a certain amount of autonomy and organizing them as separate internal service units. When setting up a clover-leaf organization (third phase) it is particularly the resources and information functions that have to be run as internal service organizations. There should be a strong motivation to render services, and the results should be made obvious to everyone through internal communication arrangements.

A question always hotly discussed is whether general services should be nationalized or not. The advocates of nationalization maintain that it is inadmissible that the profitable services should be run by private enterprise while the rest are left to the state. Their opponents in the argument point out that nationalized services soon become bureaucratic, are very expensive, and give little or no personal service.

### (c) *Industrial Organizations*

We have already described this form of organization in detail in Part II. Only industrial organizations comprise the whole sequence of planning, production process, and tangible end-product which leaves the organization and becomes visible in a market.

The 'products' of professional and service organizations are invisible, if one discounts the paper on which they are written down.

In what way are transverse models useful? They can help in making a diagnosis of a situation: 'concepts to describe and analyse phenomena'; and they can also help in solving conflicts.

As an example of their use in diagnosis, the problems of banks can be understood only if one sees how they arise out of the professional work of the traditional 'banker' and the services rendered by his employees. The general tasks of the banker have become professionally differentiated and are carried out by a team of highly specialized financial experts. They form a professional elite which it is hard for a newcomer to enter. The tasks of the employees, on the other hand, have developed into a comprehensive service organization with strictly standardized processes of action and uniform treatment of the public. Only about twenty of the most important clients are still given personal service by one of the directors. The former status of the employee still attaches to this service organization. The lines of promotion in the two halves of the bank are separate. It is difficult to switch from 'service with the troops' to 'service with the officers' corps'. It is because the directors behave as professionals and practise their specialities at the highest level that the internal management of banks is located at too low a level and has advanced little.

In large research establishments the problems are similar. At the top there are the academic specialists and below them comes a large 'service organization' of laboratory assistants doing the work assigned to them by the specialists. Both in banks and in research establishments illusions of status play a considerable role.

The conflicts that arise in these mixtures of two organization systems are usually blamed on specific persons, representatives of the two sides. The depersonalization of these conflicts is the first step towards their solution.

## MANAGEMENT'S RELATIONSHIP WITH THE FUTURE

How can management find leading concepts for the future of an organization? The paths the manager (and with him his whole management team) can take can be of various origins, kinds, and methods.

Let us start with methods based on intellectual considerations and rational thinking. Two paths become obvious:

1. Rational thinking: (a) prognoses, trends (within predictive models); (b) developmental models.

(a) *Prognoses and trends* are useful when studies can be made of the movements and quantitative changes of variables within one and the same 'real world system' in which there is *no appreciable change*. For instance the development of a market can be predicted by trend calculations only if the degree of *technical* development and also the *social structure* remain basically the same (the introduction of essentially new technical methods would lead to an immediate mutation of the system, and the sudden introduction of communism, for example, would upset any market predictions).

So quantitative prognoses are useful within certain temporal and geographical limits. They presuppose that the *basic policy structure remains the same*. This also sets the limit to forecasting macro-social developments decades in advance, an activity so keenly indulged in by futurologists.

(b) *Developmental models*, on the other hand, focus on just these basic patterns and on *changes of policy structure* resulting from growth.

This book has been written to further the ability to think in developmental models. If one knows how to handle developmental models one can foresee future structural changes and be aware of their general character. Thus it becomes possible to envisage *developments of policy structures* much further ahead and to include these in prognoses of the future. 'Development' thus leads to an open future.

Even where prognoses of development have of necessity to remain general, the fact is that the one variable which is itself always developing, the human being, is capable of moving with social developments and of living at higher levels of maturity in more complex situations.

The only difficulty with very complex social structures is that, as time goes on, people will increasingly have to be older and more mature before their own development reaches the standard of their environment. This makes for growing tensions among the younger generations, who in their discomfort would rather turn to more simple, comprehensible solutions.

With these remarks we have made the transition to a quite different source of action towards the future. Man is not only a thinking being. He also feels and experiences, and it is from this sphere that other criteria come for choosing possible solutions and decisions for the future. Once again these can be summarized in two groups:

2. Judgement on the basis of feelings and emotions: (a) action programmes arising out of dissatisfaction with a situation; (b) desirability programmes in the form of policy choices; the establishing of criteria; even the election programmes of political parties.

(a) *Action programmes:* Dissatisfaction with the existing situation is the basis for the feeling that 'something ought to be done'. In companies, this is what leads to many of the drives (economy drives, punctuality drives, cutting down personnel, etc.) which often descend like brief tornadoes on the heads of employees, usually with not much more result than the necessity to clear up the debris afterwards.

Campaigns organized with the help of modern mass media can lead to mass reactions quite beyond any rational thought about their usefulness. The sobering-down after such campaigns is often accompanied by a slight sense of embarrassment with regard to the question of follow-up.

(b) *Desirability programmes* are rather more orderly. They are a matter of choosing priorities out of possible actions. This is what the quantitative model-builder expects from management as a decision variable of the model. There is no accounting for tastes and therefore many different possibilities of choice are thinkable and legitimate.

Programmes based on a choice of priorities are possible in the form of implicit or explicit *policy*. Policy is a concretized conceptual model which states which decision variables must be given priority in concrete situations. An 'implicit' policy is *not* a policy! In the pioneer phase the personality of the pioneer was the policy of the company. This lingers on even after the death of the pioneer in the 'image' of the company. (I remember that, after the death of a certain successful pioneer, his son and the various heads of department used to sit round the table asking themselves what the 'old man' would have to say about the problem under discussion, were he suddenly to appear.)

*Genuine policy is explicit policy*: formulated, communicated, and constantly critically assessed as to whether it is still alive, whether it is being applied, and whether it is still feasible:

— thinking in developmental models provides the basis for long-term objectives
— choosing priorities and criteria for action provides the basis for the individual physiognomy of a group of people working together; policy shapes the individual model of the company.

The image of a company is the expression of its policy. Boulding[2] has said: 'An image acts as a field.' It shapes the social reality of the future. We live surrounded by the consequences of the images our forefathers had. (Marxism is an example of this on a world scale.) Our successors will live with the effects of *our* choice of policies.

Choosing policies is a matter of great responsibility and it is important that managements should be more explicit when they select the policies to which they wish to commit themselves.

The choosing of policy is also expressed in society at large in the choice of a political point of view or party. The social and political life of human beings unfolds in the dispute over policy choice. And the policy choices of civilization are laid down in legal systems.

Finally, there are concepts for the future which are rooted in the unconscious depths of the human psyche, where instincts, desires, and will impulses flow into our actions. In so far as these can be summarized as action models, two directions can be distinguished:

3. Will impulses: (a) utopia – a model of a *future* in which one

believes; (b) ideology – a model of a *past* which must be preserved.

(a) A *utopia* is a model of an ideal future in which one believes if one is among its adherents. It could have the apocalyptic character of divine providence (Teilhard de Chardin's Omega Point) or the utilitarian character of man's expectations of a paradise on earth, free of poverty, fear, etc. Once it is formulated, a utopia has a compellingly 'closed' character. It has an inherent intolerance. It is an absolute model about which there can be no argument. Either one believes in it or one does not. The strength of a utopia lies in the belief that faith can move mountains (an image acts as a field).

At the present moment two great utopias are fighting for supremacy. On the one side we have the American way of life, the 'only way of life suitable for the whole world', and on the other side there is Marxism with many nuances. It is an illusion to suppose that, if some of the centres of communism were to lose power, country after country would as a matter of course embrace a Western utopia.

(b) An *ideology* is a social model which has grown within a certain culture and been proclaimed as a set of absolute values and norms.* It, too, works as a closed model. Thus one finds a state ideology side by side with the ideologies of various classes and professions.

The entrepreneur has an ideology still rooted in the days of growing industrialization. The entrepreneur was the benefactor who provided wages, and hence bread, for others by means of his often risky initiatives. These others were expected to be grateful in return, and, if they were, he was prepared to treat them well. He had, after all, risked his personal fortune in order to create prosperity. This ideology was diametrically opposed to the utopia of the labour movement: a classless society in which everyone would equally share the ownership and revenues of the means of production.

Ideologies and utopias like these are still present in the social life of today. They are deeply rooted in the earliest experiences of childhood and thus work unconsciously in spite of new superstructures. Only if one can become conscious of the ideologies and utopias working in oneself can one view these forces rationally and include them in a developmental model which can examine the factors of structural change and the nature of new structures.

---

* We realize that this is a restriction of the term ideology but consider it justified so long as it is clearly stated.

As a result of utopias and ideologies, a number of values and norms are effective in our civilization which lie outside the rational sphere. Whether one turns exclusively towards an ideal future or builds on the foundations of the past, either attitude prevents one from assessing the 'now' of one's existence. To be oriented in the *present*, situated in the stream of development between the past and the future, is possible only if one lives with a developmental model in which values and norms evolve with the development. What was good yesterday is an obstacle today, and what may be good tomorrow is not yet possible today.

It has already been explained that management needs conceptual models for future external and internal developments so that it has a framework within which it can sort information, ask questions, and create long-term policies. The central conceptual model with which management must become familiar is the model of *development in general*, which has already been briefly described.

Development takes place in all systems which are above Boulding's fourth level. Development is a process of quantitative growth which is accompanied by discontinuous, periodic structural changes. These structural changes:
— are irreversible in time (the good old days never return)
— proceed from a general beginning
— via differentiation with specialized organ formation (subsystems)
— towards integration at a higher level of complexity.
In this process a new phase of development cannot be predicted out of the structure of the previous phase, but it can be understood in retrospect.

If the metamorphosis is incomplete, which is always the case in psychological and social development, elements of previous structures remain as subsystems in the new structure. Thus a layered structure emerges in which later (more complex) levels govern earlier (more general) levels (hierarchization).

This process takes place in the central nervous system, in the layers of our consciousness, and in social developments. As the development of social systems is practically always accompanied by incomplete metamorphosis, vestiges of earlier stages remain as historical anachronisms. These vestiges are the cause of many social tensions.

As has already been shown, development can be described as a *process* taking place in time, as a *situation* of a layered structure of subsystems or policies in one or several cultures, or as the *content* of the various levels, i.e. the variables which play a dominant part, and the subsystems which are led.

In the external and internal problems of a company which is growing and becoming more complex in structure, management will recognize these phenomena: development as a process and development as an increase of content.

Type models, systematic descriptions of development found in reality, can make concrete for management the general concept of development in the context of the company concerned.

## REFERENCES

1 GROSS, B. M. The coming general systems models of social systems. *Human Relations* 20(4), 1967, pp. 357-74.
2 BOULDING, K. *The image*. Ann Arbor, Mich., 1956.

## CHAPTER TEN

# Working with Conceptual Models

Thinking in conceptual models is above all necessary for the assessment of *objectives, policy, organization*, and *innovation* in a company.

## Objectives

The objectives of a company can never be unequivocally defined. This is seen when a group of managers discuss objectives together. Usually profit-making is mentioned first. But as the conversation continues, other questions arise. If profit-making is the main objective, then over what time-span, and at what cost? And is profit-making an end in itself or a means to an end, and so on?

It seems that a *hierarchy of objectives* must be established so that action in the real situation can be appropriately varied. Such a hierarchy of objectives *is* a conceptual model. One can find in it the rational elements, the elements of preference, and the utopian elements.

Given the criteria for selecting objectives (they arise out of the above-mentioned background), the further elaboration of the hierarchy of objectives is a matter of a systematic approach. For the third phase, for instance, the primacy of the external objectives is concretized in marketing (1). From this the internal objectives are derived, namely to steer the throughput process (2) towards the output, to give optimal support to this throughput with a minimum of resources (3), and to provide the whole with adequate information (4) at all levels in order to make it manageable.

The hierarchy of objectives of the third phase is essentially different from that of the first two. But once the concept of a particular phase has been adopted, the other objectives can be derived from it. Moreover, every objective is split up into further sub-objectives within its own section. For instance with resources management, which consists of two main branches, material resources and human resources, the main objective with regard to the development of people could be the creation of an alert and dynamic management; and a number of sub-objectives could be derived from this.

Thus the objectives shift on their way from the top to the bottom: from all-embracing objectives to increasingly concrete but at the same time narrower objectives which gradually become specified in the form of tasks. In his book *Prospectief bestuur* Van Duyne[1] has developed the public administration of a country out of what he calls a 'tree of objectives'.

### Policy

The policy of a company (and of any other organization) is also a conceptual model. In this case the model does not embrace the objectives but the mode and principles according to which the objectives are achieved 'in our company'.

The policies of a social system cannot be thought of as separate from the policy structure of the society in which the system functions. If an organization's policies differ markedly from those of the environment, then the organization will be a revolutionary cell. This would apply equally to a capitalist organization in a communist country and to a communist organization in a capitalist country.

On a smaller scale the same applies to a company. Within the general policies of a company, it is hardly conceivable that one department could work according to quite different policies of its own without causing recurrent disturbances or at least inefficiency in the work flow. And yet this is more the rule than the exception! It occurs when:

(a) there is a vacuum at the top with regard to explicit policy-making; policies then emerge at lower levels for each department;
(b) policies are formed at the top, but policy formulation, policy communication, and the safeguarding of policy execution are insufficiently developed;
(c) historical anachronisms exist in various parts of the company where policies of the previous phase of development live on and are often stubbornly defended.

Policy-making begins with reflection at the top on the two areas of external and internal policy. The next difficult step is the formulation of the policy. It is difficult because each formulation has to be checked with regard to its operability, its consequences, and its comprehensibility at the level for which it is intended.

Then comes the communication of policies, first in writing and then verbally at every opportune moment. In order to make this communication effective, it is recommended that when a policy is formed for a certain sphere it should be further concretized by working groups at the level to which it applies.

If the policies of a company are thoroughly worked over, this promotes the creation of a common language, which is good for the functioning of other communications as well. To form policies is to determine decision criteria.

Once we realize the significance of a company's own policy structure as a basis for the collaboration of a group of people, we can also understand the crucial problem of a merger between two companies, namely, how two different policy structures can be integrated to form one new one.

For instance, if the board members of the larger partner repeatedly say to their new colleagues: 'Have a look at how our Mr X does this or that, then you'll know how it should be done', then understandably those who belong to the smaller partner will avoid further contacts and rigidly defend their own policies, so that the merger will fail. In cases of this sort the fault lies in the fact that though the boards of the two companies have discussed in advance what their common objectives will be after the merger, *they have given no thought to a future common policy*.

Policies are differentiated according to the following general areas:

(a) external: marketing policy, financing policy;
(b) internal: product policy, production policy (process routes), resources policy (acquisition, depreciation), social policy, and information distribution policy.

Each of these policy areas needs further differentiation. The closer one gets to the operational level, the more difficult it becomes to distinguish between policy and the regulation of normal work. However, *thinking in terms of policies means thinking in terms of qualitative conceptual models*, in terms of criteria and a choice of principles, *not in terms of planning and regulation*. The latter are *applications* of policies in concrete situations in which quantitative models become possible because the decision criteria are known.

*Organization*

When we talk about organization we usually mean the organization of a company as it is laid down in its organization chart depicting the various interdependencies.

However, this is a later step in the history of an organization. It is preceded by a qualitative conceptual model, for example a clover-leaf organization, which comprises the choice of organizational principles. Often these are implicit. But, as has been shown in previous chapters, it is just these organizational principles that are themselves developing. It is in this field that type models can provide a guide for diagnosing development ('Which phase has our organization reached?') and for developing the organization towards the next phase.

No more need be said here about organizational policy, since reference can be made to earlier chapters. The organization of the second phase is based on the primacy of organizing resources; and that of the third phase on the primacy of organizing the process flows.

*Innovation*

Little has so far been said about policies for innovation, apart from the observation that an alert and dynamic management is necessary in a time of rapid changes in technology and in the social environment. Innovation can come only from *people* who are motivated to direct their innovative ability towards their work.

In order to build up an innovation-conscious management, from the board right down to the foreman, and including the workers, it is necessary in the first place to create *space* in which innovation is possible. This is done through the form in which leadership is given and through an organization that is flexible.

In the second phase, *leadership* is based on direction and control. One aspect of this is the 'span of control'. Job description gives the exact content and limit of the work of each person in the hierarchy. It is the duty of management to give instructions within the task description and to ensure that these are properly carried out.

Fifteen years ago, Drucker[2] was already pointing towards another possible style of leadership, which he called 'management by objectives'. The setting of an objective is primary, not the giving of instructions for work to be carried out. By being given an objective, the subordinate receives *a degree of freedom of action* and works his way towards the objective in the manner which is *optimal for him*. Drucker added that this makes it necessary for the subordinate to compare the result of his work with the objective. He was the first to write: 'Self-control is always more efficient than control from outside. Only I can know whether I have worked marginally or well.'

A second point made by Drucker was that management must be

ready to assist in the achievement of the objective. If it is not achieved, management is there not to punish but to ensure that training is available so that next time it will be achieved. Drucker's statement in full is 'management by objectives, assistance, and training'.

Span of control is replaced by 'span of assistance'. This span of assistance changes. If a superior has inexperienced subordinates who require a great deal of help, his span of assistance can encompass only a few. But as they gradually gain experience and become more independent, he can begin to extend his range. If many new and inexperienced people join later, his span of assistance will have to be narrowed down again.

This step proposed by Drucker was conceived as being within the rigid organization of the second phase, when the management of individuals was vertical.

In the third phase as described in this book, Drucker's principle remains valid, but work is even more oriented towards objectives, work done by groups in *horizontal joint consultation*, on process lines which cut straight across the vertical resources organization. Those who accompany the process flows set the *objectives for groups*, who understand fully *how* they are connected and interdependent in the sequence of activities. The 'vertical' manager and the 'horizontal' process manager will in joint consultation take care of training and development. The information centre sees to it that information for self-control is available at the level of the horizontal work groups.

The superior also functions in joint consultation, with the throughput between input and output as guideline. This brings us to the field of *organization* which must make room for and even promote flexible managing. In contrast, the task descriptions of the second phase form a fixed structure of interdependencies which can collapse like a house of cards the moment one task is changed or omitted.

Giving objectives to groups of people makes for a far more flexible form of organization. Small adjustments or absences are taken care of by the group itself. Newcomers with little practical experience learn in the group and are given more responsibility as soon as they are ready for it. In this the group is more tolerant and at the same time more strict than the best superior could possibly be.

Experience has shown us that, particularly at shop-floor level, there is great tolerance for the 'weaker brother' who is doing his best, but absolutely none for the experienced shirker. Asked why they refused to get rid of Pete, one group's answer was: 'Why should his wife suffer because his fingers are all thumbs? He's doing what he can!' How this puts to shame the social attitude of the so-called·'higher' levels.

But also at these higher levels horizontal consultation leads to an improvement of motivation and communication, though initial resistance is greater, not least from the older managers. This is why this form of organization has to *start at the top and be carried downwards.*

New patterns of leadership and flexible organization can be a part of a conceptual model which is alive at the top and is effective all the way down via policy formation, policy formulation, and policy communication.

The original and still general conceptual model of a certain pattern of organization becomes concretized in groups of co-workers *because they work at it themselves.* There can be no blueprint of a mobile and agile organization, but its *point of departure* can certainly be described. Starting from there, a process is set in motion, a process of development which encompasses more and more people and which causes the organization itself to be set in motion, so that any chart would be no more than a cross-section of a flowing river.

From the point of departure a number of unique subsequent situations develop, shaped by real people working together at a particular moment of their development. Despite the uniqueness of every development, it is possible to summarize it in 'typical' steps. To be able to think and act in terms of these stages of development will be the new conceptual skill of the manager.

REFERENCES

1   VAN DUYNE, D. *Prospectief bestuur.* Arnhem, 1964.
2   DRUCKER, P. F. *The practice of management.* New York, 1954; London, 1955.

# Recommended Reading

*Chapters 9-10*

NEUMANN, E. *Depth psychology and a new ethic*. Trans. London, 1969.
HARRIS, DALE B. (ed.) *The concept of development*. Minneapolis, 1968.
CHIN, R. The utility of systems models and developmental models. In W. G. Bennis, K. D. Benne, and R. Chin (eds.), *The planning of change*. New York, 1961; revised edition, 1969.

# PART IV

# Capita Selecta

## CHAPTER ELEVEN

# Human Development

A responsible personnel policy in management development in the phase of integration calls for a complete view of the way in which human capacities develop. One of the most important facts about human development is that it takes place in typical stages during the course of a lifetime. However, development is full of uncertainties. Only one thing is inevitable in life, namely that it will one day come to a visible end. Just because this is so obvious one thinks about it as little as possible.

The life of a human being has a time of ascending and unfolding, a time of blossoming and balance, and a time of ripening and decline. This is the biological unfolding consisting of evolution and involution: blueprinted growth. It is significant how man himself and his environment react to this biological law.

A second form of development takes place in the psychological structure of the human being as he passes through infancy, childhood, adolescence, young adulthood, and so on. Here too there are laws which, despite individual differences, show that man passes through a series of typical stages. The general laws of development apply here too:

— psychological development is *irreversible* (youth does not return)
— development progresses in steps from *level to level*, whereby different layers appear in the psyche (if we can find the child in ourselves we can understand children)
— *hierarchization* can then be seen to mean that the highest level determines the total psychological reaction and rules the lower, subconscious, earlier levels (which can, however, rebel against this)
— *differentiation* in this context means that every subsequent level is more complex than the preceding one and creates specialized subsystems
— *integration* means that after the transition from one stage to the

next, a single complete psychological personality is formed once
again; the actual transitions are critical phases in man's psychological development (attainment of school age, puberty, etc.).

A third factor of a human being's development is his own biography,
his unique path through life. Here we are concerned with spiritual
potential, which does not develop as a matter of course but is dependent on the interrelationships resulting from his confrontation with
other human beings. Without this 'encounter' with other people, man
cannot develop. In childhood he is dependent on education, and as an
adult on self-development. As soon as he neglects this activity of self-
development he begins to free-wheel, stagnate, and decline rapidly.

Prior to adulthood, man develops mainly in terms of biological–
psychological influences; then the older he grows the more individual
spiritual–moral development comes to the fore; in other words, the
more obviously does man in his psychological–spiritual maturing become independent of biological development.

Since spiritual development, urged on by the potentiality of the
personality, takes place above all in the interactions of human encounter and creativity, and since the possibility of innovation in turn
depends on spiritual development, it is understandable that the environment has a certain freedom either to promote this aspect of development by making true encounters possible, or to curtail these possibilities. To foster such development means to encourage self-
development and to create circumstances that will assist this. As the old
Russian proverb says: You can lead a horse to the water, but you
cannot make it drink! It is the same with the personal, spiritual development of the human being.

In the following we shall start with biological development. The
rising curve in the diagram below indicates a surplus of vital forces, and

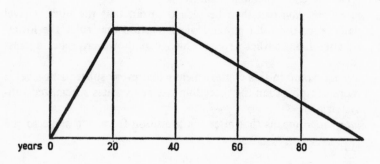

years 0      20      40      60      80

the falling curve the prevalence of impairment, or involution. We see that by and large life passes biologically through three main phases:

— phase of biological growth and development:    0 to ± 20
— phase of biological balance:               ± 20 to ± 40
— phase of biological decline:               ± 40 to ± 80

In this brief summary we cannot discuss the more subtle differentiations of this curve or the remarkable fact that several human organs and organ systems have their own curve. The above is merely an average.

This curve depicts a fact that no medical progress has hitherto been able to change. It is quite possible to postpone the moment of death by creating biologically suitable circumstances. The result is more old people in a tolerable state of health in relation to their age. But how many of them can manage without spectacles after the age of about forty? Growing old brings with it a decrease in the suppleness of tissues (lenses, lungs, blood vessels, etc.) and finally their degeneration and decay.

The significance of the biological life-curve in relation to work is obvious. The more the work calls for physical exertion, the more it is dependent on age. Much research has been done into this over the last fifty years, for example with reference to railway workers, miners, etc. Obviously in these occupations there is a problem for workers over the age of forty or fifty. The same applies to other occupations requiring physical exertion, such as that of the travelling salesman.

The next important question in connection with personnel policy is whether psychological development runs parallel with biological development. Does one have to reckon with a decrease in performance after about forty or forty-five here too, or does psychological development have its own curve? The answer to this question cannot be unequivocal.

In a very small child, psychological development is heavily dependent on biological development. For instance, the beginning of an illness is often first manifested in behaviour and mood. As the child grows older this direct dependence decreases. A second force now begins to influence the psychological development of thinking, feeling, and willing. This is *individuality*, which gradually starts to show itself in the way in which difficulties are overcome. In the second half of life this individual attitude has a greater effect on psychological achievement than has biological involution. This influence can be increasingly felt after the age of forty or forty-five.

Thus after this age the development of the psychological personality can reach any level between two extremes: on the one hand, a curve following biological involution and, on the other, a curve which can bring psychological achievement to a high plane of qualitative functioning. Though it is nonsense to try to express this development with a curve which suggests quantity, nevertheless for the sake of simplicity let us first include psychological and biological development in the same diagram before going on to examine the structural changes. We

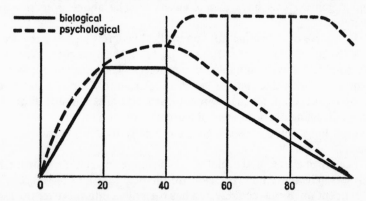

see here that after the age of about forty the human being faces two possibilities on his path of psychological development, and his course is determined by spiritual activity and effort.

If he continues to drift with the stream of vitality which has carried him so far, if he bases his self-esteem on physical achievement or on his work routine, then he will irrevocably set out along the lower path. He will have to apply more and more effort just to remain at a constant level; he will find it more and more difficult to take in new things, for as biological rigidity increases he will also become psychologically more and more set in his ways. He will be on the defensive and build up a 'maginot line' around his position; he will delegate less and less and take more and more work home in order to prove to himself and others that he is still fully needed and cannot yet be bypassed, and so on. We have all come across such people in our work situation. They are like a blockage in the organization and stand in the way of any innovation.

On the other hand, we find people who, after a crisis in their forties (to be described later in more detail), rise to a new level of creativity in their fifties, based on experience, a wider horizon, and a greater time-span of foresight. A person like this, at the height of his individual capacity, is able to conceptualize, to guide policy, and, after a period of activity and accomplishment before his fortieth year, to mature to real thoughtfulness and wisdom. This level of creativity can last for a long time before it finally succumbs to the onslaught of old age or actual physical infirmity.

Looking at the lives of really great men we usually find one of two extremes: those who are child prodigies or really creative in early manhood, and those who start being creative after forty, when they have been through many years of struggling and learning. Only those of tremendous genius are creative in both phases.

The direction a man chooses after his fortieth year is a very individual matter. Nevertheless, circumstances and the human environment do have a great influence on it. Since creativity, mobility, and innovation are of enormous importance in management in the phase of development facing enterprises today, what has just been said really pinpoints the basic issue of personnel policy and management development. How can we prevent employees from taking the lower path? An answer to this question calls for a closer look at the earlier periods of life.

Naturally, the first twenty years have a great influence on later development, especially by means of education. Education that concentrates on the reproduction of fixed subject-matter teaches the pupil to rely on his memory, on 'what he already has'. Education that focuses on problems and questions, and on ways of solving and answering them, gives pupils confidence in their own ability to find solutions and helps them to take pleasure in facing new problems. Many young people entering their first job at about the age of twenty are, like Epimetheus, capable only of hindsight and will never make the grade of Prometheus, whose foresight enabled him to look ahead. However, to change the educational system can be only an indirect task of commerce and industry. Others are making great efforts in this direction and there is some progress.

An enterprise should never be tempted by the fact of inadequate education to accept an 'Epimetheus' and use him gratefully as a stopgap in the technical system. Though people may have an unsatisfactory start, it is never too late to begin to challenge their ability and strength of character or, in short, to develop the human resources of the enterprise.

For the sake of greater detail we shall now divide the phase from about twenty to about sixty into shorter periods.

The first of these covers the years between twenty and thirty. It is still characterized by strong vitality and psychological striving. There is an expansive attitude towards the world. A great deal of social creativity is expected of a young person at this age. He has been given a place in the occupational world, but he still has to prove himself. This means he has to make sure that he is accepted by his superiors and colleagues on a basis of both real achievement and interpersonal relations.

Outside the work situation he will usually set about creating a milieu, an atmosphere, and a life-style with another person in which a new generation of human beings can grow up. This, too, is an exercise in creativity. Every personnel officer knows that a visit to a person's home often shows that person in quite a new light.

At the beginning of his twenties a person is still or has only just stopped being an adolescent. He still has the emotional instability and the dogmatic judgements of this earlier period, which cannot be discussed here, and his self-esteem is still dependent on how the world reacts to his initiatives. Praise from the boss merits a celebration at home, but a word of admonition 'makes life unbearable'. At the age of twenty-seven, Goethe described his feelings as being 'in the seventh heaven of delight or in the depths of despair'. However, as vitality is normally still strong at this age, these ups and downs do not usually last long. Life continues to demand its due.

In order to evaluate his own achievements, a normal young person in this period of life needs the appraisal of others. To help him means to tell him the truth and show him how he can improve. The content of his work must be an obvious challenge. A supervisor once said: 'You have to keep the lads on their toes.' One might say that a task should demand 105 per cent of their present capacity. The challenge must be *achievable*. To demand 150 per cent of current capacity would not be achievable and would therefore discourage.

The surest way of having difficulties with men after they are forty is to give them work when they are young which takes hardly any time to do, and to let them carry out this work year after year. The best will leave. But the great majority, who are people with average ability who *could* develop in more suitable circumstances, will adapt to the qualitative 'free-wheeling' of their work and will later swell the ranks of the 'normally frustrated', whose only connection with their work is the wage packet.

Job rotation, group tasks, training, and developmental leadership lay the foundation for the subsequent creative ability and flexibility of experienced workers.

Around the thirtieth year, sometimes sooner, sometimes later, a change takes place in a person's inner constellation. Many experience this as a definite farewell to youth. Emotional instability decreases. One is no longer totally immersed in one's situation but can stand back and observe things objectively. The rational element gains the upper hand. One has some life-experience to look back on and some things in the future seem more concrete. (With reference to this period Martha Moers[1] speaks of 'objective impulses', whereas for the earlier period she uses the term 'vital–psychological drives', and for the period after forty 'spiritual–psychological impulses'.)

The period of the thirties is a time of consolidation, in which one's own career is made visible, matter-of-fact judgements are formed, and actions are carried out in a considered way. In the terminology of personnel policy one could call this the *organizational period*. General life problems, work, and plans for the future are handled in an organizational and rational way. One feels at home in the logical organization of scientific management, but not in the static tasks it demands. During this period a person must have learnt to organize and carry organizational responsibility, so that later he can conduct policy.

At thirty-five a man has reached the middle of his life. His vital forces still support him, his mind is fully developed, and his will is directed towards activities with concrete content. Problems at the social level are solved in a rational and organizational way. Talking to workers and also middle-management people of this age, one notices that they feel they have got life 'nicely sorted out'. They know what they can get out of it, and also approximately their own level within the hierarchy of the organization. It is interesting that this does not give rise to any problems.

Not until the following years do they encounter, at first incidentally and then more often, a *crisis of values*. 'I have achieved what I have been seeking for years. What now? Another twenty-five years in this town, with this firm, till I retire?' A feeling of *uncertainty* arises which did not exist a few years earlier. What once seemed of value is now no longer attractive. 'There must be something more!'

Many seek it in external change — of house, work, or marriage; in the old days people used to emigrate, to make a new beginning far away, to be twenty once again, to go through the expansive period once again, but this time in a different and better way.

The crisis at the beginning of the forties, drastic for some, creeping for others, is a crisis into which man is thrust so that he can once more take stock of his values. His 'objective drives' have brought him to a certain point, but now they are suddenly found to be empty and no longer give real satisfaction. Where does one go from here? Where can one find new values and new aims?

For the whole of the phase of expansion (from the age of twenty to the age of forty) man is carried by experiencing his vital forces and placing himself at the centre of his environment. This does not mean that he is unsocial, but the emphasis is on the self: '*I* am successful', '*I* am managing the department very well', '*I* made a success of that transaction'.

The crisis now leads from *I* to *we*, from subjective ego-centredness to objective social awareness. At thirty-five a man will ask in a certain situation: 'How can *I* solve this problem?' A man of fifty-five, if he has weathered the crisis in the right way, will ask in the same situation: 'Who is the most suitable person to solve this problem?' or even 'How can I delegate this task so that the person concerned can learn something from solving it?'

We shall therefore call the periods between the mid-forties and the mid-sixties the *social phase*, the phase in which *one sees oneself as one of the factors* within a wider context. Life-fulfilment then lies in taking on tasks which fit within this wider context and also in giving others the possibility of development.

For people who have great responsibility or who do creative work, their fifties is the period in life when their creativity is qualitatively at its highest. Indeed, not until now can real policy be conceived. Much of what is termed policy is merely forecasting or an extrapolation of developments within a limited system. For genuine policy a totality must be created out of data of entirely different orders for which there is no common denominator. There is a juxtaposition of differing value systems. One's own preference for a certain area must not be allowed to interfere. Only in an objective situation with varying dimensions can a responsible choice be made which will determine the careers of large groups of employees.

For others, their misgivings about former values and about their own expansiveness come as a shock or as evidence of weakness. They become more rigid than ever in their insistence on their own pet solutions to problems, their own ability to organize and their own excellence. This can happen to people like foremen, departmental heads, matrons, directors, etc. At first only their immediate colleagues notice it. But by the time he or she has reached the age of fifty-five the person concerned is a source of gossip for the whole enterprise and a headache for the rest of the management. Some forms of reorganization can only take place 'over his or her dead body'.

Management faced with a problem of this kind must in the first place ask itself: What mistakes have *we* made so that *he* has become like this? When he was between forty and fifty did we not profit from the fact that his department ran on oiled wheels? Did we leave him there because we could not be bothered to make a change? Did we overlook the symptom that no promising young men emerged from his department ready to move on to higher levels?

Many people, particularly those who are very active and full of vitality, are in danger of taking this path, and yet they could be released from this kind of cramp with the help of a deep-reaching conversation, a transfer, or a special assignment.

In his sixties a man enters calmer waters. He has to accept that much of what he would have liked to achieve will remain fragmentary. For everybody, but particularly for the best, life becomes an unfinished symphony. By resigning from many tasks and choosing only a few

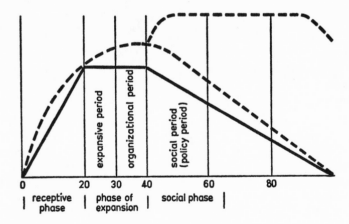

important matters, one can retain one's creative forces, though these now converge on the essence of the task for the sake of others. The knowledge that one will no longer actively have to bear the consequences of one's efforts brings about a mellowness which contrasts sharply with the self-assertion and stubbornness of those who do not wish to lay aside their expansiveness. Many a successful pioneer has ruined or at least damaged his life's work by adopting this attitude.

In order to develop the human capital of an enterprise to be alert, flexible, and directed towards continuous systematic innovation, one needs at least a general knowledge of the development of the human being during the productive years of his life. This material will have to be treated in much greater detail so that it can form a basis for the working out of task assignments, systematic promotion policies, and so on, over several decades. This is the intention of the author.

REFERENCE

1  MOERS, MARTHA. *Die Entwicklungsphasen des menschlichen Lebens.* Ratingen, 1953.

## CHAPTER TWELVE

# Organizational Development

## C. J. ZWART

### SOCIAL DYNAMICS

Change is as old as mankind. Whoever has an eye for man's typical capacity of setting himself goals which he is able to realize will also discover that nothing is more human than the desire to strive for a change in existing conditions. Change is the wave that carries man forward in his development. 'From these experiences in exerting our power to shape and refine our environment emerges an image of fluidity. Nothing is static.'[1]

It is in a certain sense an optical illusion if we think we can observe no changes in the world around us. Stagnation can be regarded as a slow form of change. Whether something seems to be changing or unchanging depends on the scope and the time-period of our observation.

However, what is new today is the speed of change. Since the sixteenth century the development of science and technology has undergone a remarkable acceleration which has now become almost explosive. So human beings and organizations are also forced to function at an increasing rate.

Products and services unheard of five years ago are in daily use today. Others have vanished over the same period. But it is not only economic life that has started to accelerate. Political and cultural life are changing as well, and in view of the enormous gap between the attitudes of today's older and younger generations we seem to be only at the beginning of a general acceleration of change.

This acceleration of change evokes fear in people because the margin of uncertainty in their decisions it constantly increasing. On the other hand, we meet the stimulating and challenging question of whether processes of social change are controllable or not. This is not only an interesting question for students and researchers but also an actual social problem because of the increasing urge in many parts of the world to seek radical solutions.

Some seek their salvation in revolutionary breakthroughs and aspire to impose their ideas for the future forcibly on the present. Others are convinced that it is possible — even given acceleration — to respect the existing situation and, starting from the *status quo*, to allow processes of change to go forward in an evolutionary manner. In brief this is a field that is covered by the theory and practice of 'planned organizational change'. We are concerned both with the nature and course of change processes as such and with the possibility of managing and controlling them. The growing stream of questions posed by practitioners in this sphere means that an increasing number of scientists have concerned themselves with the question of how people and organizations change.

Anthropologists, economists, sociologists, psychologists, educationists, and also technologists have made the phenomenon of change the object of their study and research. So it is not surprising that the volume of literature on this subject has increased enormously in the last few decades. Seeking to organize this abundance of literature one finds considerable discrepancies in methodology and terminology. As Van Doorn[2] rightly remarks, there is as yet no solid basic theory on the phenomenon of social dynamics.

Despite the differences in the varying approaches, it can be stated that the change processes under discussion here must always be associated with human activity. People stand at the beginning and at the end of a change process, they are its initiators and its target. One could speak in this connection of the 'population' of a change process and thus differentiate between change in individuals, in small groups, in organizations, and in whole societies.[3]

In the following we are concerned with processes of change in organizations, particularly industrial enterprises, in so far as these changes are brought about with the help of an external expert. Let us call the organization asking for help the 'client system' and the external expert the 'change agent'.

The term 'change' does not tell us much. At most it suggests that one state of affairs changes into another state of affairs. However, from the viewpoint of organizational development, not every change in the state of affairs, not every movement, action, or reaction in an enterprise is significant. Changes never appear as isolated phenomena;

they have a definite sequence and are interrelated. We can look upon change as a process taking place in time. The question whether processes of change in organizations can be controlled cannot be answered without insight into the nature of the relation between the different stages of the process.

Emery and Trist[4] point out that in studying organizational change one must take into consideration not only that organizations and their environments are changing at an increasing rate but also that the changes lead to ever greater complexity. In our opinion this is an irreversible process in which each new stage is more differentiated than the previous one.

An analysis of closures and mergers of enterprises shows that the continued existence of an enterprise today is not threatened in the first place by seasonal changes or economic fluctuations but by the loss of markets and sales channels, by modifications in patterns of consumption or distribution, by new products and techniques, or by more efficient production methods. The difference between continuity and bankruptcy is not usually determined today by 'doing good business' or 'having bad luck'. The great question is whether an enterprise allows change to be forced upon it or whether it can anticipate structural changes with the help of up-to-date technical, economic, and social strategies. This is a question of modern business strategy. Lippitt *et al.*[5] are right when they see a connection between planned change and the current pressure on enterprises to keep changing their structure.

The controllability of change processes, which is of essential importance for the continuity of an enterprise, is therefore linked with management's ability to manage a constantly increasing complexity. For this reason we prefer to speak in this connection not of change but of development. Development implies structural change, and it is the characteristic task of modern management to initiate timely and fundamental changes in the organization structure. Servan-Schreiber[6] even regards this ability to bring about rapid changes as the distinctive difference between American and European management.

It is the task of the change agent to internalize the principle of development in the client system as a permanent attitude of management. As Chin[7] points out, it is his task to teach the client organization to think in developmental models. Developmental models make it possible to recognize the past, the present situation, and the future of the organization; to pinpoint transition areas, and to describe symptoms which indicate that a certain constellation of the system has entered a 'critical' stage.

The change agent starts from the assumption that the client system has a basic potential for development. He will help it to select a dominant direction for development and will seek to promote the creative participation of all members of the organization.

Let us now ask ourselves whether there is a difference between organizational development and reorganization.

In their interesting article, Emery and Trist[8] note that the relationship between an enterprise and its environment is determined to a large extent by the structure of the environment itself. They call this structure the 'texture' of the environment and they distinguish between 'placid randomized environments', 'placid clustered environments', 'disturbed-reactive environments', and 'turbulent fields'. These turbulent fields, they say, are becoming the characteristic environment for more and more organizations. For many organizations this trend means a great increase in the area of 'relevant uncertainty', a situation hinted at by their remark that 'the ground is in motion'.

In view of what has been said, it is no coincidence that many enterprises are seeking for more flexible, less hierarchically structured, forms of organization, and that high priority is given to flexible management. Innovation in almost all fields of management is valued highly and reorganization is the order of the day. Although we recognize the great importance of innovation, we would point out the danger that conflict can arise in the organization if a general policy of innovation and the internal structure are not integrated.

Organization theory, particularly in its practical implications, is still mainly concerned with analysing and improving the internal organization structure. Many enterprises, thanks to their impressive and costly staff departments, have gained control of the current production process and considerably increased the efficiency of the operating production system. But there is a danger that the promotion of internal efficiency may become more or less an objective in itself. In many cases the existing production apparatus or at least parts of it are still being refined and streamlined long after the board has discussed and renewed its objectives. The fact that the internal structure lags behind the new external objectives means that reorganization usually takes the form of incidental, heavy-handed intervention which is supposed to set the ponderous and sluggish internal apparatus moving, usually in too short a time.

Thus the structuring and restructuring of the organization become strategies with conflicting objectives and criteria. Innovation is forced and not enough time is allowed for the system to start functioning again in accordance with new criteria. Or, if a new constellation of criteria really comes into a state of balance, in many cases this happens at the cost of much resistance and of a decrease in motivation on the part of the people working in the organization.

Management has two essentially different dimensions, which, however, complement each other. On the one hand its task is to initiate the innovation process, which means planning and shaping new production capacity. On the other hand there is the task of managing and controlling the existing production capacity of the enterprise. In other words this is the difference between 'navigating' and 'running' the ship.

If we look at an enterprise as a system with an input and an output, we may come to the conclusion that the output is the input of the control system. Starting with the external objectives, there is constant correction inwards. The internal apparatus originates in the external objectives. As a whole it is an instrument by which the demands of the market are being answered. It is never an end in itself. The existing production capacity of the enterprise is doomed in advance to disappear because new objectives replace the old.

Schumpeter[9] found an excellent way of expressing the relation between these two dimensions of management when he spoke of a process of 'creative destruction'. He regards capitalism as a process of development. For him the core of management's tasks is the creation of new methods of production and transportation, new products, new markets, and the development of new patterns of organization. But all this means that what exists must perish. Economic structure changes inexorably from the inside outwards as the old is demolished and foundations are laid for the new.

If, as Emery and Trist remark, 'the ground is in motion', what has just been said means that the distinction between organizing and reorganizing disappears. The innovation process and the structuring process overlap as the external objectives change rapidly in a turbulent field. We could also say the opposite, namely that, through a continual process of reorganization, management must preserve the system from becoming too rigid.

Speaking on reorganization methods, E. C. H. Marx[10] described and showed the connections between organizing and reorganizing. He said:

Organizing embraces an element of change and an element of stabilization. Thus organizing can always be described in two ways: as a process of organizational change and as the stabilization of the organization process. Reorganizing is organizing seen as a process of change. Reorganizing embraces both the definition of the desired organization and that of the process by which, on the basis of the existing organization, the desired organization can be discovered and realized.

If, as in the above, we emphasize a dynamic view of an enterprise and place changeability in the foreground, we do so because this corresponds with social reality in this century. At a time that confronts us more intensely than ever before with the dynamic aspects of society, the dividing-line between statics and dynamics is becoming artificial. Organizing is an activity aimed at the reduction of dynamics. Organization structures are momentary snapshots of this structuring process.

We may look at organizations as partly material and partly non-material forms, which arise in time, and change between innovation process on the one hand and structuring process on the other. They may be compared with the sandbanks that appear in a flowing river. Organizational development therefore always contains an element of interference with reality and it is regarded here as a concept of action.

We shall now deal separately with some objectives, strategies, and models of organizational development.

OBJECTIVES OF ORGANIZATIONAL DEVELOPMENT

We have stated that in our discussion of developmental activities we shall restrict ourselves to organizations and in particular to enterprises. We have not yet defined what we mean by the concept of 'organization'. There is probably hardly a term in the social sciences which has been interpreted in so many ways and has caused so much confusion.

The history of scientific management, of human relations and of revisionism, bears the marks of the different scientific disciplines which have been interested in the phenomenon of organization. Technologists, economists, sociologists, and psychologists have produced quite different attitudes and methods in the field of organization theory. Sometimes organization is regarded as an activity, sometimes as the result of activity.

Hitherto organization as activity has usually been described as the direction of people and resources towards an objective or as the creation of appropriate relations. It is a more recent idea to include in organization as activity the creation of a team of people who wish to work together continuously towards a common goal.

Organization as the result of activity is found to have the following meanings: an organized group, a functional association, a social construction, and a form of cooperation. Finally, the term organization is also taken to denote the internal organization structure.

By organization we understand certain types of group such as enterprises, schools, hospitals, societies, prisons, armies, and so on. Such a group is formed according to a certain plan and consciously directed towards achieving a specified objective or serving a specific purpose. In this it differs from groups such as families and friends, tribes, ethnological groups, etc.

It is a feature of these so-called formal organizations that the basis of their existence is in the first place the realization of a specific objective. Furthermore, it is characteristic that their continuity is guaranteed irrespective of changes in membership.

On the other hand, in our opinion differentiation, specialization, hierarchization, and functionalization are not characteristics of all organizations. They appear only in certain phases in the development of an organization. Thus larger organizations may usually be characterized by considered division of labour, central and peripheral positions, differentiated and well-defined responsibility and authority, and a multiplicity of material, social, and information processes. But with small organizations, such as pioneer enterprises, this is often not the case.

In certain circumstances other groups, such as tribes or families, can be seen to undertake the planning of activities or differentiation and hierarchization. But this usually occurs to a far less degree than in formal organizations; moreover, in most cases it is the result of tradition or habit rather than of purposeful ordering.[11]

Organizations can be regarded as systems. Characteristically they are of a pluriform nature in which a distinction can be made between various elements and the relationships between them. Every system has a structure. The difference between system and structure is not always clear from the way in which terminology is used. If we say 'This is an excellent organization', we could be referring either to the functioning of this particular group among other organizations, or to the internal structure of the organization.

Structure means literally 'building', 'framework'. The structure of an organization can therefore be described as a particular pattern of relationships. An organization model is valid only within a particular structure. A change of structure implies a change of model.

Looking at systems has the advantage of protecting us against too great a simplification of reality. By distinguishing and defining elements and their relationships one can express the fact that parts of a functioning organization have their own characteristics but are at the same time interdependent.

We can now ask about the objectives of organizational development in a different way: Which system variables are influenced by the change agent?

Katz and Kahn[12] point out that 'to disregard the systematic properties of the organization and to confuse individual change with modifications in organizational variables' is a mistake often made in connection with organizational change. The behaviour of people within organizations, they say, remains the behaviour of individuals but has another set of determinants from that influencing their behaviour outside the organization. They also emphasize that 'systematic change' with lasting results cannot take place unless the organizational variables change. It is worth noting that the first systematic change activities, which started with the work of Frederick Taylor, were directed not towards changing the attitudes of individuals but towards changing technical and organizational variables.

Management consultants of the classical school concentrate on measuring and analysing existing production processes — the technical subsystem — and then on the basis of the data obtained they design a new organization model. The new blueprint still has to be introduced. The significant point is that people in the organization actually remain outside this process. Ready cut and dried, the changes appear, the people being in a certain sense their object.

Policy consultants are a more modern variety in the advising professions. Instead of turning their attention primarily towards the technical system, they seek to change the policy system. At board level they put forward new ideas which could become new objectives of the organization. Here too the people are in fact left outside the process of change. The new policies are introduced from above, possibly in a 'democratic' package.

The complete opposite of this approach appears in activities designed to bring about a change in the attitudes of the members of an organization. Examples of these activities are those arising out of the human relations school and group dynamics. By training and personality-building — mostly undertaken outside the enterprise — an attempt is made to bring people to a new way of thinking. The immediate objective is to give the members of the organization increased understanding of the motives behind their own behaviour.

The most general form this approach takes is in conferences designed to broaden people's horizons; a series of interesting lectures is arranged, with or without discussion. More specific forms are unstructured and structured group methods such as sensitivity training and problem-solving. In practice these methods do not seem to produce the desired effect because there is no suitable follow-up in the work situation. Participants in the conferences and training programmes return to the same functions, and the role expectations of their subordinates, colleagues, and superiors have not changed. Any results therefore depend on their perseverance in trying to overcome the barriers in the organization.

Leavitt and Colthof categorize the objectives arising in practice in a somewhat different way.

Leavitt[13] differentiates between 'structural approaches', 'technological approaches', and 'people approaches'.

Structural approaches are concerned with changing the hierarchical system, the communication system, and the work-flow system. They involve distributing and describing tasks, determining competencies, fixing duties and responsibilities, and improving relationships between functions and departments so that overlapping is prevented. Technological approaches primarily serve the purpose of bringing about changes in technology and production processes with the help of methods and techniques which themselves have clearly technical characteristics. Leavitt includes among these both the classical efforts of scientific management and modern methods such as operational research. People approaches aim at bringing about change by altering the behaviour of individuals belonging to the organization. This approach is concerned above all with the human process of change. Leavitt regards the first two approaches as 'unhuman' because they concentrate on finding efficient solutions to problems as such, completely bypassing the fact that the solutions have to be realized and integrated by people.

Colthof[14] distinguishes three levels at which change activities can take place. A certain depth of penetration of change corresponds with each level.

Activities at the first level are aimed at changing the work processes, for instance working methods, administrative or financial processes, etc. Activities at the second level are directed towards the organizational role pattern. According to Colthof, this level is 'below' the previous one because organizational roles are usually less clearly visible. Activities at the third level are designed to change the behaviour patterns of persons and groups. This level is still more difficult to perceive and lies below the second.

From what has been said it is clear that the objectives of a process of organizational development and the values underlying them can differ considerably. What objective one chooses in a concrete case of organizational development, and what value one attaches to it, seems to depend to a high degree on the phenomena one thinks one can distinguish in an organization.

We shall now attempt to make a basic inventory of these phenomena, distinguishing between three modalities, i.e. three different modes of being of an organization. An enterprise appears in the form of instruments, in the form of concepts, and in the form of relationships. Referring to the system concept mentioned earlier, we can describe these modalities in the following way.

Instruments are material elements of the system. Among these are buildings, capital, machines, land, forms and documents, raw materials, tools; and people also are looked upon as instruments in this sense. The characteristic of all these instruments is that they can be perceived with the senses.

Concepts are non-material elements of the system. They include values, norms, expectations, objectives, and policies. Concepts are ideas or interpretations of how things are or should be, or what one expects or strives for.[15] Their characteristic is that they cannot be perceived with the senses. They cannot be expressed in number, weight, or measure, but they are of a realistic nature.

We called the third modality that of relationships. In an organization there are relationships between things, between things and people, and between people. There are also relationships between concepts. The totality of these relationships between elements is the structure of the organization.

We could summarize by saying that an organization as a system consists of an instrumental subsystem, an ideational subsystem, and a relational subsystem.

In thus making an inventory of organization phenomena with the help of the three modalities mentioned, we arrive, as it were, at a momentary snapshot, because we ignore the time-factor. As soon as we include the time-factor, we have to add that in a functioning organization there are also processes. Thus we can perceive, among others, material flows and information flows, and processes of interaction and communication. These two points of view do not contradict one another. We have described the structure of an organization as a pattern of relationships between variables. A process is a totality of relationships which change with time. Barber[16] makes the following interesting remark about this: 'There is nothing static in either concept system or structure, except in the sense that all process is assumed to have an analyzable structure at any moment in a time series.'

Earlier we described 'organizing' as an activity aimed at reducing dynamics. It would therefore be better if we spoke not of 'structure' but of 'structuring'.

We can look upon the form aspect and the process aspect of relationships as two dimensions. If we observe and take an inventory of the relationships of a system at a particular moment, the form aspect comes to the fore. However, the change agent will have to handle both dimensions. Depending on the nature of the actual or potential problems of the client system, he will have to wear alternately either his structuring or his dynamizing 'spectacles'.

One cannot speak of organizational development unless the aim is to bring about the development of the whole system. Approaches like those made by Leavitt and Colthof have only partial objectives because they are directed towards parts of the organization.

The change agent regards the client system as 'a moving total'. Though his entry is always through the people — the social subsystem — he will also have to concern himself with the instrumental and ideational subsystems.

Since innovation can only arise in people and since no organization can change more rapidly than the people wish to develop, enterprises are in many cases termed 'social systems'. There is nothing wrong with this, so long as the change agent remains aware that the complex reality of the enterprise comprises more than people and the relationships between people.

The change agent who wishes to change a whole system will discover, further, that his work will not be limited to the relations between the elements of the system, but will also be concerned with each of these elements separately. Changing a single norm or expectation can be just as important for the progress of the change process as changing the whole policy system. A therapeutic talk with one individual can sometimes mean more than changing the communication network between departments. The position of a single machine or the path of a single document can prevent changes taking place elsewhere. Alternating concentration on people and on the context of the organization means that organizational development and management development go hand in hand.

### STRATEGIES OF ORGANIZATIONAL DEVELOPMENT

In the process of organizational development we are concerned not only with the objectives of the activity but also with the way in which the objectives are reached. The client system and the change agent are faced with the task of defining their respective roles for the duration of the change project. We call this the determination and formulation of an action strategy. According to Dale, the literal meaning of the term 'strategy' is: 'The art of warfare in so far as this consists in the making and execution of plans for movement on a large scale.' Hutte[17] points out that strategies refer to the whole role relationship between the consultant and the organization as well as to the course taken by the consultant through the organization.

The following problems are central to most discussions[18] on the role of the change agent. First, does the change agent become part of the client system during the change project, or does he remain an outsider? And second, does the change agent share the responsibility for the progress and consequences of the change process or is this borne by the client alone? Those with experience of change projects in enterprises know that these questions cannot be answered unequivocally.

It is true that the change agent is not a part of the hierarchical system of the organization to be changed. He can give no formal commands. On the other hand, he can and must occasionally be included in the change process in such a way that he is in fact encapsulated in the existing network of power and authority of the client organization. In such cases, which are sometimes unavoidable or even desirable in the interest of adequate assistance, he can hardly be regarded as an outsider.

Many consultants feel that they are responsible for the quality of their advice while considering the client responsible for its introduction and implementation. This view is not wrong in itself, but it is incomplete and insufficiently subtle. The change agent is, after all, concerned with a reacting field. As soon as a relationship has been established between client and consultant, the latter, whether he wants to or not, will influence the decisions of the client through both the nature and the timing of the advice he gives. Every process of organizational development consists of a chain of advice, strategic decision, and new advice. Each new piece of advice contains an evaluation of the previous advice. *This is impossible if the change agent does not feel that he shares the responsibility for the progress of the change process.*

Gouldner[19] sees a connection between the different professional attitudes of change agents and the condition that 'applied social scientists' cannot and may not formulate objectives for the client. He points out that this condition, which has the character of a guideline for action, offers no solution for numerous problems encountered by the change agent in practice. On the grounds of a difference in basic attitude, Gouldner divides strategies into 'engineering approaches' and 'clinical approaches'.

'Engineers' base their work predominantly on the concept of a value-free social science. They take the client's problems at face value. They restrict themselves to studying and analysing, and start with the assumption that resistance to their findings is not their concern and that in principle the client will react sensibly to new insights.

'Clinicians' start with the assumption that the statement of the problem will usually have to be reformulated, in conjunction with the client, and that resistance to new insights will remain even if perfect investigation methods are used. They consider it their responsibility to trace the origins of this resistance and they will help the client to overcome it.

Gouldner is obviously pointing here to the difference between analysis and therapy. We leave open the question of whether the concepts of engineering and of clinical work provide a good indication of the difference between an analytical and a therapeutic approach. What is more important is that he considers a clinical strategy to be closest to reality. He gives high priority to the creation of a good relationship between the client and the change agent, and holds that the change agent cannot fulfil his function as a helper through fact-finding and data-collection alone.

Bennis[20] goes even further than Gouldner when he states that planned change is a carefully considered process based on cooperation, wherein change agent and client together plan and achieve an improved way of functioning for the client system.

Miles[21] makes the following interesting remark about the relationship between consultant and client system: 'The consulting system formed by a consultant and a client group or organization can be thought of as a temporary arrangement: a permanent organization has a newcomer attached to it for a period of time, thus forming, in effect, a new system.'

It is our view that in a process of organizational development the client and the change agent form a temporary system. *The expert is one element of this system.* His responsibility will have to be determined from situation to situation by defining with precision the boundaries of the system and by setting up the rules of play for the functioning of the system. Elliott Jaques[22] gives a good example. He says that during the first months of the change project in the Glacier Metal Company much attention was devoted to the joint establishment of rules of play for the research team and that these rules of play were to be found displayed on all the notice-boards in the factory.

Miles's view enables us to delineate strategies of organizational development more sharply. We differentiate between exclusive and inclusive strategies.

Exclusive strategies exclude the joint responsibility of the client and the change agent for the progress and realization of the organizational development. The change agent is the consultant in the traditional sense. Consultant and client organization are regarded as two separate systems. Interaction between the two systems comes to be, as it were, a mechanical process. Rational solutions to problems are sought after; and the client is expected to accept and introduce, in a sensible way, reasonable proposals based on expert knowledge.

Inclusive strategies include the responsibility of the change agent for the progress of the change process. He helps the client to achieve new objectives. A prerequisite for inclusive strategies is that the change process is promoted to a high degree through the good relationship between client and change agent. Together they form a temporary system and their cooperation is a slow, organic process of growth. One could speak of a functional relationship of trust in so far as the nature and frequency of the contacts between client and change agent are determined by the demands made by the process itself. Furthermore, it is realized that rational solutions are often accepted in theory but not put into practice because of psychosocial resistance.

As the above shows, in the light of practical experience we have opted for an inclusive strategy of organizational development. A more practical specification of such an inclusive strategy is given below:

— The relationship between client and change agent is voluntary; this implies that each openly makes the other aware of his motives.
— The objectives of the process of organizational development must be formulated and accepted jointly.
— There must be agreement both among the members of the client organization and between client and change agent as to the method of decision-making during the change process.
— Optimal participation of the members of the client organization is striven for; they are encouraged to make creative contributions.
— The methods and techniques used by the change agent must be explained; this means that they are always transparent to the client.
— The change agent is prepared to have his role-playing evaluated by the client; his manner of functioning during the development project thus comes under discussion.

## MODELS OF ORGANIZATIONAL DEVELOPMENT

The strategy and the goal of a process of organizational development can be combined in a model of change. Such a model serves in every case to describe the characteristics of each stage of the process and the main activities of the client and the change agent.

The number of change models discussed in the literature is not great. Furthermore, the discussion is usually restricted to a general description of the different stages of the change process.

Lippitt *et al.*[23] use a model adapted from one of Lewin's. They distinguish the following five phases of change:

— developing a need for change (unfreezing)
— forming a change relationship
— working towards change (moving)
— generalizing and stabilizing the change (freezing)
— achieving a terminal relationship.

Van Doorn[24] mentions the following sequence: the stage of equilibrium disturbance, the transition stage, and the stage of re-establishing equilibrium.

Hutte[25] works on the basis of a sequence of so-called strategic phases:

— entry and introduction into the organization

— orientation on the problem
— further detailing and localizing of the problem
— setting-up of action campaigns
— structuring the process of terminating the role relationship.

Following Benne and Muntyan, Colthof[26] speaks of change as a 'three-step procedure', and distinguishes in sequence: the preparation stage, the shift stage, and the consolidation stage.

We shall not go further into the characteristics of these models since they are hardly operational. There is usually no methodological elaboration; also, the connection between the phases of the process and the corresponding activities of the client and the change agent is unclear.

In the following we discuss a model of change which has arisen as a hypothesis on the basis of a process of organizational development that we have observed closely over a period of several years (see diagram, p. 175 below). The basic material will be published in the form of a dissertation at a later date.

The model describes the process of organizational development as a joint path taken by client and change agent, though their activities are not of the same nature at every stage of the process. The model also shows that the actual stage of realization is preceded by a number of preparatory stages. Every change situation is a field of forces placed between new future concepts on the one hand and the pattern of present activities on the other. In the social system this polarity is experienced as tension between new possibilities and existing limitations. The problem is that at the beginning of the process these new possibilities seem, as it were, to lie outside the client system. They still have to be incorporated into the client system as ideas for the future. The preparatory stage is therefore concerned with the internalization of the new concepts. Here the change agent provides the means of making the polarity of concept and situation operational in a way that allows concrete innovation to arise out of the social system. This is depicted in the model as a transformation process with three stages. *Each stage has its own character and a specific objective.* It is essential that, through this transformation process, concept and situation should gradually approach each other so that finally they can meet in the stage of actual realization.

As has already been said, innovation can arise only out of the social system, and therefore it is the task of the change agent in the preparatory stage to create a 'space' for change in which the client can creatively choose a dominant direction of development. Not until the initially alien ideas for the future have been conceived anew within the system, and not until the client consciously 'wills' the new direction of development, can genuine implementation begin to take place in attainable steps.

There is at the outset no cut-and-dried recipe for the joint path of the client and the change agent. It must arise consciously, and appears as mobile activity in a social 'space'.

The first stage of the development project moves between a general explanation of future possibilities on the one hand and a general explanation of the situation on the other. The first step in a process of organizational development consists in recognizing *an unsatisfactory situation* and deciding to do something about it. This unsatisfactory situation can be the result of actual or of potential problems. Either the client experiences that his enterprise is not functioning well, or he foresees that external shifts will affect his organization in the future and decides to anticipate this. New technology, the emancipation of employees, the penetration of other firms into one's market, shifting consumer habits, mergers, changing professional interests, increasing prosperity, the raising of the school-leaving age, rapid growth, a malfunctioning communication system, ageing personnel, etc. — all these can lead to an unsatisfactory situation and become an impetus for change. The change project must begin at the top because it must be decided whether the problems are of a structural nature and could have consequences for the organization as a whole.

The process is set in motion because there is a need for an answer to these problems. Uusually the help of an expert is needed. The great question now is whether out of the tension between 'is' and 'should be' a *positive dissatisfaction* can arise which will be strong enough to make the process viable. This tension can emerge only if new future concepts are confronted with the realities of the existing situation. This means the confrontation of the general exploration of the future with the general exploration of the situation. The new concepts can arise within the client system itself, or they can come from outside. If the client system works with an external change agent, the latter will always have to begin by passing on his concepts, for instance with regard to social development, organization, management.

The purpose of this process of communicating concepts, which is best done in the form of a management conference lasting several days with the whole of top management, is twofold. On the one hand, the tension necessary for change is created. On the other, a completely voluntary relationship can arise in this way between client and change agent. The change agent must feel the client's reaction to his concepts. And the client has the right to know the basis of the change agent's approach to his task. Therefore at this stage the change agent will explain his way of working and state the strategy he intends to follow if a change process is set in motion. Only when this reciprocal acquaintance has been made can a decision for mutual action be taken.

From the concepts given by the change agent, the client system forms its own relevant image of the future. This image of the future is still general, but its effect is to widen the horizon. Boulding[27] is right when he says: 'An image acts as a field.' The client discovers new possibilities and a future direction for development.

Also, however, the client system must come to recognize the limitations imposed by the existing situation. It must learn to regard this situation as a realization of past concepts. Working methods, technology, features of the end-product, and so on, have come about as a result of ideas held by designers and planners at an earlier stage. In a large differentiated organization, a so-called policy of not making strict descriptions of functions can in fact turn out to be nothing more than a relic of a pioneering attitude which places personal informal relations above all others. Such a policy from the past can then be experienced in the present as a chaotic communication network.

The activities of the change agent and the client do not have the same character in this first stage. The change agent creates a field of tension by passing on his concepts. We call this the 'polarization' of the system. The client system strives to assess to what extent the 'alien' concepts are relevant to it, and it creates its own picture of the future. We term this activity of the client 'conceptualization'

To sum up, we can say that the objective of the first stage is the conscious assessment of possibilities and limitations. It is essential that sufficient enthusiasm for the process of change should come about among a representative group at the top of the enterprise. This enthusiasm must make the client system strong enough to overcome the unavoidable resistance that will arise.

The dangers of the preparatory stages are 'illusory thinking' and 'acting by force'. Illusory thinking arises when the new concepts are not confronted with the real situation. The client may be very enthusiastic but have an insufficient sense of reality. As a result the process of change remains an illusion which is never realized. Acting by force is the client's attempt to force the situation. The limitations of the existing situation are forcibly pushed to one side and the change is 'simply' introduced.

The polarity of general exploration of the future and general exploration of the situation has its own characteristic. Viewed as psychological processes, changes of attitude can appear in the thinking, or in the feeling, or in the willing.[28] The essence of the first stage is that new ideas must arise and old ones be broken down. This process takes place through perception and thinking. We call the result a cognitive change of attitude on the part of the members of the organization. If the preparatory process were to end here, there would be a danger that the process of organizational development might remain in the theoretical sphere. The new possibilities are described as 'interesting', 'vague', 'illogical', 'important', etc., but in fact the concepts of the future are still partly outside the client system. The client system has not yet really allied itself to them, and the resistance that arises at this stage is therefore usually still of a good-natured variety.

The second stage of the development project is concerned on the one hand with choosing the operational objectives and on the other with reviewing and analysing the actual functioning of the organization.

This polarity brings about a new field of tension. At the end of the first stage the new concepts are still at the periphery of the client system. The client system has accepted the new picture of the future intellectually, but the process can only really get under way if in the following stages the members of the organization succeed in making an inner identification with this picture of the future. They must be able to accept the picture at the emotional level as well. They must not only *think* of the change process as a possibility, but at the same time *experience* it as desirable.

Thus the second stage is essentially a 'motivating' process. The change agent creates a field of tension between operational objectives and operational analysis in which the motivation for the client's inner acceptance can be born. The objective of the second stage is therefore to achieve a change of attitude at the emotional level in the people concerned. We call this an 'expectative' attitude change.

As regards method, this means that the joint path taken by the change agent and the client is not in effect a straight line. We spoke earlier of mobile activity. In fact the development process oscillates between the polarities in the tension field. But each new swing is a little smaller than the previous one until finally the oscillation is at its smallest in the realization stage, when concept and situation meet.

After the movement of the first stage, the general concepts of the future, which are really ideas, can be transformed into operational objectives. This means in practice that new objectives are formulated for parts of the total enterprise, for sales, for research, for the personnel department, etc. The objectives could be, for example, a new market strategy, a new style of consultation, new criteria for the establishment of work situations, and so on. The operational objectives make apparent the subsequent steps in the process of organizational development. But this is possible only if the change agent has presented his concepts in the form of developmental models.

In addition, it is necessary that there should arise in the second stage an increased awareness of how the system operates. It is not enough for the client to understand the system as a realization of earlier concepts. The 'what' and 'how' of procedures must be objectified. This is achieved by means of a self-survey, which reveals how the system functions in practice.

This self-survey is not a technical intervention by an external expert. It is not the task of the change agent to turn the whole organization upside down with the help of ingenious methods and techniques. The change agent gives the client system assistance of a kind that enables it to make its own analysis and find its own therapy. Self-survey is therefore limited to the group or groups which have already started moving in this stage of the process, and is directed, as far as is relevant, to the various modalities of the system: the instruments, the relationships, and the concepts. The investigation must reveal what work processes there are, what processes of interaction and communication take place, and what interpretations of the general style of management are current.

The phases of the self-survey are: observation, inventory, and analysis.

The purpose of the observation, which is undertaken by the change agent, is to select the actual tools for the analysis. It is with the phase of observation that the change agent really enters the organization for the first time, and this is made possible because the basis for a relationship of trust has been laid in the first stage.

In the inventory phase the material for the actual analysis is collected. This is done by the client himself.

The analysis proper, or the diagnosis, has two aspects, namely individual development interviews and a group meeting.

A developmental model for planned organizational change

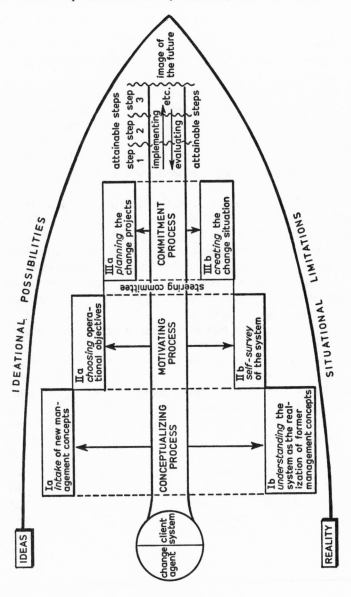

In the individual interview the change agent reflects back the material collected by his partner, interprets it with him in an open discussion, and then tries together with him to find problem statements for change projects.

In the group meeting the whole picture is reflected back to the group, and problems are formulated that are relevant for the group as a whole. Through confrontation with the operational objectives it is now possible to select actual change projects. Since this meeting must lead to decisions it is very important that people should know in advance what kind of decision-making is to be employed. This applies particularly to the top group of the enterprise, which usually consists of the board and the top management team, who are joined in this case by the change agent.

The third stage is concerned on the one hand with planning change projects and on the other with organizing change situations. Here what matters is that changes are really *wanted*. The objective of this stage is also to achieve among those concerned a change of attitude at the level of the will. We call this an 'intentional' attitude change.

The main feature of this stage is that client and change agent together begin actively to take the first steps along the path towards the new objectives. We call this 'commitment'. For the client the process is existential, but the change agent is also involved in it to such an extent that he in fact shares in the commitment.

It is at this stage that real resistance will arise, and the change agent must help to overcome it. In some cases he enters into a personal consultant relationship with certain people. This makes him vulnerable because he loses his role of objective outsider.

In order to ensure that the process does not become rudderless and thus uncontrollable, a steering committee must be formed between the second and the third stages. This committee, whose members should ideally be drawn from all management levels, guides the change process on behalf of all the other people in the organization. The steering committee does not constitute a new hierarchy beside the existing one. It does not give commands, but stimulates initiative and suggestions; it describes, times, and measures the practical progress made by the process against previously determined criteria. The steering committee bases its work on the rules of play drawn up and accepted by the members of the organization.

The setting-up of a steering committee serves a double purpose. In the first place it enables the change agent to be of real assistance, without allowing the process to become uncontrollable and thus no longer assessable. In the second place the client system learns how to steer its own process of organizational development. It can practise what it will later have to do all the time when its relationship with the change agent has come to an end.

The planning of change projects must fulfil the following conditions. There must be a clear formulation of purpose and a clear statement as to who is going to participate and in what roles. There must be a time schedule. An assessment must be made of the help and support — for example in the form of training — that will be required in order to carry out the project. Finally, evaluation criteria have to be formulated. (Experimental change projects in experimental situations can be undertaken as preliminary exercises on a limited scale; these serve the purpose of gaining experience, of revealing side-issues and difficulties, and of giving the client system confidence that it can achieve a change.)

After this third stage the actual realization stage begins in attainable steps. Once it has been planned, each attainable step has two parts: implementation and evaluation. After evaluation, corrections can be made and objectives reassessed. Then a new step begins. During the realization stage the change agent gradually withdraws until the client system can continue on its own.

In the above, attention has been given almost exclusively to the top management group. In practice, other groups would be included in the process during the preparatory stages. They have the same right to learn about the change agent's ideas, for example in a suitably adapted management conference. Their creative contributions must be promoted as far as possible.

## REFERENCES

1 LIPPITT, R., WATSON, J. & WESTLEY, B. *The dynamics of planned change*, p. 5. New York, 1958.
2 VAN DOORN, J. A. A . & LAMMERS, C. J. *Moderne sociologie: systematiek en analyse*, p. 280. Utrecht, 1959.
3 LIPPITT, WATSON & WESTLEY (see reference 1 above), p. 5.
4 EMERY, F. E. & TRIST, E. L. The causal texture of organizational environments. *Human Relations* 18(1), 1965, pp. 21-32.
5 LIPPITT, WATSON & WESTLEY (see reference 1 above), p. 9.
6 SERVAN-SCHREIBER, J-J. *Le Défi Américain*. Paris, 1967. Eng. trans. *The American challenge*. London, 1968.
7 CHIN, R. The utility of systems models and developmental models. In

W. G. Bennis, K. D. Benne, and R. Chin (eds.), *The planning of change.* New York, 1961; revised edition, 1969.

8   EMERY & TRIST (see reference 4 above).

9   SCHUMPETER, J. A. *Capitalism, socialism, and democracy.* London, 1943.

10  MARX, E. C. H. Een bijdrage tot organisering van reorganiseringsmethoden. Public lecture, Leiden, 1966.

11  For the concept of organization see, among others:
VAN DOORN, J. A. A. *Sociologie van de organisatie.* Leiden, 1956.
ETZIONI, A. *Modern organizations.* Englewood Cliffs, N.J., 1964.
MAYNTZ, R. *Soziologie der Organisation.* Hamburg, 1963.

12  KATZ, D. & KAHN, R. L. *The social psychology of organizations.* New York, 1966.

13  LEAVITT, H. J. Applied organizational change in industry: structural, technological and humanistic approaches. In J. G. March (ed.), *Handbook of organizations.* Chicago, 1965.

14  COLTHOF, H. *Veranderen en aanpassen in de organisatie van het bedrijf.* Alphen a/d Rijn, 1965.

15  For expectations, norms, objectives, and values, see VAN DOORN & LAMMERS (reference 2 above), p. 86.

16  BARBER, B. Structural-functional analysis: some problems and misunderstandings. *American Sociological Review* 21(2), 1956, pp. 129-35.

17  HUTTE, H. A. *Sociatrie van de arbeid.* Assen, 1966.

18  LIPPITT, R. Dimensions of the consultant job. In Bennis, Benne, and Chin (see reference 7 above).
GARDNER, B. B. The consultant to business. In A. W. Gouldner and S. M. Miller (eds.), *Applied sociology.* New York, 1965.

19  GOULDNER, A. W. Engineering and clinical approaches to consulting. In Bennis, Benne, and Chin (see reference 7 above).

20  BENNIS, W. G. A new role for the behavioral sciences: effecting organizational change. Seminar, North Carolina State College, April, 1963.

21  MILES, M. B. On temporary systems. In *Innovation in education.* New York, 1964.

22  JAQUES, E. *The changing culture of a factory.* London, 1951.

23  LIPPITT, WATSON & WESTLEY (see reference 1 above), p. 129.

24  VAN DOORN & LAMMERS (see reference 2 above), p. 286.

25  HUTTE (see reference 17 above), p. 77.

26  COLTHOF (see reference 14 above), p. 33.

27  BOULDING, K. *The image.* Ann Arbor, Mich., 1956.

28  See, among others, VAN DOORN & LAMMERS (reference 2 above), p. 44.

## CHAPTER THIRTEEN

# Decision-making: Joint Consultation, Negotiation, Conflict

In the three subsystems of an enterprise, economic, technical, and social, one finds oneself in three different worlds with their own laws and their own methods of decision-making. It is important to be clear about these differences in order to avoid overstepping the boundaries.

## THE TECHNICAL SUBSYSTEM

This is a causal, deterministic system. This means that models within the technical system are of the logical and rational kind, with or without feedback.

Designing such models is a matter of choosing a path for achieving a defined goal. Given the same resources and the same goal (e.g. a machining process), various designs are possible, all of which, if they are good, approach the solution of the task in question. The selection of one possible design will then depend on a judgement of the value of certain aspects of the design.

A technical construction becomes a *problem* if it can no longer satisfy the set goal. In that case it has to be repaired if the structure produces deviations, or adjusted if the function shows deviations. The path to the repairing or adjusting is again logical and analytical.

This path begins with a diagnosis of the cause of the disturbance. Thus it is a path of *problem analysis*. Not until the final real cause has been found is it possible to determine the path towards restoring the former condition.

Next there is a *decision road*, when all alternative solutions are explored as to their consequences. Then the measures to be taken emerge as the optimal solution within several required standards relating to length of standstill, hours of work, replacements, and so on.

Finally comes the *assessment* of whether the construction once again complies with the set standards.

Since the technical system permeates the whole enterprise, and therefore no problem can arise which does not *also* have a technical or organizational facet, even if only of a procedural kind, it is always possible to adopt a technical method of problem-solving for all problems. But this method can solve only the technical and not the economic or social aspects of a problem. Nevertheless, the logical, causal, deterministic method of problem-solving is so fascinating and simple that there are schools of thought currently advocating it for the solving of *all* problems.

We may refer here, among others, to the method of Kepner and Tregoe, which is at present attracting attention in German commerce and industry. Kepner and Tregoe[1] begin their book with two axioms which they make their point of departure:

(1) every problem is a deviation from a (known) standard;
(2) every problem consists of sub-problems and every sub-problem has only *one* cause.

Building on these axioms they construct a path of seven steps of logical problem analysis, which leads to the single cause of the problem. From this, the direction of the action to be taken is determined. Then follows a second path of seven steps, called the decision road; here the target, and the alternative solutions and their consequences, lead to the planning of the measures.

This way of working is obviously useful where the technical aspect of a problem is predominant. But the axioms stating that every problem is a deviation from a norm and that every problem has only one cause are no longer applicable when, in the economic or social subsystem, there are arbitrary or fluctuating norms, together with a complex of connected causes, sometimes called a 'systems cluster' in American literature.

If this method *is* applied in situations involving people, the social aspect of the problem is reduced to an unacceptable degree. The solutions found mean that symptoms of an economic or social nature have to be swept under the carpet, and they then simply reappear elsewhere in a different guise. Moreover, in recent years many problems that have arisen within the technical system can no longer be described unequivocally in a deterministic way. This makes *stochastic* or *probability models* necessary.

With these, various possibilities can be shown, each with its degree of probability. In the natural sciences, many nineteenth-century deterministic models have been replaced by probability models. Problem-solving can then be analogous to that already described. But instead of *one* cause there are *several* possible causes which have to be named, each with its degree of probability.

## THE ECONOMIC SUBSYSTEM

Coming from the technical to the economic subsystem, we find that here more than one type of model-building is possible.

In the first place the economic sphere is familiar with a number of deterministic models, such as market mechanisms, cycles, etc. As reductions of economic reality these can be made clear in analogous models comprising, for instance, communicating containers with coloured liquids, or meshing cogwheels depicting accelerations and decelerations, and so on. One can also make abstract mathematical models of these mechanisms.

In addition, economic activities take place within *finalistic, normative models*, of which *strategic models* are a sub-category.

In a strategic model various subsystems may be found as *action centres* within a single system. Each action centre operates normatively within the same field and with *incomplete information* about the other action centres. The behaviour of the other action centres can be analysed, the effects of different 'moves' studied, and the most probable chosen. But one of the rules of the game in this system is that it is improbable that the other action centres will in fact take the most probable line of action.

Wherever rival social organizations operate together in the same field, it is a *strategic model* that is involved. Action within a strategic model can be directed towards maintaining the *status quo* or towards changing it in order to improve one's position. By analysis of the situation, possible actions and their consequences can be calculated exactly or approximately. The decision road is different from that of the deterministic model where all variables are known. The decision road goes via the acceptance of *risk* and *uncertainty*.

The concept of 'acceptable risk' is clearly a normatively loaded concept which can be judged in various ways in a strategic model. It is difficult enough to determine the *probability* of an effect (especially when there are more than two action centres), but in addition one also has to determine the *desirability* of an effect. This is indeed a difficult proposition, particularly when the side-effects lie outside the economic sphere.

It has already been suggested that the game of chess is the best-known example of a strategic model in which the strategy of conflict is practised. A strategic game theory has been developed which has a scale of possibilities ranging from 100 per cent conflict to 100 per cent collaboration. Between these two extremes lie the mixed games with some conflicting and some coinciding interests.

The commercial game of an enterprise is always of the mixed type. Under cover of mutual interests, the conflicting interests are fought out. Both parties are thus tied to certain limits, since in a situation of total conflict no business could be done.

The tensions between the departments of an enterprise should also always be seen within the same mixed strategic model. These tensions can thus never be rationally organized out of existence. One can of course rationally solve the technical or organizational components of the problem; but there is then a danger that one of the action centres in the strategic model will experience this as a threat to the *status quo*; the result would then be 'illogical resistance to logical changes'.

## THE SOCIAL SUBSYSTEM

The technical subsystem has to be approached deterministically; the economic subsystem requires in addition a normative approach; and the social subsystem adds *development* to these. So the social system has to be understood and steered at the three levels of logical, strategic, and development thinking.

Simple causal models can be built for all situations in which basic subsistence plays a part. This is the area of quantifiable material needs and their satisfaction. This approach is admissible in situations such as that of the developing countries, where large sections of the population live below subsistence level. The human being is here reduced by circumstances to a physiological system with measurable needs.

As soon as a certain degree of prosperity has been reached, other variables come into play. Psychological needs always have to do with interpersonal relations and they are shown in mixed strategic models. They appear in multivalent situations where values of different categories contend with each other for precedence.

Finally, development both of individuals and of groups means a progression from simple general structures to structures with more differentiation and greater complexity. Therefore purposeful action within the social subsystem of an enterprise always has to give consideration to development, which leads to far-reaching structural changes.

In the context of a deterministic model one speaks of social techniques, and in that of a normative model of social skills. In connection with a developmental model one must speak of developmental skills, because the variables in the model are human beings who develop. This is why the social system has the possibility of maturing. The problems involved have been discussed in Chapter 12.

## Social Skills

Decision-making, which involves human activity, takes place within a mixed strategic model. Acting within this model is one of the *social skills*. In contrast to dealing with inanimate things within a deterministic model, one has to take account here of more than one cause of a problem and more than one way of problem-solving.

Any interpersonal problem can be given a place on the continuum shown here:

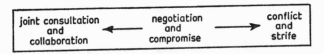

The mixed situation between consultation and conflict enters the situation of negotiation if the partners have a main common interest and a less important conflicting interest. This is the case with all price and wage negotiations. With wages, for example, negotiation takes place in the area between the wage on which the worker cannot live and the wage that would mean the folding-up of the company. Within these margins all the arguments for determining higher or lower wages can confront each other.

Every negotiation swings back and forth between consultation and conflict. In a situation of *total conflict* the harmonizing common interest no longer exists: 'I don't care what happens to the others as long as I get what I want.' Cold war is very near conflict; whereas association is an attempt to approach joint consultation.

Social skill in this respect is the knowledge and ability to act and react in an appropriate way in all these different situations.

Social skill in general has three aspects:

— social insight
— social sensitivity
— social technique.

Insight can be acquired through study. Sensitivity can be practised in specially created situations in which a person is made conscious of his own behaviour within a group. Social technique can also be practised in role-playing and other exercises.

Here we can deal only with a few aspects of social insight, so let us look at the procedure of joint consultation in a group.

*Joint Consultation*

This is important because, as we shall see, the procedure of joint consultation also provides the foundation for action in situations involving negotiation and conflict.

A group can meet in order to analyse and formulate a problem, or in order to find a solution for a given problem. Sometimes the two activities must be done consecutively. In every case there are three aspects — the group, the path it takes, and the objective:

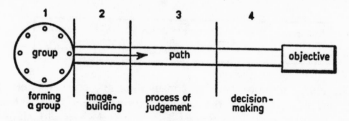

The group is on a path to an objective. This path has a number of stages:

1. At the *group-forming* stage, the group must be motivated to *want* to operate *as a group*. Necessary conditions for this are:

— a feeling of *freedom* to express one's own opinion and to make a contribution without fear of reprisals
— a situation of *equality* of all the participants in relation to the problem awaiting solution; this means that each person takes part in the group because his potential contribution will be of value in the solution of the problem
— the style of leadership in the group must be accepted by all the

participants, and each must know that he is accepted by the others as he is, with all his characteristics, good and bad.

An introductory talk can ensure that these basic conditions are fulfilled. (If this stage is not carefully handled and if the participants are uncertain of the basic conditions of joint consultation, then they will not open up and from the outset the situation will be one of negotiation and not of consultation.)

2. The group, now that it *is* a group, sets to work to compose a joint *image* of its task.

For this it is necessary that every piece of information bearing on the question, the task, the side-issues, and so forth is brought forward and assimilated by all the participants. The purpose of this stage is to ensure that in the subsequent discussion and related activities everybody is completely informed, so that at least one knows that one is talking about the same thing. One must also make sure that the available information is sufficient for the discussion of the problem. In some cases it may be necessary to reduce a general question to an operational objective.

At the end of this stage of the group process, the participants have an agreed image of the point of departure and of the task of the group.

3. The next step is a *process of judgement*. What is the value or weight of the given or collected information? What binding conditions and criteria are given, and what criteria does the group itself wish to establish for possible solutions?

These criteria must be clearly formulated because possible solutions will have to be checked against them. This searching for criteria, for *judgements*, is really the core of joint consultation, which can only be undertaken in a group. If these criteria are all already available there is no need to form a group, since the problem could then be solved technically or even by computer.

4. *Decision-making* is the last step taken by the group on its way to its objective.

In the first part of this stage the group seeks a number of possible alternative solutions all of which comply with the criteria set up by the group.

In the next part the consequences of the various solutions are examined, and here a step backwards is sometimes necessary so that in a new process of judgement the *desirability* of certain consequences can be discussed.

Then comes the selection of the most desirable solution, involving possibly the consideration of more than one solution with its associated consequences.

Finally, it is necessary to communicate the chosen solution to other parties as well as to arrange for the implementation of the agreed measures.

For the efficient functioning of joint consultation it is necessary to adhere to a clear procedure.

If the group has not been successfully formed, the participants will retain uncertainties and tensions; if the image of the task does not emerge clearly, discussions will be endless and confused; if judgements are not carefully made, there will be conflict at the decision-making stage; and in the end the group will be so pleased just to reach a decision that it will forget to examine the consequences or plan the necessary implementation.

The leadership function of a group on its way to an objective has the task among others of guarding this procedure. An experienced and mature group can manage itself, and the leadership function can be spread informally within the group. But an inexperienced group needs firmer leadership. Otherwise some members might immediately produce a solution and compel the group to discuss it before the judging process has taken place. Others might stubbornly continue to argue on the basis of a faulty image, and so on.

The traps that group consultation can fall into are numerous. But as the group gradually learns to operate 'cleanly' and efficiently, group consultation can become a useful instrument for the solution of complex problems requiring various specialists.

Not every group has the task of solving a problem or even of proposing a solution. There can be groups with image-building as their objective, or the communication of information, or the assimilation of information by the members. There are also study groups whose objective is a deepening of the judgement process.

The work of group consultation could be expressed as: shared information, joint consultation, and joint decision-making.

*Negotiation*

Those who are experienced in group consultation can, with a change of emphasis in the technique, handle negotiation as well.

There are situations where negotiation as such is justified. But it can also happen that a planned consultation session suddenly deteriorates into negotiation if one of the participants refuses full cooperation. In negotiation the parties are not prepared to reveal all their information, to place all their cards on the table.

In a situation of negotiation the group is 'polarized': each party presents only information that is favourable to its own position; its own criteria, its 'hidden agendas', are kept dark as long as possible. A successful negotiation leads to a compromise instead of a shared process of judgement.

### Conflict

A guideline for survival in a conflict situation would be to take the opposite of all the rules of procedure for joint consultation. The following points could serve in a conflict situation:

— never let the group unite; divide and conquer
— ensure that confusing information is brought into the discussion
— let the others argue about information and criteria and fix your attention on the solution you want
— suddenly suggest a solution which you do not want and which you know the others will not want either
— when they start opposing your suggestion, present them with the solution you really want, as a compromise
— criticize the criteria put forward by others and at the same time upset the balance with new information
— and so on...

It may be surprising to find these hints for the devil's advocate published here, but it is necessary in life to strive for good while being prepared to meet evil. Furthermore, these hints may serve to reveal an opponent's techniques.

However, situations of total conflict hardly ever appear in practice. Nearly always the situation is one of negotiation verging on conflict. Even a war is waged with certain reservations concerning the situation that will exist when the war is over, and during the most violent offensives contact is usually maintained somewhere in the background via a neutral country.

Thus it is immensely important to take every opportunity of returning to a situation nearer negotiation. 'International consultation' is in reality always negotiation. And if an official involved in such a situation tries to conduct matters for his part as if he were taking part in joint consultation, then he will fail — which is something he cannot often afford to do, in view of the interests he represents.

The ability to switch rapidly from negotiation to consultation and vice versa belongs to the social skills that every manager should possess. Where forced to do so he should be able to fight adamantly, but he should also be flexible in negotiation, and open and honest in joint consultation.

Some professional deformity has arisen here as a result of much negotiation. Thus one finds many managers who cannot relinquish their negotiation tactics even for internal consultations, who consciously or unconsciously withhold information so as to remain 'in control', or who start consultation when they already have a solution in mind. In this way 'consultation' can become 'manipulation'. To vary a well-known phrase one might say 'manipulation doesn't pay'.

Those who substitute manipulation for joint consultation in their own firm reduce the result of consultation and undermine their co-workers' motivation for full participation. Worse still, manipulation becomes a code of behaviour and 'a spanner in the works'.

REFERENCE

1  KEPNER, C. H. & TREGOE, B. B. *The rational manager*. New York, 1965.

## CHAPTER FOURTEEN

# Developing Social Skills

During the transition from the second to the third phase in the development of an enterprise, the frequency and intensity of joint consultation increase. If resistance to the increasing amount of consultation arises, it is mainly because there is a general lack of practice in effective and objective discussion. Thus there is a common need to practise the social skills of collaboration in learning situations created for this purpose.

The first to tackle this problem systematically were a number of young American social psychologists working with Kurt Lewin, who died shortly after the Second World War. They developed sensitivity training in what they called a social laboratory situation, in which the participant could experience (his own) behaviour in groups. Their organization, the National Training Laboratories (NTL), specialized in group training for all sectors of organization needs. In Europe this work was taken over by the European Institute for Transnational Research and Studies in Group and Organizational Development (EIT).

Those who have taken part a few times in the three-week training groups of the NTL in America will have noticed that their technique and style have grown out of the American social situation and are closely adapted to it.

The behaviour of the individual in the group is given precedence, and the open experimental situation is carried to the extreme. In addition, the training group (T-group) is placed in an unstructured situation without leadership, goals, or procedures. The course leaders remain firmly in the background, helping only with brief explanations during the group meetings (which last about two hours), and with brief introductions to sociopsychological phenomena given after the session in the second half of the morning. The frustrations that come about during the group discussions are experienced and assimilated in a different way by each participant. The group as a whole is occupied above all with itself and there is no common objective outside the group. In the afternoons more clearly structured role-playing and group exercises take place.

The whole of the learning process is accompanied by considerable tension, and it enables many individuals to acquire greater insight. Whether it also leads to better *work*-oriented consultation still remains to be seen.

Participants in the American courses, and in the Laboratories introduced in Europe, have opted to take part in such exercises voluntarily. They are therefore responsible for their own decision. However, if in the course of larger structural developments in an enterprise whole groups of personnel have to learn how to function better in work-oriented consultation, then participation is no longer, or only partly, on a voluntary basis. In such circumstances the participants should be protected from the stress of enforced self-knowledge, and the learning process should be directed more towards work-oriented consultation and to the behaviour of the individual in a work-structured situation. Each participant is then free to achieve some self-awareness and self-development according to his abilities and needs.

The primary aim of the group is cognitive learning and the fostering of perceptiveness and social skills. Furthermore, a group of teachers in a school, or a group of people working in the same department, differs from a mixed group of widely differing participants in that they have to meet each other again in the same configuration in their work situation once the course is over. Unreleased tensions which arise if the laboratory situation is completely open must not be allowed to affect the work situation; therefore the participants have to be protected during the learning process and the organization concerned has to be sure that it is sending its personnel to a course which will bring about a growing measure of collaboration.

Faced with the task of developing a course in social skills suitable for European conditions and work situations, NPI (Institute for Organization Development) carried out its first group courses in 1955, initially for people in industry and in technical teaching. Since then these courses have undergone development from year to year, in the light of wide experience. Except during the holiday season, courses take place constantly, often several at a time in various sectors of adult education.

These courses have a basic design, which derives from the view that social skill has three components:

— social insight: knowledge and understanding of sociopsychological codes
— social sensitivity: the ability to appreciate social situations (empathy) and to appraise them fairly
— social technique: the ability to behave in different social situations in a way appropriate to the situation.

Any of these alone leads to one-sidedness. It is a balance of the three components that constitutes social skill.

In the specific situation of an enterprise there are some particularly important facets of social skill: for example, the ability to make realistic plans for group activity; flexibility in leading and being led; the capacity to form clear judgements; the ability to participate in changing groups with changing objectives.

NPI's courses in social skills usually take a fortnight; but their design and objective are adapted according to the time available. The course is composed of a number of elements:

— a triad of planning, implementation, and evaluation
— information on sociopsychological codes
— some practical exercises
— follow-up in the work situation of what has been practised during the course; this is done in organizations undergoing general organizational development.

This basic design allows for any number of variations and combinations brought about either by the course leaders or by the participants themselves.

The following is a brief description of the main elements of the course in social skills run by the NPI.

## 1. *The Triad of Planning, Implementation, and Evaluation*

*Planning:* Realistic planning is one of the first social skills to be practised. A major part of the frustration engendered in group consultation is the result of unrealistic planning of activities. Taking part, for instance, in a weekly consultative meeting, one can experience how unrealistically the agenda is compiled. Often there are twelve to seventeen urgent points to be discussed, although only one afternoon is available for the meeting. The points are so important that by the time number six is reached the afternoon is over and the remainder have to be postponed to the following week. Such an unreaslitic agenda may in turn be the result of unrealistic distribution of the tasks of a group within a larger organizational structure. To be able to diagnose the source of unrealistic planning is a part of social skill.

During the course, then, the group makes plans the previous evening for the free group activities to take place the next morning. This planning is the responsibility of the group itself and is carried out under the group's leadership. The organizers are simply present at the first meetings in order to supply information on request.

For example, a plan might be made for a group discussion involving the whole group (usually twelve to fourteen people). In addition to selecting a *theme*, a clear *problem* within the theme should be determined in order to avoid embarking on a discussion which might lead nowhere. The course leaders do not interfere even when there are obvious omissions in the planning; the group must experience and later evaluate the results of its own decisions.

In addition, decisions have to be made on questions of procedure. For instance: whether there should be an introduction; whether there should be a chairman; whether the group should pause at regular intervals to see what headway it is making; and so on.

After some exercises, the group is likely to choose forms of activity other than plenary discussions. Some of the participants may decide not to take part in the activity but to follow the process from outside as observers. Or the group can split into two: first, Group A discusses and Group B observes, and then Group B discusses while Group A observes. Or every group member taking part in the discussion can have another member assigned to him, to keep him informed of how things are going, and so on. In the second week of a two-week course in particular, one can find ever freer forms of activity, observation, and communication, so that these can be practised in various situations.

It is important to make plans the day or evening before an activity is to take place. Night often brings a new point of view or a change of motivation— a fact that can be included in the exercise so that people become aware of it.

*Implementation:* The discussion itself, in whatever form it has been planned, takes place the following morning. The seminar leaders do not intervene, but are present as observers; they make notes or use a tape-recorder as required. This exercise usually takes an hour and a half.

*Evaluation:* With a more advanced group, evaluation can take place *ad hoc* during the course of the discussion; but usually it is done at the end of the afternoon and takes about as long as the morning discussion itself. Experience has shown the usefulness of the interval between the morning session and its evaluation late in the afternoon. The participants have had time to view their performance from a distance and can thus be more objective, and yet the distance is not so great that they have forgotten the details. Even so, participants usually have little more than a general opinion about their morning's work: it was 'satisfactory', or 'not much good', etc.

In order to assist the evaluation process of the group, the course leaders provide a framework for the evaluation session. This can be simply a summary of the morning's discussion; or it can be a time-schedule, describing what took place in each consecutive five minutes. This is a kind of first reflection of what happened: Where did certain themes appear? Where did they disappear? Where did they reappear? And so on.

On one of the days the procedure of consultation can be highlighted: How successful was the joint building of an image? How was the process of judgement tackled? Was a decision made?

On another of the days the discussion may be used more for the purpose of reviewing the interaction, the group process as such: How did leadership function in the group? Did this influence the discussion and the outcome? Who participated and how? What tensions were there? What blocked certain contributions? How did the group handle this?

It may be sufficient in some cases to make a detailed analysis of a critical five-minute period in the morning's discussion, emphasized if necessary by playing back the tape.

To support the evaluation, the essence of the discussion can sometimes be summarized by the course leaders in the form of a humorous drawing. The evaluation, especially the humour, will not be forgotten, and so the learning process is deepened.

The general object of evaluation is the confrontation of planning and implementation: Did we achieve the aim we set ourselves? If not, why not? During the next planning session the group tries to avoid previous pitfalls, only to discover that it encounters new difficulties instead.

The group wrestles in turn with content, procedure, and group interaction; gradually it gains a certain amount of experience and is able to move more freely in these areas.

## 2. *The Morning Lectures*

The lectures given in the morning after the group work give the members an opportunity to switch from active participation to listening and assimilating. The lectures first of all introduce the concept of development, then describe some aspects of the social development of a group, of an organization (its phases of development), of society, and of man himself during the course of his life. In short, they deal with the main themes of this book; indeed, in a sense one could say that this book was written as an answer to the questions, needs, and problems arising in the group discussions. As a rule the person who gives the lecture in the second half of the morning is present during the morning discussion, so that he can often deal directly with the questions to which it gives rise.

It is therefore important that while certain fundamental topics are dealt with in these lectures there should nevertheless be great flexibility of content, sequence, and form.

## 3. *Afternoon Activities*

The afternoon is reserved for various more structured activities. Ideally these should be of an artistic nature: exercises in dramatic expression, modelling, and painting; also role-playing in familiar social situations which participants frequently encounter in their workplace. Artistic activities can cure all sorts of inhibitions, quite apart from the fact that they are enjoyable. There is definitely no need for a course in skills to be a gruelling experience.

Some evenings are free while on others guest speakers talk on subjects relevant to the group.

This brief description will have shown that a course in social skills can be both strenuous and relaxing. The alternation between active participation and listening, and between different kinds of activity, makes a composite whole which is healthily acceptable. Moreover, after the first few days the group has considerable freedom to participate in the planning of further events.

## 4. *Follow-up*

After the basic course, NPI is able to offer follow-up possibilities of various kinds.

For people who often have to lead discussions, and also for personnel and training officers, a continuation course on evaluation techniques can be organized. This provides practice in evaluating group activities and in presenting the evaluation to the group.

A seminar on creative collaboration offers a follow-up to the general course in social skills and answers the need for deeper personal development in a group context.

Those involved in large reorganization projects, as described in Chapter 12, can employ many varieties of social skill and corresponding ways of working in their own organization. Where firms have their own internal courses, small groups can be assisted within their actual work situations.

Organizational development can also be studied in mixed groups. A 'change game' is then built into the seminar, based on a practical case. In other instances one of the seminar participants will have done a small piece of research; he then provides the data and the others act as his external consultants. In this way, quite detailed internal investigations can be carried out by the group, and their work will be evaluated. Naturally the enterprise involved has to take part, but it receives in return some support for its own change projects.

Thus the teaching of social skills, which began with external courses for mixed groups of participants, has developed into a great variety of mutual learning processes for concrete work situations.

The experience gained in commerce and industry can be usefully applied in other areas of society — schools, hospitals, national and local government, etc. — for social institutions present similar problems of development even though they have different objectives.*

---

* For a description of the various courses mentioned in this chapter, see the Programme of the Conference and Study Centre of VNO (Verbond van Nederlandse Ondernemingen), Koningin Astridboulevard 23, Noordwijk aan Zee, Netherlands.

## CHAPTER FIFTEEN

# Mergers and the Clover-leaf Organization

At the present time mergers, and other less complete collaborative arrangements, are the order of the day. The reasons for mergers are manifold.

Ideally, a merger should come about as a free decision on the part of two healthy expanding enterprises who see the merger as a means of strengthening both their positions. In practice, however, the freedom of decision of the partners varies according to whether both are healthy or both are undergoing difficulties, or whether one is strong and one weak. In the latter case a merger is a cover-up for a takeover.

Whenever a merger takes place, two enterprises, two systems with their own often different policies, have to grow together to form a new, larger enterprise, a single system with new policies and new organizational principles. A merger is therefore always a process of intensive social change; and in practice it is usually unplanned social change.

Whether the merger is carried out horizontally, vertically, laterally, or in the form of a chain merger, the expectation is always that the result of integration will be greater than the sum of the parts. Mergers are made according to the formula $2 + 2 = 5$; but this does not become reality unless the merger is carried out as a planned revolution. On the morning after the night before, when the ceremonial pen has been laid aside and the champagne glasses have been cleared away, the new combination faces the task of realizing the expectations.

A merger shows everything in a clearer light: the seeming security of submarginal enterprises, the over-ripe pioneer phase, the rigid phase of differentiation — all these are highlighted by the need to develop into a new and larger entity. In addition, it becomes painfully obvious that the forward vision, the horizon and the time-span of the management, which may already have been too small for the separate firms, are unquestionably too small for the much larger new entity.

A merger often means a jump not only to a quantitatively larger totality but above all to a qualitatively different market and to different technology, financing, and information-processing. This means that a new kind of human capital is needed in the new situation. Some people are made redundant by duplication; for many of the new positions there will be a need for at least some retraining and very often for a considerable change of attitude; and for some positions new people will have to be taken on who have knowledge and experience of a kind not available in the merging enterprises. Most important of all, however, is the concept of the new organization structure and the new policy.

In Chapter 12 we were concerned with planned change and organizational development taking place in an evolutionary manner. But in the case of a merger, organizational development takes place in a revolutionary manner. Within a short period of time a series of co-ordinated reorganizations have to be achieved within the framework of a well thought-out plan, if the advantage of the merger is not to be lost. And if the new internal and external policies have been insufficiently worked through in advance, this is where failure will occur. It is obvious, moreover, that classical organization theory cannot meet this situation.

An answer to the situation can be found, however, in the clover-leaf organization and in the path from the classical second phase of organization to the third phase.

First of all, the place and task of the top management must be clearly defined in a merger. This gives rise to a number of practical difficulties. Taken together, the merging enterprises have too many directors. Also, particularly in the early years the new top management must be able to make quick decisions and to carry out policy without disagreement. A board of three directors working as colleagues, as described below, or a chairman and three directors, are appropriate for the task.

Experience shows that it is not effective to leave the boards of the partners as they are, simply letting them meet from time to time as the new joint board. The clash of roles is so great that conflicts cannot be avoided. Important decisions, which could 'hurt' one or other of the partners, are often not made. Whether it is necessary to engage anyone from outside at director level depends on the talents of the two former boards. But it is no use appointing a chairman from outside if the existing directors are split because:

— within the new combination the partners adhere to their former policies
— there is a power struggle between persons or groups
— one of the partners feels superior to the other.

This is why it is so important that the partners should establish more precisely than usual, *before* the merger, who will be the new directors, how the tasks will be divided, and what policy will be introduced. If agreement is not reached about these things beforehand, it is better not to go ahead with the merger.

The policies of the new board can be systematically worked out on the basis of the clover-leaf organization.

## 1. *New Commercial Policy*

The pioneer phase had as its commercial objective the *selling of products* to known customers within a familiar market. In the second phase this objective often changed to *selling for turnover* to an anonymous market. In the third phase the goal must become *marketing development*, where account is taken not only of existing products and known or conquerable markets but also of the needs of existing or potential consumers which could be solved by the enterprise with the help of current know-how, relations, or technology.

The moment the merger takes place can be the moment to start in principle with this form of marketing by formulating new commercial objectives and reshaping the commercial organization. At the same time, there must be an overall analysis of the situation of the two merging partners and a general investigation of the personnel position, including an estimate of training requirements and of the need for new personnel.

## 2. *Processes*

The next step will be the investigation of the technical processes within the two companies. In the case of a horizontal merger these will be almost identical. In a vertical merger the two will join within a larger process flow. With a lateral merger, many techniques will be the same although the companies are making different products.

Here again an overall joint opinion pertaining to the new throughput of the merged companies must be reached. A decision will also have to be made on the separation of units with their own technical objectives, or even on the departmentalization of the new organization according to products, geographical location, or market areas.

## 3. *Resources*

The resources brought in by each partner have usually been estimated and assessed at the time of the merger. The financial resources are often the only ones that have been explicitly allocated. In addition there are the various properties, the buildings and machines. What approximately will be the position and function of these in the new situation?

The human resources are a problem on their own. Any merger, as a form of accelerated growth, leads to uncertainty about being able to keep up with the new situation. What degree of uncertainty is morally justified? To give categorical assurances that no one will become redundant is a form of deception. And even if the total number of employees does not decrease, the increase in scale and the acceleration of development will still mean a significant change in all management positions. Now all unsuitable appointments made in the past, all merely nominal functions, all those who have been shunted into sidings or kicked upstairs into harmless positions will be revealed.

For this reason a training programme and a rough estimate of critical positions must be made beforehand. One may offer all the help one can, but no promises should be made which cannot later be fulfilled.

Much will depend on a realistic and yet inspiring personnel policy, supported by a united top management which sets an example in that it comprises new skills. The new commercial policy may need new technical processes and resources. How can the enterprise achieve a rapid expansion of the know-how required for uninterrupted development? A general estimate will have to be made of this too. It will be necessary to know what working groups to establish and what tasks to give them.

In this way, once the merger has taken place, workers and management will notice that the new board knows what it wants. This gives them the motivation they need if they are to put their hearts into their work. Conversely, uncertainty at the top about all these problems will lead to a resistance to change at the lower levels.

## 4. *Information*

The increase in scale of the new combination will result in great changes in internal communication channels. Many of these will grow longer as the distance from decision centres increases, and information will begin to travel along different paths.

The merger may show up the need for a central data-processing service. The correct place of the information centre in the organization must have been broadly agreed upon, otherwise there may be a tug-of-war later.

The geographical location of the new board must also be decided in advance. It is definitely undesirable to compromise by selecting a meeting-place for the board half-way between the original centres, while the members remain in their former offices for day-to-day work. This problem is important because the psychological status of the company near the board is higher than that of the other companies further away. For the period immediately following the merger it is important for the board to be located where it can have real contact with the largest possible part of the future enterprise.

All these matters are reviewed and discussed in advance, and then, as soon as possible after the merger is announced, the management must be shown the general plan of the new organization structure, including the approximate timing of its realization.

This brings us to a model of planned development which differs somewhat from evolutionary development. This developmental model (see diagram) shows us the following:

1. Before the merger takes place there is a general concept of the future. This can be created by the partners at board level, possibly with the participation of a few trusted managers or with the help of an external consultant.

2. When the merger is announced, the steering committee, which has the task of effecting the merger in practice, is introduced to personnel.

With the general concept of the future as a basis, the committee begins to set up a number of operational objectives (e.g. commercial concentration; in the technical sphere, provisional exchange and improvement of work methods; unification of administration; establishment of an information-processing centre).

This is followed immediately by an operational analysis of: the extent of changes, staffing, critical areas, areas where change is likely to be easier, and so on.

These two investigations lead to a still quite general plan of implementation, showing priorities and approximate timing.

It is important that already at this stage a broad network should emerge, showing sequences and interdependencies. Then comes the

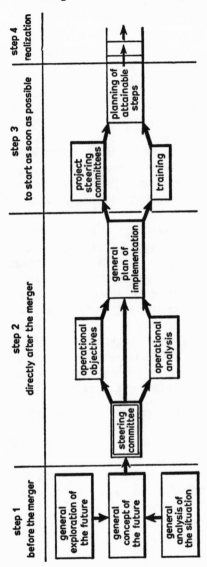

approximate assessment of timing, which shows the probable critical path. Particular attention is paid to the latter. It is likely that at this point the steering committee will wish to call in an external (independent) consultant to help with the elaboration of the first network.

Thus the general plan of implementation is made visible on a chart for all concerned, and can be seen and understood *in its totality*. This last point is most important: people accept the necessary change in their own area more readily when it is seen as part of an overall plan rather than as a disaster befalling only themselves.

3. A number of projects emerge from the overall plan. It is useful to set up a smaller steering committee for each project, to plan its execution in attainable steps.

At the same time, the main steering committee considers the training requirements for effective functioning in the new situation, and the training departments are mobilized to tackle the task of adapting training activities to the organizational changes, either internally or with outside help.

The main steering committee then withdraws and retains only the function of supervising progress. For this purpose it receives summaries of the monthly plans for the various projects, and progress reports evaluating what has actually happened. This main steering committee can, if possible, be installed at the level directly below the board.

If, at the time of the merger, a top management team is formed, representing the merger board and the directors or assistant directors of the departments in the fields of commerce, processes, resources, and central services (e.g. information-processing, personnel, training), then the board itself will be free for its proper tasks and yet will be sufficiently informed about the progress of the merger.

Most of the literature on mergers deals only briefly with the concretization of mergers as described above, and for this reason we have gone more deeply into this aspect. We conclude with a few remarks about the organization structure once the merger is completed.

Each of the original enterprises had, for better or worse, a complete board with a complete management task. As a result of the merger, the tasks and areas of competence unavoidably overlap, and there are too many directors for the future board. This means that a merger always leads to a form of group structure. Large companies that already have a group structure have, therefore, far fewer difficulties with a merger. They are already used to a layered structure at the top, and divisional management within the group policy.

When medium-sized enterprises merge, the situation is rather different. Here the level below the board can hardly be called general management; the tasks are really functional.

When companies merge, the board members should understand that it is not a disgrace in the new structure to be the director of a division of the merged group, having a general management task within the group policy. Indeed it is a new and invigorating experience to contribute as much as possible to the total result within the framework of the general policy. The members of an efficiently functioning top management team in a group that has area directors are certainly less likely to die of heart attacks than are members of an over-populated board with duplication of positions, poor delineation of tasks, and power struggles.

The merger board is therefore well advised to organize itself as a group board. This means that at the top there is no longer room for a technical, a commercial, and a financial director, each with well-defined tasks not to be infringed by others. The members of a group board are colleagues in their responsibility for the totality of management. However, each of the directors does have a main area to which he acts as a point of entry for the rest of the board, so that they know who they must turn to in the first instance in respect of any area.

Thus the members of the board have a number of joint responsibilities and, in addition, their separate tasks (see Chapter 8, p. 117). Depending on the complexity of the tasks, the board must be supported by its own specialists accommodated in a large secretariat or a number of small staff departments. These staff give assistance on the more technical problems arising from the establishment of the new objectives and the new policies.

Communication with the area directors takes place via a top management team which meets regularly to discuss both the information from the top and the information from the various areas.

A merger is a planned revolution. The unfortunate thing is that usually everybody imagines he can achieve a compromise by pouring water into someone else's wine. But the revolution is either complete or it fails. A failed merger brings about a maximum of human suffering. A successful merger can bring a new lease of life.

Apart from a complete merger, collaboration in certain areas is also possible. Van der Wolk[1] has collected a number of examples from practical experience.

For instance there can be formal collaboration in purchasing, in personnel administration, medical services, exports, imports, personnel policy, advertising, and building activities. The advantage of these forms of cooperation and association is that each enterprise retains its individuality but at the same time reaps the benefit of an increase of scale in the relevant areas. These examples apply mainly to small and medium-sized enterprises.

A merger is final and means that the individuality of an enterprise is absorbed into the spirit of the larger entity. An association leaves an enterprise much freer, so that collaboration can be terminated if it is no longer advantageous.

### ORGANIZING THE TOP OF A GROUP STRUCTURE AFTER A MERGER

The top management of a group manages a number of companies or units. The management of the companies is carried out in accordance with the clover-leaf organization, whereby it is understood that the primary function within the sphere of external relations (selling and marketing) moves within the framework of the group board's marketing policy. The same applies to product policy and production policy.

It is the task of the company boards to participate in the group board's policy-making by submitting proposals in these fields. Within the framework of group policy, *the autonomy of the companies is as great as possible* in the fields of marketing, product policy and production allocation, financing, and social and management development policy.

### Tasks

*The chief function of the group board consists in: initiating (objectives), integrating (policies), and evaluating.*

In carrying out its function, the group board is supported by a number of small staff departments with highly qualified staff whose task it is to share the board's work in policy-making (but not to provide services for the companies). These staff departments cover (as necessary):

— commercial matters: sales policy, market research
— technical matters: product development policy and production allocation
— economic and financial matters and internal accountancy
— social matters: management development
— communication policy, including information-processing policy
— possibly also legal matters, public relations, etc.

The four main tasks of the group board are:

(i) strengthening and developing the *commercial basis* of the group
(ii) *management development* (development of the human resources in the group)
(iii) *financing* of commercial and technical developments
(iv) long-term *development policy* (internal and external).

*Organization*

(a) If possible there should be collective management (but in times of extensive reorganization it can be desirable to have a chairman).
(b) The top should be as small as possible in relation to the extent of the task.
(c) There should be no 'super' specialists at the top.
(d) Three kinds of task can be distinguished:

— A number of tasks (see below) are the joint responsibility of the whole board.
— Other tasks (see below) are the concern of a particular group director who acts as a point of entry to them for the group top. This director also deals with the appropriate functionaries on behalf of the board as a whole.
— Each director maintains special personal contact with the company or companies allotted to him. The company problems with which he is primarily involved are commercial, personnel, and financial–economic matters pertaining to the *development policy*.

*Joint Tasks of the Group Board*

1. Policy questions:
— long-term planning of commerce, personnel, technology
— political relations, annual report, etc.
— group organization (among other things, appointment of directors, top-category salaries, etc.)
— market allocation, products, manufacturing technology
— expansion plans, mergers
— communication policy, including information-processing.

2. Communicative functions:
(a) Meetings of the group board should be frequent (e.g. weekly); in the case of a collective body the function of chairman should rotate. Participants are: the group board, the board secretary, and the directors of the staff departments.

The members of the group board can meet together as often as they think necessary.

(b) Meetings of individual members of the group board with the directors of the companies will be less frequent.
— Form (i): a member of the group board discusses the general situation with 'his' company.
— Form (ii): a member of the group board discusses his 'special attention' area with a number of company directors responsible in the same area (e.g. commercial, technical, financial, social issues).

(c) Group conferences should take place several times a year. Participants are the group board and *all* the directors of all the companies.

(d) As required, working groups and policy groups can be formed: they can be anything from *ad hoc* committees for the solution of temporary problems to permanent committees meeting regularly and joined when necessary by board members, directors, and staff.

*Separate Task Areas of Board Members*

As a rule, in group boards, with or without a chairman, each member is allotted a number of special areas of attention. These areas are distributed according to the main functions of the clover-leaf organization:
— supervision of commercial functions (marketing up to and including selling)
— supervision of process flows, the throughput (product development, production grouping, technological policy)
— supervision of resources organization (finance, capital goods, personnel)
— supervision of communication and information policy.

Each member of the group board has his most important supervisory task within one of these four areas. In order to prevent one-sidedness, however, he also has a number of ancillary tasks in other areas.
   These include the following:
— observing external developments in the area in question, with the help of the staff department
— pursuing the group's internal answers to these external developments
— asking stimulating questions to promote investigations and the submission of proposals to the board

— together with the staff department, assimilating proposals and integrating these with personal points of view, thus providing *policy information* for the whole group board.

**REFERENCE**

1   v.d. WOLK, E. *Samen sterk*. Alphen a/d Rijn, 1964.

# Recommended Reading

## Chapter 11

BÜHLER, CHARLOTTE. *Der menschliche Lebenslauf als psychologisches Problem.* Göttingen, 1959.

STERN, E. *Der Mensch in der zweiten Lebenshälfte.* Zürich.

BALLER, W. R. & CHARLES, D. C. *The psychology of human growth and development.* New York, 1961.

SCHELER, G. *Die Problematik der Lebensalter.* Stuttgart, 1963.

RÜMKE, H. C. *Levenstijdperken van de man.* Amsterdam, 1963.

LAUER, H. P. *Der menschliche Lebenslauf.* Freiburg i/Br., 1952.

KÜNKEL, H. *Die Lebensalter.* Constance, 1957.

GUARDINI, R. *Die Lebensalter: ihre ethische und pädagogische Bedeutung.* Würzburg.

## Chapter 13

BLAKE, R. R., SHEPARD, H. A. & MOUTON, J. S. *Managing intergroup conflict in industry.* Houston, Texas, 1964.

DRUCKER, P. *The effective executive.* London, 1967.

FOKKEMA, S. D. De begripsvorming en het probleemoplossen in de hedendaagse denkpsychologie. Lecture, Groningen, 1961.

GROOT, A. D. de *Het denken van de schaker.* Amsterdam, 1946.

HAIRE, M. (ed.) *Modern organization theory.* New York, 1959.

KAHN, R. L. & BOULDING, E. (eds.) *Power and conflict in organizations.* London, 1964.

KOONTZ, H. (ed.) *Toward a unified theory of management.* New York, 1964.

MALOTAUX, P. C. A. Subjectiveren en objectiveren. Lecture, Rotterdam, 1968.

NEWMAN, W. H. & SUMMER, C. E. Jr. *The process of management.* Englewood Cliffs, N.J., 1961.

RICE, A. K. *Productivity and social organization.* London, 1958.

SIMON, H. A. *Administrative behavior.* New York, 1957.

VERBURG, P. Besluitvaardigheid. Lecture, Wageningen, 1962.

VAN BEUGEN, M. *Sociale technologie en het instrumentele aspect van agogische actie.* Assen, 1968.

v. d. WOESTIJNE, W. J. Organisatie en voorbereiding van beleidsbeslissingen en de controle daarop. *Maandblad voor accountancy en documentatie,* July 1960.

*Werkgemeenschap voor vernieuwing van opvoeding en onderwijs: samenwerking en conflict.* Report of a conference, November 1967.

Chapter 14

BENNIS, W. G. (ed.) Twenty years' National Training Laboratories. *Journal of Applied Behavioral Science* 3(2), 1967.

BERKHOUT, W. C. Overijld toegepaste wetenschap. *Sociologische Gids* 1, 1954, pp. 12-14.

BOS. A. H. Ervaringen met meerdaagse cursussen voor volwassenen. *Mens en Onderneming* 14, 1960, pp. 341-50.

— The evaluation of groupwork. *Management International* no. 3, 1962.

BRADFORD, L. P., GIBB, J. R. & BENNE, K. D. *T-group theory and laboratory method.* New York, 1964.

TEN HAVE, T. T. (ed.) *Vorming.* (Handbook for social-cultural work in adult education.) Groningen, 1965.

KOCK VAN LEEUWEN, J. A. C. de, SCHRÖDER, M. & V. d. VEGT, R. Vier jaar ervaring met training voor tussenmenselijke verhoudingen in Nederland. *Mens en Onderneming* 18, 1964, pp. 226-32.

KRAAK, J. H. Group methods in management development programs. *Management International* no. 3, 1962.

MARROW, A. J. *Top-reacties.* Rotterdam, 1965.

MILES, M. B. *Learning to work in groups.* New York, 1967.

Studiekring voor groepsarbeid: een Amerikaans vormingscentrum voor groepswerk. *Volksopvoeding* 2, 1953.

THELEN, H. *Dynamics of groups at work.* Chicago, 1954.

TRIST, E. L. & SOFER, C. *Explorations in group relations.* Leicester, 1959.

Chapter 15

KREKEL, N. R. A., V.d. WOERD, T. G. & WOUTERSE, J. J. *Ontwikkeling, samenwerking, fusie.* Alphen a/d Rijn, 1967.

TOWNSEND, H. *Scale, innovation, merger and monopoly.* Oxford, 1968.

ALBERTS, W. W. & SEGALL, J. E. (eds.) *The corporate merger.* Chicago, 1966.

# PART V

# Looking Ahead

CHAPTER SIXTEEN

# Shaping the Future

Contemplating the future involves the designing of finalistic, normative models, since the future of a society is not determined by the facts of its past or present. Every situation in a society has *many future possibilities* within a wide sector of freedom, and this sector of freedom increases according to the degree to which a higher standard of living has freed people from the constraint of direct physiological requirements. As Gross[1] has noted, development progresses from 'quantity of goods' to 'quality of life'.

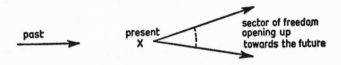

Thus 'designing the future' has become just as urgent as controlling the economic situation in the present.

Where is the future already being consciously designed? Apart from the 'think tanks' serving the military staffs of the world powers, which keep their criteria of choice secret 'for security reasons', there are some university and semi-academic institutes and foundations. The Rand Corporation, MIT's Institute of the Future, and the 'future' workshops in Tokyo, Berkeley, France, and Holland, to name only a few, are centres of the new science of futurology.

Considering the enormous amount of information and the intelligent staff at the disposal of these institutes, it must seem almost arrogant for a single individual, even if he has a small institute with a staff who share his thinking and his work and who act as a 'sounding-board', to venture any further comments on this subject. Indeed, in a way it is arrogant; but on the other hand we should remember that we could slide into a future controlled by technocrats if we were to leave everything to 'those who know better'.

213

To work out possibilities and to design concrete models for a near and a more distant future is certainly a job for specialists, but *determining the criteria of choice* is a democratic matter. We must not allow ourselves to be paralysed by the complexity of existing structures and by the quantity of information to be sifted and digested. If we did, we would have to leave the fundamental choice of our future to a small elite of super-specialists.

A small incident that occurred during the London Symposium of Biogenetics Specialists in 1963 might serve to demonstrate what could happen. The discussion panel, consisting mainly of Nobel prizewinners, made it known that within twenty years it would be possible to control heredity sufficiently to produce supermen. Asked by one of the audience what such supermen might look like, the panel fell into embarrassed confusion. At last one of the group looked around at his colleagues and said, 'Oh, rather like us'.

This incident clearly shows the situation in which we find ourselves with all our plans for the future. Nobel prizewinners and super-specialists are needed for the control of heredity. But people with plain common sense are required to determine the criteria for the aims and application of these new techniques. For this to be possible, many people must concern themselves with the overall concept of a possible and desirable future.

One way of achieving this would be for the various 'think' workshops to employ 'translators', who could transform the highly specialized information into pictures that others could understand. They would have to describe the *possible* future in such a way that those who would have to live in it could decide whether it would also be a *desirable* future.

The work required for the technical part of the future can only be done by people who 'believe' in their ideas and thus have sufficient motivation to overcome the endless train of difficulties which obstruct the path of realizing an idea. As they proceed they naturally fall in love with their brain children and expect everyone else to receive them with open arms. This is why it is essential that others should decide whether a technical possibility has a place in a basic model of society or not. It has already been suggested that 'previsional forums', which would engage in public discussion of models of the future, should be established alongside existing political parliaments.

Realists may remark here that this is all well and good, but the military think tanks have accumulated such a stock-pile of potential destructive force that the little bit of future that still remains to be governed is not worth bothering about. With Martin Luther, I should like to say this: 'If I knew that the world would come to an end tomorrow, I would still plant a tree today.' In the following, then, let us plant a tree in the form of a possible (normative) model for the future.

In his book *Le Défi Américain* (*The American challenge*), Servan-Schreiber[2] describes the near and the more distant future of Europe from the standpoint of industrial development. Parts of his book confirm much that has been said in earlier chapters of the present volume, but at the same time the very different emphasis of his work, with its enormous amount of documentation, is apparent. The post-industrial world is described exclusively from the macro-economic aspect, and post-industrial society is expressed in average income per head of population.

As I have already pointed out (p. 16 above), it has been calculated (by the method of extrapolating certain trends) that by the year 2000 only four countries will have reached the post-industrial state: the United States of America, Japan, Canada, and Sweden. Europe, including the Soviet Union and the Eastern bloc, Australia, and New Zealand will have advanced industrial societies. And the rest of the world will still not be fully industrialized. In terms of annual income per head of population, the three groups would have, respectively: from 4,000 to 20,000 dollars a year, from 1,500 to 4,000 dollars a year, and from 50 to 600 dollars a year. (These are the figures cited by Servan-Schreiber. Other futurologists have arrived at somewhat different results, but the principle is the same.)

Servan-Schrieber says that post-industrial society will be characterized by man's unprecedented freedom from physical, economic, and biological constraints: manual labour will have virtually disappeared, there will be a large amount of leisure-time, distance will be annihilated, and there will be spectacular new methods for the diffusion of culture and information. He goes on to ask: 'Will this be a happier society? That is another question.' What is certain is that this society will represent the avant-garde of human history, and 'that is what concerns us'.

Before going into Servan-Schreiber's book in more detail, let us enlarge on one of its fundamental theses.

He is concerned exclusively with the economic aspect, whereas we take other aspects into account as well, which have to be balanced with the economic aspect. Let us assume that the external circumstances of life in post-industrial society have been described accurately; and let us note that Servan-Schreiber also says that an important aspect will be the very large increase in education for everyone, and continuing education for adults; the only decrease will be in competition for educational resources. There will be, then, an enormous spread of culture and information and a great deal of leisure-time (it has been estimated that four seven-hour working days a week will be sufficient). In addition, a much higher level of education for everybody is to be expected. The question prompted by all this is: in what models will this abundance of information be arranged? Will it be merely a bewildering 'noise' or will it be relevant information for those who receive it? What will be the form and content of all this extra education?

The picture painted by Servan-Schreiber, and by the Denison report[3] from which he quotes, gives the impression that it will be scientific and technical instruction for the purpose of maintaining the highly developed technology of a post-industrial, cybernetic society. But a better-educated population will be more mature and thus more troublesome and less inclined to accept central cybernetic guidance. Have the prophets taken into account that a more mature population might one day arrive at quite different decisions? That it might even take 'unwise' decisions and saw off the economic 'branch' on which it is sitting?

Quite apart from the question of whether it is technically possible for 6 to 10 per cent of the world's population to live in plenty while 75 per cent are on the brink of starvation (50 to 600 dollars annual income), will this *economic* development in the future also be *politically* acceptable? Or will it lead in this form to a war of all against all?

Following this introduction, let us attempt to describe the problems of a post-industrial society in terms of three subsystems which can guarantee continued existence only if they are *integrated*.

It has already been said that the model we have chosen starts from three subsystems: cultural–moral–spiritual life, socio-political life, and economic life. We refer in this connection to the writings and actions of a non-politician, Rudolf Steiner,[4] who as early as 1919 was advocating a threefold social order.

Every human being stands in all three of these subsystems, though usually, through character and profession, in one more than the other two. Nobody can be entirely outside any of the three. Without the cultural–moral dimension he would be an imbecile; outside a political–

national life he would be a stateless person, a condition that would draw him very firmly into the political field; and if he were to place himself outside the economic life he would die of starvation.

We shall now describe these three subsystems in terms of their development towards and place in post-industrial society. They must be distinct from one another and yet not separate. A post-industrial society is acceptable only if the three subsystems are integrated in a single social structure, though this structure can take many different forms.

## THE CULTURAL–MORAL–SPIRITUAL SPHERE

On the way to a post-industrial society the average level of education and development will rise. Everybody will receive basic schooling; a large majority will receive further education (general and occupational); and a large percentage, probably more than half, will receive higher education in one form or another. With this prediction we find ourselves in the midst of the problems of which today's student revolts are mere outpost skirmishes.

What *form* and *content* should be given to this quantitative increase in education?

Will the young people of the future be satisfied with the world view, the scientific theory, and the values that are implicit in the foundations of education today? Will they, for instance, understand and value 'objectivity', as scientific empiricism (a relic of the nineteenth century) tries to teach us? Already today young people are beginning to reject the ethics of pre-industrial and early-industrial society, as well as the ascendancy of the natural sciences over the humanities. They are demanding new values of their teachers, values that are applicable in a modern society; and they are seeking the basis for a world view that can give them new life objectives.

In the student riots of the 'progressive' American universities, young people are rejecting the one-sided experts who wear the blinkers of their own discipline; they want to meet complete people with whom they can wrestle intellectually in order to win through to an opinion of their own. It is interesting to see whom the students choose as teachers so that they can develop themselves.

In a more mature society there is also a demand for earlier responsibility. In a speech during the celebration of the 125th anniversary of the Swiss Pharmaceutical Society, Professor Portmann of Basle remarked: 'It is strange that we are prepared to call up young men of twenty for military service and even give them the opportunity to undergo an officer's training with all the responsibility that involves, and yet regard others of the same age-group as too immature to carry responsibility in other fields.' But the cultural revolution required to lay a foundation for post-industrial society will not be achieved simply by reorganizing the universities. In addition to the fact that they are not allowed to have any social responsibility, young people also have profound doubts about the absolute authority of the scientific system itself.

Are the variables that have been chosen and those which have been left out of the models of the various sciences still the right ones? Will a new science, which will come to the foreground under future conditions (cybernetic society) and even dominate the whole cultural pattern, be acceptable with the limitations chosen for it today? Or will young people turn towards interdisciplinary forms of scientific exercise? Does the play *Oppenheimer* depict an exceptional situation or one that will become the rule? Calling attention to this problem reveals the gigantic task that will have to be accomplished within the next thirty years.

Another point is the omnipresence of information and the annihilation of distance, with the accompanying loss of an intimate, peaceful, and enclosed life. Information is on tap everywhere, and the taps are the knobs of radio and television sets and of other apparatus still to be devised in connection with the central information storage units of gigantic computer brains. At a CIOS Congress in Rotterdam, Diebolt said things that make the inventions of the cybernetic society seem a nightmare, though he reported objectively and without emotion on what exists already and what is still being developed.

Is any privacy still possible in a cybernetic society? If one thinks about this one comes to the following conclusion: To possess information means to possess power; and the centralization of information about every citizen means the centralization of power.

What ethics determine the use of this power through information? Into what conceptual model can the citizen integrate this avalanche of information? Who will keep a watch on the systematic influencing of public opinion by the mass media emanating from the military think tanks and the industrial 'future' workshops? Who will create a balance to counteract the enthusiasm of scientific technocrats wanting to foist their brain children upon us?

These are not academic questions; they are already being asked by young intellectuals on both sides of the iron curtain; and on both sides the teachers and leaders are unable to give an answer.

Here is another gigantic task for the next thirty years. Looking at this problem alone out of all the many that exist in the cultural–moral–spiritual sphere, one can see that the 'great society' of a post-industrial culture will be standing on feet of clay. The threat comes not only from outside but above all from within. In sum, we can draw the provisional conclusion that, for an acceptable cultural, moral, spiritual life, not only is it necessary to have *resources* provided by the economic system, but above all new standards and values and a new image of man and the world must be created so that these resources can be guided and utilized.

## THE SOCIO-POLITICAL AND STATE SPHERE

The telescoping of distances and the penetrating force of information make an isolated political and national life impossible.

Politics has become an intellectual battle of ideologies which are organized in spheres of influence and power blocs. No one can escape from this. Development towards world citizenship continues, a world citizenship which is deeply longed for by many and which again makes young people especially feel involved in all political and national developments throughout the world. For these same people it is self-evident that one should be concerned about others. (It is less a matter of course that others should be concerned with them.)

In his above-mentioned speech, Professor Portmann remarked that interesting history books would one day be written by non-Western peoples.

Since political direction is a question of a social model and since in a post-industrial society there will be enough time and maturity for political involvement, questions about the social structure and about the rights people have within it will play an important role.

In the foreground there will be the problems of *authority* (the granting of authority, from below, for the building of social models) and of *power* (the monopolizing of this model-building by a small section of the population). If we assume that the equality of everyone before the law is the basic principle of a constitutional state, the question immediately arises whether this is no more than what we understand today as a legal issue or whether it is not also a principle for the whole social structure. Hierarchy, which is necessary in a highly developed social organism, is then only acceptable 'from below'.

These questions of interpersonal equality and of power centres constitute the principal problem of our present social unrest. It is particularly difficult to perceive where and by what means power comes about. The shift that has taken place is illustrated by the remark that if Karl Marx had lived a hundred years later he would have written not *Das Kapital* but *Die Information*. It is indeed a fact that the possession of information is more important for power formation than is the possession of money and the means of production.

One could call Marx's life-work a critique of the phase of the industrial pioneer. In this phase it was the pioneer who took the initiative and who still owned the means of production he had purchased with his own money, and it was labour, bought on the labour market according to supply and demand, that was the last item on the balance-sheet.

As a neo-Marxist, Herbert Marcuse[5] provides a critique of the second phase, the 'one-dimensional society' of scientific management. For him, communism is as despicable as capitalism.

It has already been said that it is interesting to see whom the students choose as their teachers, to enable them to develop themselves. Herbert Marcuse is one of these teachers, though recently, during a conversation in Germany, he complained that the radical Left had made him their idol and quoted his words without having read his books. Those who do read his books will find, in *One-dimensional man* for instance, a brilliantly one-sided interpretation of our affluent society. He begins by saying that efforts to prevent an atomic catastrophe overshadow the search for its potential causes in contemporary industrial society. These causes therefore

> remain unidentified, unexposed, unattacked by the public because they recede before the all too obvious threat from without — to the West from the East, to the East from the West.... We submit to the peaceful production of the means of destruction, to the perfection of waste, to being educated for a defence which deforms the defenders and that which they defend.

And the 'containment of social change is perhaps the most singular achievement of advanced industrial society'.

In acrimonious sentences like these he formulates his critical theory, without ever pointing the way to a positive solution. Marx still had the dialectics of capital and labour, of employer and employee, to point to. A hundred years later Marcuse feels he must show that any polarity has disappeared. Man and society have become one-dimensional: the workers have become citizens and the entrepreneurs have become servants of the system; both have been flattened by a social form which knows only the technical–economic dimension.

The way in which this civilization comes about is because one choice is made, of one 'project', one design. The technological universe becomes a political universe:

> As the project unfolds, it shapes the entire universe of discourse and action, intellectual and material culture. In the medium of technology, culture, politics, and the economy merge into an omnipresent system which swallows up or repulses all alternatives... Technological rationality has become political rationality.

Chapter by chapter, this society formed by deterministic–technological thinking is investigated, starting with its control systems: 'This is the pure form of servitude: to exist as an instrument, as a thing.'

After the first two parts of the book, 'One-dimensional society' and 'One-dimensional thought', comes the last part, 'The chance of the alternatives'. It is this third part in particular that is disappointing to a large extent. The critical theory of society offers no alternatives but the 'Great Refusal' and hope without meaning. In the final sentences of the book this alternative without an alternative is summarized as follows:

> But the chance is that, in this period, the historical extremes may meet again: the most advanced consciousness of humanity [he means here the young intellectual elite], and its most exploited force [he means the starving masses]. It is nothing but a chance. The critical theory of society possesses no concepts which could bridge the gap between the present and its future; holding no promise and showing no success, it remains negative. Thus it wants to remain loyal to those who, without hope, have given and give their life to the Great Refusal.

In conclusion, Marcuse quotes Walter Benjamin: 'It is only for the sake of those without hope that hope is given to us.'

At first sight it is amazing that such a pessimistic philosophy can arouse a wild enthusiasm in young people. This enthusiasm is nourished by the fierce criticism of an affluent society, which brings about feelings of alienation, powerlessness, and futility in young people — a criticism, therefore, that speaks as their own hearts speak.

The lack of an alternative suggestion worries the older generation rather than the younger, who feel that everyone can suggest his own solution; people will not again be tucked up and rocked to sleep by an infallible system of the future. It is precisely the openness of the final words, together with the one-dimensional and thus uninhibited critique, that is the secret of the book's success. A more subtle and differentiated investigation and critique requires the foundation of a more subtle and differentiated life-experience.

In our discussion of the transition from the organization structure of the second phase (criticized by Marcuse) to that of the third phase, we mentioned the level of individual maturity that is necessary in order to be able to function in this third phase. A speedy realization of this maturity in other fields of society is dependent on its development in the concrete situation of people at work.

Socially, a long path of development will still be necessary before we arrive at a society in which the cultural–moral, the political–legal, and the economic subsystems are in balance. The problems exist in the small group, the working community, and among nations and peoples. One cannot, however, use the same yardstick to measure the deeds of nations and the deeds of individuals. This statement crops up regularly in the newspapers. But what *is* the yardstick to be used?

Will our present model of international law and supranational organizations be able to meet the demands of a future world order, with three levels of prosperity? Is it not so that in the United Nations Organization nations are judged as though they were free individuals rather than as groups interrelated by a common destiny, which they cannot accept? And in a conflict does it not often happen that both parties fight with their backs to the wall?

These are questions which show again why the static model with its three groups of prosperity is explosive in itself. And is this problem, too, supposed to find a satisfactory solution within the next thirty years?

When Servan-Schreiber himself protests so strongly against America's economic penetration into Europe, though the two share the link of a common culture, one can get some idea of how unacceptable the economic supremacy of one country over another must be when large cultural differences are involved.

## THE ECONOMIC SPHERE

When we speak of an industrial society we mean that industry as a subsystem holds a dominant position in the total life of a country.

It is understandable that economic planning should play a primary role in the determination of national policies. But this can be healthy only if the economic sphere knows its place and serves to free man from material cares; thus it creates prosperity in order that in the created prosperity it can serve the wellbeing of mankind.

This means that policy-making in industry is economically, technically, and socially the touchstone that determines which aims and social values are achieved in reality.

Every civilization has its dominant bearers of culture: at one time it was the priests, later the military leaders, then the demagogues, the orators, the scholars, the politicians. Today it is managers at all levels who bear the heavy task of creating, through example in their organizations, the values and standards for mature social systems, thus paving the way for a renewal of society.

It should be remembered in connection with this statement that in an organization in the third phase of development every individual decides for himself whether he wants to be a co-manager or a wage-earner, whether he wants to share in the responsibility for achieving an optimal value increase between input and output, or merely do what he is told in return for an agreed wage.

In leading up to the description of the phase of integration in the development of an enterprise, we showed how in the pioneer phase the first task of creating a market is achieved and how in the second phase the technical and organizational task is accomplished.

The next task is the one facing industry at the moment (in America too): to create, in the already developed economic and technical subsystems, integrated social systems that are essentially humane. This task, which originally rested on initiating entrepreneurs, belongs in the third phase to the whole industrial community.

Economic life is based on the division of work: we work for others, while living on what others do for us. Economic life is built on working for others *and* on having confidence in others. Without this trust in others (that delivery will be made as arranged, that payment will be made as agreed) economic life ceases to function. It may seem that the opposite is the case, that egoism and deception are the basis, as one is only too willing to believe. However, economic reality is different. And just because trust is the basis, economic life can and must be *the first*, within the present hierarchical structure of enterprises, to practise and learn about the reality of educational leadership, of shared responsibility, of humane attitudes.

From here, the other subsystems of society can be penetrated: the cultural and the political organizations. But this is a task for which the time between now and the year 2000 is short indeed!

We can be relatively brief in this discussion of the economic sphere, since the earlier chapters of this book have been leading up to this point and have already dealt with the material. Everything that has been said about the third phase applies in principle also to post-industrial society. Industry in this society will have an associative attitude in its external relations. True marketing is solving problems for others.

True solutions are found not because one party dictates what he thinks is best for another; they come about when there is joint consultation under the auspices of a common interest. This applies to the triad of entrepreneurs, co-workers, and consumers. Joint consultation in external relations often involves some mutual education, so that both parties are in a position to choose freely between the various alternatives.

Once the economic sphere has created the post-industrial society it will have reached the end of its primacy as a culture-forming factor. It will then be taken for granted, just as is the availability of postal services, water, bread, and transport. It will exist, but it will have become a *dissatisfier*. People will be angry if its services are not available, but they will not praise it if it works well.

In post-industrial society the dominant factors will once more be of a cultural–spiritual nature; but instead of being borne by a few charismatic personalities they will be carried by the whole population. We are therefore convinced that *all predictions based on a direct extrapolation of our present economic society into the future fail to recognize the true nature of development.*

Development is a discontinuous process. The growing and unfolding which take place in one phase of development create the conditions for the next phase. Thus the dominant subsystem that has achieved a step of development then merges with the many serving subsystems and another subsystem takes the lead. This was the case with the spiritual leadership of the theocratic states and later with the military–political leadership of the national states. Economic life has always transcended the borders of national states and is the only system that could pave the way for a worldwide social structure. When it has achieved this, it will be reduced once more to its proper task of service in the next phase of development.

What we have described here is the normal process of development. This process is frustrated by forces that delay it. These are at the moment:

— *the persistence of national states* with their political–military way of thinking which belongs to an earlier, pre-industrial phase, and their illusion of national glory;
— *the conservatism* of vested interests, which want to maintain old social subsystems by means of power centres (pressure groups); they resist innovation because it is felt to be a threat;
— *the short-sightedness* of many individuals whose horizon is narrow and whose time-span is short; this leads to hostility towards anything that is above average, a kind of anti-intelligence; in leadership, too, it will tolerate only the average (the good is the enemy of the better);
— *inertia of the heart*, a lack of feeling for one's fellow-men, a why-should-I-care attitude 'so long as it doesn't happen to me'; too great a willingness to compromise; lack of initiative and involvement.

Nations, enterprises, and groups who know how to avoid these four dismal companions will be the ones who blaze the trail for a fully developed post-industrial society.

With regard to annual income per head of population, it may well be possible for some countries to achieve such a society economically. But if the other problems of a post-industrial society are not tackled and the solutions implemented at the same time, then internal revolutionary forces of protest will make it all illusory.

The third phase of industrial development has only just started. This phase provides the transition from an industrial to a post-industrial society. We are convinced that *this is where the problems are to be found that we can grasp with our hands and that can motivate our hearts.*

Not until this third phase has to some extent become reality will it be time to talk about the problems of the 'great society'. Nevertheless, now is the time to concern ourselves with the conceptual model of a post-industrial society, so that our activities in the coming decades and our work towards the realization of an integrated industrial structure can be given a more concrete perspective. For this reason let us look again from another angle at a possible model for a post-industrial society.

The French Revolution, a clarion call heralding a new age, posited as the leading image for a new society the demand for liberty, equality, and fraternity. The origin of this concept has not been discovered, but this does not detract from the brilliant simplicity of the slogan. Many people have since proved that these demands cancel each other out, for instance absolute liberty and absolute equality are mutually exclusive. It is, however, possible to see these principles as qualifications of different subsystems of society, and then the way they are formulated becomes meaningful.

If we recognize *liberty as the inherent principle of cultural–spiritual–intellectual life*, this means that in the coming society these aspects of life can only evolve in freedom. History in the last fifty years has made us so familiar with this problem that it hardly needs further elaboration here. The fight for the freedom of belief, of art, of scientific practice, of individual cultural creativity, though generally acknowledged, is not yet won. The struggle for freedom in these areas continues.

In education in particular there is a great lack of freedom. The state provides the money, but only with strings attached. An educational battle still has to be fought to gain freedom for parents and teachers.

To see *equality as the inherent principle of the socio-political and judicial spheres* is generally acceptable. The equality of everyone before the law, in all its facets, is a value that has been won by the Western world. Violent emotional reactions occur wherever this equality is threatened by state despotism or the misuse of ideological power.

But in the industrial sphere this equality is not yet fully implemented. Where real joint consultation takes place (see Chapter 12), it is based on the freedom and equality of partners working towards a mutually acceptable goal. The fact that each person has something different to contribute as far as content is concerned does not detract from their equality as people in the consultation situation. Joint consultation is the training-ground where one can learn to practise equality in the real social situation.

Equality does not apply to the sphere of the intellect, of the mind. To preach equality here is to destroy these facets of life and devalue them to an average mediocrity. Indeed, in the intellectual and spiritual spheres *inequality* reigns. One person can have more knowledge and understanding than another. One person's judgement may be more valuable than that of another. But if a person who is more highly developed in these respects were to construe from this the right to feel more developed humanly as well, and if he were to derive from it the right to *rule* in the social sphere, he would be making the mistake of not distinguishing between the three subsystems. Someone who is spiritually more developed may work only through spiritual conviction and has to wait and see whether others will freely recognize his point of view.

That freedom does not apply in the social field is also commonplace in our civilization. It is just in the social subsystem that for the sake of others and oneself one has to adhere to social rules which apply to everyone. Road-users in particular know how difficult it is to put this into practice. In the socio-political system, equality is anchored in the foundations of Western democracy.

It may be difficult to understand how *fraternity can be the inherent principle of the economic subsystem*. But if instead of fraternity or brotherhood (words that had a powerful ring in the days of the romantics) we use modern terms such as collaboration, joint consultation, cooperation, association, then our feet are firmly on the (economic) ground.

We have already explained that the future of economic life in its fully developed industrial form lies in the collaboration of partners who are of equal worth, however different they may be. The concept of brotherliness might also remind us of the brothers who were enemies, seeking to ruin each other. But it is fraternal collaboration, not fraternal strife, that brings advantages to both. And in the economic sphere everyone depends on everyone else.

There is a historical point in the development of every subsystem at which it becomes visible as a subsystem of society as a whole. Emancipation from a centrally organized hierarchical spiritual life began in the sixteenth century with the rise of Protestantism, and since then this liberating process has continued in all other spiritual and intellectual fields, even those which still adhere to the old model. This process cannot be halted; a new spiritual hierarchy can come about only through recognition from below. The wiser man cannot place himself above those who are less wise, but they are free to recognize his wisdom and acknowledge him as their teacher.

This is also a deeper reason for the current student unrest: they want to seek and choose their own teachers. It is up to the teachers to see that they are chosen. Teaching at a university, one notices clearly the difference between lectures that are compulsory and those that are on optional subjects.

The French Revolution pinpointed the outward visible moment at which the socio-political system was born. 'Citizen' was the slogan. That the peasant could address the marquis in his palace as 'citizen' proved his equality as a human being. The Restoration was an attempt to reverse this first breakthrough, but the smaller revolutions of 1848 and later were enough to bring about new forms of socio-political life everywhere. The labour movement at the beginning of this century was the next wave; and the demand for equal opportunity in education up to and including university education is the present wave.

There will be other new waves, for many old forms cling tenaciously to life. The recent developments in enterprises, which we have tried to describe in the model of the third phase, are symptoms that began to show around the year 1955 and since then have developed to a conviction, not to be ignored, that 'the time has come'.

At first, collaboration developed *externally* in mergers of 'competing brothers' and in efforts (in spite of relapses into strife situations caused by the economic situation) to achieve joint consultation with authorities and trade unions, though as yet hardly with consumers. Mutual collaboration with consumers is still difficult because of the lack of representative consumer organizations willing to grasp their important task for the future.

*Internally* collaboration is developed through a change of attitude from command to consultation and participation in decision-making. This process is still being obstructed by an organizational structure belonging to the second phase, built on directing and controlling. As soon as the internal organization allows for more joint consultation or even demands it, this process too will commence properly, for an organization with four functional subsystems that touch each other at every point can only provide results through flexible and fair (dare we say 'brotherly'?) consultation.

We have arrived at a historical moment in the development of our Western civilization. The economic system, generating many forms of enterprise, has the possibility and the challenging task of being the first in which the three subsystems of society can live together in an integrated form. This is a trail to be blazed and at the same time a path of exercise and practice for the benefit of many other social systems, including socio-political systems on a global scale.

The French Revolution postulated a utopia with its demand for liberty, equality, and fraternity. This call continued to work as a leaven for a whole century, particularly in socio-political developments. Immediately after the First World War, in the great confusion of a conquered Germany which was seeking a new form of society and suffering on the one hand under communist putsches and on the other under the rise of national socialism, Rudolf Steiner, already referred to as a non-politician, suggested a model of society based on the integration of three qualitatively different subsystems. After an abortive national-socialist attempt to assassinate him in Munich in 1922, Steiner refrained from further socio-political activities and turned his attention towards developing the free educational movement of the Waldorf or Steiner schools. If one reads today what he wrote at that time about a threefold social order, one can understand why the model he described not only could not then have been realized but indeed had to be entirely forgotten.

The time was not yet ripe; the idea of a social order with three distinct areas — a free spiritual life, a political–civil life based on equality, and an economic life based on fraternity — could not be comprehended during the time of transition from over-ripe, paternalistic, pioneer enterprises to the first beginnings of scientific management. Today for the first time development has progressed to the point where these thoughts can be understood from reality. For this to be possible a whole generation had to live through the triumphs and limitations of the second phase. It is important to study these writings again; those who do so will be astonished at the relevance of this conceptual model today.

While working on this chapter, I heard a radio programme which included a report on the heroic battle of the Czechoslovak people for their spiritual freedom as well as an item on the convention of the American Democratic Party in Chicago, which had to be protected by riot police and the National Guard, and was hindered by telephone, taxi, and bus strikes. The latter situation is a clear demonstration of some of the things said here. In 'God's own country', which is on its way to a super-affluent, cybernetically controlled 'great society', a normal, democratic, political institution can function only if the most powerful protection is available.

To turn once more to Servan-Schreiber, it is just this that needs to be said in general criticism of his brilliant book *The American challenge*. There is indeed an American challenge, and, as Servan-Schreiber rightly says, it is not of a material but of a non-material nature. Let us say it is of a spiritual nature. The challenge lies in the development of the human resources in enterprises, of know-what and know-how, of research and development, but above all of management as a group of people working together towards innovation. To express this once more in terms of the concept of development one could say: the economic objective of an enterprise develops from customer orientation to price competition and thence to service competition. The next step on the path to a post-industrial society is via innovation competition.

In part we can agree with Servan-Schreiber. But he depicts the problems in a too simplified black-and-white form. This is obvious from the following quotation:

> There is no way of leaving the 'economic area' to the Americans so that we can get on with the policitial, social, and cultural areas in our own way, as some people would like to believe. There is no such compartmentalization in the real world.

And then his picture of the future: 'The European elite would be trained at Harvard, Stanford, or Berkeley, continuing a precedent that has already begun.'

The subsystems of society are certainly not separate in the real world. This means that we must accept the challenge in the field of management development as well. But does this also mean that Europe has the task of striving with all its resources for a one-sided, super-affluent civilization, a race in which we would certainly be outstripped by America? Europe is the very place that still has the chance of building a well-balanced civilization with a large degree of diversification both in the spiritual–cultural and in the socio-political sphere. The drama of Czechoslovakia is a sign of this.

It could very well be that in thirty years' time the leading younger generation of Europe will not be trained at Harvard, Stanford, and Berkeley; but rather that the leading younger generation of America and other continents will seek their education at European institutions and universities because that is where they will find the teachers who can help them out of their spiritual–cultural and socio-political impasse.

This is a better objective for European efforts than an exclusive imitation of the American way of life, however much the development of human resources in enterprises remains a direct task. We do not need a development of exclusively rigorous economic thinking and action, leading to a kind of economic imperialism that would arouse the hatred of the rest of the world, but rather one of economic thinking and action that is integrated with the spiritual and social needs of a *truly* 'great society'.

I have confidence in the openness and spiritual strength of young people and trust that they will find their way to the teachers they seek. May Europe be prepared at that moment to receive them and give them their due.

At the beginning of this final chapter I said that I would plant a tree today even if I knew that the world would come to an end tomorrow. Is this picture of the future therefore an ideal, a utopia, which 'realistic scientists' can push aside?

Our modern science-oriented picture of the world is based on a number of assumptions which have grown historically as a reaction to a spiritualism which had become decadent. As late as the beginning of our 'modern age' a realist was still a person who placed mind first and saw material reality as having been formed by the mind. And a nominalist was a person who accepted material phenomena at face value, formed his ideas about the material world, made norms, and created concepts and theories.

But man is not only a creature who knows and explains; he also chooses, and thus shapes the future. Realism and nominalism are not only basic philosophical attitudes, but also moving forces in respect of the future: 'an image acts as a field'. The choice is not whether we want idealism, whether we want a design for the future, but which idealism, and which design.

This view of the future is only one of the many possible designs for the future that the margin of freedom from the past offers. It is a view that is based on an image of man and an image of society at the centre of which stands the concept of development with its discontinuity. The path to this future leads quite practically towards a striving for the integration of the social subsystem in the work situation and towards the practising of *human* relations within the actual groups in which we are placed.

A common path towards the next level of society will be found only through such concrete experience, and not through manifestos demanding action of others or through structures forcibly imposed by Left or Right.

Others will throw other designs for the future into the arena; it will be up to all of us to make a choice.

REFERENCES

1 GROSS, B. M. The coming general systems models of social systems. *Human Relations* 20(4), 1967, pp. 357-74.

2 SERVAN-SCHREIBER, J-J. *Le Défi Américain*. Paris, 1967. Eng. trans. *The American challenge*. London, 1968.

3 Servan-Schreiber refers to Denison's doctoral thesis, written in 1964 while Denison was connected with the US National Council on Economic Development. See also:

DENISON, E. F. & POUILLIER, J-P. *Why growth rates differ: postwar experience in nine western countries*. Washington, 1967.

4 STEINER, R. *The threefold social order*. Newly revised translation of *The threefold commonwealth* (1923). New York and London, 1966.

5 MARCUSE, H. *One-dimensional man*. London, 1964.

# Recommended Reading

*Chapter 16*

GALBRAITH, J. K. *The new industrial state*. Boston, Mass., and London, 1967.
DRUCKER, P. F. *Landmarks of tomorrow*. London and New York, 1959.
STEINER, R. *World economy*. London, 1933.
GROSS, B. M. *The managing of organizations*. London and New York, 1965.
BOULDING, K. E. *The meaning of the twentieth century*. New York, 1964.
RIESMAN, D., with N. GLAZER and R. DENNEY. *The lonely crowd*. New York, 1950.

# Appendix

# The Use of Quantitative Models

## A. F. G. HANKEN

### INTRODUCTION

Natural scientists have been successfully using quantitative models for several centuries. Perhaps the best-known examples are the cosmological models developed by Kepler and Newton. But their application in other fields has taken a long time. This is particularly the case with regard to socio-economic systems such as commercial enterprises; here the application of formal methods had little significance until after the Second World War. That they were accepted in the end was partly the result of operational research activities that went on in England during the war. These showed that many logistic and tactical problems could be solved with the aid of a mathematical approach.

Moreover, the step from military organization to industrial enterprise was not a large one, since a variety of operations can be similar in character, i.e. they can be formulated in the same way.

For instance, if the problems of time spent in waiting are to be studied, it is possible to use the same formulation in respect of the waiting of ships to be unloaded, the waiting of patients in a doctor's waiting-room, and the waiting of customers in a shop. For the study of these problems a waiting-time theory or queueing theory has been developed, by means of which the average cost of waiting-time, of queue length, and so on, can be calculated, provided sufficient information is available for the definition of the problem. A further example is inventory theory, which has led to the elaboration of a number of general models concerning the problems of relating supply to demand. With these models it is possible to calculate the optimal amount of supplies to be ordered, the optimal time for placing the order, the optimal reservoir of supplies to be maintained, and so on. Yet another example is the linear-programming model. This is a much-used method for determining the optimal allocation of limited resources. Thus linear programming can be applied to discover the most profitable solution of transportation problems caused by the availability of only a limited number of vehicles.

The list of available techniques, theories, and methods is by no means exhausted by the above examples. We could add probability calculation, information theory, simulation, game theory, decision theory, industrial dynamics, dynamic programming, communication theory, and many more. In a greater or lesser degree all these have contributed to the management sciences. In some cases, for instance game theory and information theory, the contribution has been small, but other procedures, such as probability calculation and simulation, have obviously been of great importance for management.

Thus a large number of models have become available for the formulation of management problems. However, problem formulation is of practical value only if it can lead to a solution within a reasonable length of time. Without additional resources this is often impossible; hence electronic computers, developed during and after the Second World War, have come to fulfil an essential need. Now we are able not only to formulate management problems but also to implement their solutions.

However, it is not our intention to present a review of the many existing techniques and their fields of application (see, for this purpose, the literature listed at the end of this appendix). Rather, the aim here is to give an impression of the methodology and background of quantitative analysis. Two concepts, *system* and *model*, will serve as the point of departure.

For the following considerations we shall assume that a system is situated in the real world; it is the object on which our interest is focused. Thus a commercial enterprise, a production department, or a machine can be regarded as a system. Naturally, it is essential that the system should be defined with precision so that later, in the course of the research period, no misunderstandings can arise as to the extent of the research project. The purpose of the research is usually the improvement of an existing system or the design of a new one that must satisfy certain conditions.

With regard to models, it is usual to differentiate between scale, analogue, and symbolic models.

A scale model has the same form as the original, but differs in dimension. Reducing or enlarging the scale can make it easier to handle, e.g. a map, a photograph, or a model of a group of buildings. Scale models are also used for the simulation of dynamic processes, e.g. wind tunnels or operational models of waterworks.

The analogue model is also physical in nature, but its form differs from that of the given system. The best-known examples of this type of model are analogue and digital computers.

In the symbolic model the main characteristics of a system are represented by mathematical or logical symbols. If these symbols refer to a specific system or to a particular type of system, the model is termed an operational model, e.g. an inventory model, or a differential equation model referring to a planetary system. A model with no physical connotations is an abstract model. It is with abstract or symbolic models that we shall be dealing mainly in this appendix.

We construct a model in order to analyse a system. At first sight this seems to be rather a devious method. What exactly happens? Instead of experimenting directly with the the system, we first construct a model which is to take the place of the system (abstraction). Then from the model we draw certain conclusions which are relevant to the problems under investigation (deduction). And finally we examine our conclusions and transform them into practical measures (realization). The progression from the system to the model and then back to the system is termed a *model cycle*:

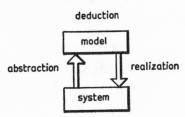

Clearly, there are two ways of proceeding: we can either tackle the problems with the help of a model or experiment directly with the system. Let us consider a simple example. We decide on the spur of the moment that we would like to listen to some classical music on the radio. To do this we can try out the different stations and choose a programme on the basis of this 'experiment'. Or we can turn to a 'model', in this case a publication giving the radio programmes, and reach a desirable goal in that way. In a situation of this kind, a direct experiment is perfectly feasible. But in many other situations it would be impracticable, too costly or time-consuming or unpredictable, or too dangerous.

For example, let us imagine that the directors of an insurance company wish to examine the financial consequences of a reduction in premiums. In order to analyse this problem they will call in an actuary, who will examine the situation with the help of a mathematical model. There will be no question of making an actual experiment at the expense of the company's clients.

There are many advantages in using models. However, in order to achieve the desired results with this analytical method, the OR worker or the systems analyst, like the craftsman, must be able to use his own tools and must, at the same time, have enough specialized knowledge of the projects in which he is involved to enable him to bring them to a satisfactory outcome. In other words, he must be familiar with a number of specific techniques, e.g. linear programming, as well as with the *modus operandi* of various parts of the firm, e.g. the production department. The diagram below illustrates this approach.

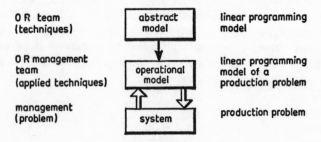

It will be seen that the operational model is situated at an equal distance from the abstract model and the system. Here theory and practice, technique and given problem meet. The OR specialist is familiar with various types of abstract model. These are the forms in which reality can be represented. The problems originate in the enterprise, the domain of the manager. The application of a technique to a particular problem results in an operational model with variables and parameters corresponding to the relevant factors in the actual situation. It is obviously no longer possible for a single person to master this whole field of theory and practice. The OR worker cannot even be expected to be *au fait* with all the scientific techniques.

In practice this difficulty can be avoided by letting the OR team cooperate with the managers and others who are familiar with the actual problems of the system. Obviously collaboration of this kind offers certain advantages, but there is unfortunately one drawback. Fruitful collaboration is possible only if both groups speak the same language, and this is not always the case. In a study of operational research activities in American industry, Schumacher and Smith[1] found that, though the importance of these methods was increasing, the lack of cooperation between OR teams and management often presented problems. Westbrook,[2] in his study of the chemical industry, came to the same conclusion, i.e. that communication problems were limiting the applicability of the management sciences. He also remarked that there was a tendency for the OR teams to adopt too technical an approach in that they would attempt to structure a given problem in such a way that it would suit the application of a previously selected technique. It goes without saying that the problem and not the technique must be the logical starting-point for the building of a model.

In the following sections we deal with the methodology of model-building and with the characteristic qualities of a management model.

## METHODOLOGY

Let us look more closely at the three phases in model-building: abstraction, deduction, and realization. It could be said that the model cycle begins and ends with observations of the real world. What happens in between is not quite so obvious. Abstraction and realization in particular are still vaguely defined processes in which the intuition of the investigator plays a far from negligible part. The deductive process is a much more stable part of the model cycle. Although in many cases several ways of solving a problem are possible, on the whole the results obtained will be comparable.

The three phases do not always occur in the same order. The dilemma of the chicken and the egg confronts us here. What information should we collect first if there is no model to serve as a guide? How can we construct a model if there is no information on which to base it? Instead of a well-defined inductive or deductive process, we resort in practice to an evolutionary development. In fact, we go through the model cycle many times, frequently beginning with a vague model and only a few data. Then, as we gradually assemble more information and the analytical method assumes a firmer shape, an increasingly clear picture emerges from these rudiments (model refinement). We can conclude this iterative process when the results we are able to obtain from the model are sufficiently exact. However, every operational model must be regarded as provisional, since it can never be proved that a particular construction is really correct. There is always the possibility that new information will become available, which does not fit in with the conclusions drawn so far.

We now discuss separately the three phases of the model cycle.

## 1. *Abstraction*

A model is a simplified reproduction of a system. Reality is always more complicated than an abstract outline. The simplification is achieved by omitting any characteristics of the system which are not relevant to the problem in hand. Thus only the essential characteristics of the system are retained as a basis for the construction of a model. To decide which characteristics are relevant and which are not is, however, often difficult.

If the management of a sales organization, for instance, wants to investigate the consequences of a reduction in the price of a certain product, it will have to take into consideration numerous factors. The sale of the product depends on the attitude of the public, the strategy of competitors, the delayed results of an earlier sales policy or advertising campaign, and so on. It is not so simple, in this connection, to decide which variables must be considered essential.

Two extremes have to be avoided: the sins of omission and commission. The sin of omission can be seen in a number of OR models which offer only a partial approach to a problem because they ignore certain important aspects (e.g. psychological or sociological aspects). In terms of reality the value of such models is often small. At the other end of the scale there are models that incorporate an extremely detailed view, for instance 'industrial dynamics' models such as those conceived by Forrester.[3] These are based on detailed investigations of the processes of industry. It is not unusual for an industrial dynamics model to consist of about a hundred equations and to include several hundred variables. This method makes it possible to evaluate the consequences of a large number of decisions. Forrester studied a number of storage and production problems in this way. The results, however, did not always concur with the real-life situation. Nevertheless, an investigation of this kind can often provide some insight into the 'mechanics' of a firm.

The choice of variables to be included in a quantitative model is not only governed by the problem to be investigated but also limited by the need to work with measurable quantities. This means that the influence of immeasurable factors or imponderables is often disregarded. For instance, the productivity of a firm is closely connected with the attitude of the workers, but it is extremely difficult to express the latter factor in a number. Or to take another example: an optimal stocking policy is to balance supply and investment costs against the costs of a supply shortage. However, the costs of a shortage are very difficult to calculate because loss of goodwill plays a part, as well as lack of profit. And yet these costs, so difficult to estimate, are necessary data in many OR supply models. If a problem is purely technical, there are usually no imponderables to be considered, but it is essential to make allowance for them when considering systems with socio-economic implications.

Summarizing, we can say that the process of abstraction is very difficult to describe and that it involves numerous intuitive and irrational factors. It is not possible to list all the points to which attention must be given, but the following are frequently very important: selection of the variables and parameters for the model; the measurability of these factors; the influence of imponderables; determination of the appropriate degree of abstraction, i.e. the model must be realistic but as simple as possible.

## 2. Deduction

One constructs a model in order to be able to draw certain conclusions from it. This is equivalent to the solving of systems equations. The question arises whether this deductive process is always possible. In this respect it is important to distinguish between approximate and exact methods of problem-solving.

The problem of the travelling salesman can serve as an example here. This problem appears in many variations and can be described as follows. A salesman has been commissioned to visit $n$ towns. He must organize his journey in such a way that between setting out from a given point and returning to that point he visits each town once and covers the smallest possible number of miles. Clearly there is an exact solution to this problem. From the starting-point he can visit $n-1$ towns, from the next town $n-2$ towns, and so on. In total there are thus $(n-1)$ $(n-2) \ldots (2) (1) = (n-1)!$ alternatives. For each alternative the total number of miles can be calculated, and by choosing the shortest possible route the salesman has 'solved' his problem.

If we assume that the salesman takes 10 seconds to calculate the length of each alternative route, then he would need approximately $4 \times 10^{10}$ years, using every second, to calculate the shortest route covering 20 towns. Naturally one would prefer a less time-consuming method. An exact method, other than enumeration, for solving this problem has not yet been found, but algorithms have been developed which usually give exact answers or good approximations (Dantzig, Fulkerson, and Johnson).[4]

A number of approximation methods, such as the Monte Carlo method, and also simulation techniques, have been devised, which are applicable fairly generally. These methods are based on a step-by-step simulation of the processes that occur in the given system. With the help of computers, only a fraction of the time taken in reality is now needed for a simulation. Thus in only a few minutes or hours an extensive experience with a system can be obtained.

Our conclusion is that for every problem that is, in principle, soluble, an exact or approximate method of solution can be found that will yeild results within a reasonable amount of time. Different methods usually lead to comparable results.

## 3. *Realization*

By realization we mean testing the solutions by comparing them with observable quantities (validation), and then introducing changes into the system or designing a new system based on the results obtained in the deductive phase (implementation). It is at this stage that the value of the quantitative method is clearly demonstrated. Contradictions are likely to come to light, which call for further research into the elements of the model.

When a systems analyst suggests a change based on his analysis of the model, he should, of course, take into account the relevant economic, psychological, and social consequences of his suggestion. That he does not always do so is shown in an article by Abrams.[5] From his study of operational research activities in Canadiann dustry, Abrams states that 25 per cent of all technically adequate research projects never lead anywhere because their implementation would bring about social and psychological effects insufficiently foreseen and catered for by the OR teams. We have already mentioned the problems of communication between OR teams and managers, and the above shows how an individual or group can be the obstacle.

The 'reacting environment' is another important matter to be considered in connection with the phase of realization. In the interaction of a system and its environment each affects the other, as is illustrated in the following example. A new hospital was built with what the planners considered to be ample bed-space for the area it was to serve.

However, since it was a new hospital with modern equipment, it attracted a particularly good medical staff. As a result, far more patients were attracted to the hospital than had been calculated for, and so, contrary to expectation, extensions had to be built almost immediately. This shows how a system can influence its environment and in turn be influenced by it.

The phase of implementation is perhaps the least suitable for systematic consideration. However, it is important to observe the process carefully in order to avoid as far as possible any unpleasant surprises during the last phase of the investigation. Nevertheless one has to be prepared for at least some unforeseen effects resulting from incorrect observations or interpretations during the model-building period. In this respect experience is the best teacher.

## THE ELEMENTS OF A QUANTITATIVE MODEL

Earlier in this appendix we referred to the connection between an abstract model and an operational model. Both models can be said to depict a relationship between variables and parameters. A variable is an element that changes in time, whereas a parameter is an element that is kept constant. In an operational model these elements have a certain significance which frequently corresponds with an observable and measurable quality in the realm of experience. A discussion of the different types of variable that are used in models is very important for a full understanding of the structure of a quantitative model.

Variables play a certain role in a model, just like actors on a stage. This role determines to some extent the possible interrelations of the variables. The classification and arrangement of a firm's information flow can often be simplified if one has some knowledge of these different types of variable. There are as yet no completely watertight definitions, but a rough classification is possible. Readers who are interested in more exact definitions may consult Zadeh and Desoer.[6]

1. *Input variables:* These comprise all the information about the environment (market) of a system (firm) that is important for this system and that the leading people (managers) in the system cannot influence. The board of directors of a firm, for example, can have no influence on the variety and number of articles produced by a competitor. Or the buying department of a small firm can have no influence on the price of raw materials.

2. *Decision variables:* These comprise all the essential decisions that are important for the system; there are a number of possible alternatives among which the board or the staff have to choose. Thus one can decide whether or not to purchase a computer, whether to increase or decrease production, or whether to engage more personnel. There are as many decision variables as there are degrees of freedom within a system.

3. *State variables:* These are variables related to the internal situation of the system; they are the results of previous inputs and decisions and they cannot be directly manipulated. The various stores of a company, or its liquid assets, can be described as state variables. These variables are the result of the number of orders received in earlier periods, or of the amount of buying that has been done, or of the number of payments made to suppliers, etc. Thus the state of the company can be indirectly influenced via the decision variables. The state variables that determine the system are also called the order of the system.

4. *Output variables:* These are the variables referring to the objectives of the system; they are determined by the inputs and the decisions. Examples are: monthly turnover, liquid assets, production costs over a set period, etc. These are indicators that receive special attention from management, who try to pursue a policy that does not neglect such output or goal variables. It may be noted that state and output variables are not necessarily different from one another, since the choice of objectives is a relatively arbitrary process from the point of view of model theory.

So far, we have used firms or enterprises as examples. We could, however, equally well have taken subsystems such as a production department or a machine.

Looking more closely we see that the four types of variable can be divided into two groups: independent and dependent. From the point of view of the model, input and decision variables belong to the first category, since data concerning input variables have to be collected in one way or another via information channels from the environment, and decision variables also have to be specified. With regard to decision variables, either management can make a decision known, or an optimization procedure can be applied, as described later. The state and output variables are dependent on the system. In other words, these elements can be derived, with the help of the model, from the history of the independent variables (and the initial state of the system). The four types of variable are set out in the table below.

| | *Independent Variables* | | *Dependent Variables* | |
| --- | --- | --- | --- | --- |
| | *input variables* | *decision variables* | *state variables* | *output variables* |
| usually related to | environment | system | system | system |
| can be manipulated | no | yes | only indirectly | only indirectly |
| quantity | number of inputs | degrees of freedom | order | number of objectives |

We shall now attempt to describe more clearly the function of management in this connection. For this purpose we define management as the group of persons who make decisions with regard to a given system (a firm). The system can be an entire firm, or a subsystem such as a production department. Let us assume that management makes decisions based on the existing situation and on influences from the environment (inputs) with the intention of achieving as nearly as possible a number of given objectives assessed according to certain norms. In this case the output variables represent the standards for the evaluation of the objectives.

We could compare this situation with that of the pilot of an aeroplane who, on the basis of his position and the available amount of fuel (state) and the atmospheric conditions (inputs), sets his course (decision) in such a way that he will reach his destination (objective) within the shortest possible time or with a minimum of fuel. The pilot cannot alter the wind velocity of the atmosphere, but he can, within certain limits, select the altitude, speed, and course of his flight, thus choosing a route which requires a minimum of time and/or fuel. His position and his fuel gauges (outputs) show him how far his decision coincides with his objective.

This picture of a system under optimal control, embedded in an environment, could be called a *cybernetic* model. The decisions influence the state and the output; the values of the state and output variables influence the decisions; thus a reaction mechanism is built into the system. There is a certain analogy between this model and an organism striving to stabilize its inner state within a changing environment (homeostasis). In an article entitled 'Self-regulation of the body', Cannon[7] writes:

It seems not impossible that the means employed by the more highly evolved animals for preserving uniformity and stabilizing their internal economy (i.e. for preserving homeostasis) may present some general principles for the establishment, regulation and control of steady states that would be suggestive for other kinds of organization — even social and industrial — which suffer from distressing perturbations.

One of the tasks of management is to ward off the negative consequences of changes in the environment by making decisions which increase the stability and life-expectancy of the firm. It is essential that the management of a firm should not only reckon with the present situation but also attempt to anticipate future external influences. A firm is always subject to a certain amount of inertia, with the result that it cannot react rapidly and effectively to influences from outside. It is therefore important that future inputs should be 'predicted' as accurately as possible so that the degrees of freedom of the system can be utilized to optimize the internal processes. For instance, if an increase in sales is expected, certain investments can be made in anticipation, so that these larger sales become possible at the right moment.

It may be asked to what extent it is possible to predict the future values of inputs (often called 'states of nature' in American literature). In order to answer this question we have to distinguish between three types of quantitative model.

In the first place, there is the deterministic model, which assumes full knowledge of what the future will bring. This is an ideal situation, hardly ever realized, but there are circumstances in which future inputs can be calculated sufficiently accurately. For instance it is possible that the orders received by a production department are of such a nature that detailed long-term plans concerning capacity, materials required, processes, and time-schedules can be made. Or the future demand for electricity, over a planning period of, say, a year, can usually be estimated quite accurately, enabling a deterministic model to be used.

Much more frequently, however, the situation is uncertain and various possibilities have to be taken into account. In this case we assume that, as regards future inputs, a number of alternatives are known, together with the chances of their being realized. To take the simple example of a bakery, we find that an ever-recurring decision has to be made concerning the amount of bread to be baked. This daily decision is important, since any surplus bread has to be sold at a loss once it has gone stale, and of course, if too little is produced, the consequence is loss of profit. Though it is not possible to estimate daily sales exactly, the chances of selling a certain amount of bread can be calculated from experience. For example, there is a 25 per cent chance of selling 501-600 loaves, a 60 per cent chance of selling 601-700 loaves, and a 15 per cent chance of selling 701-800 loaves. Knowing this and knowing the cost of over- or under-production, the baker can come to an optimal decision with the help of probability calculus.

In the third type of situation, the future alternatives are known, but not the chances pertaining to these alternatives. In principle it is possible to calculate an optimal policy for each alternative, but it is not known whether the future will take a favourable or unfavourable turn. This type of problem occurs frequently in practice, especially when a new situation is encountered. Let us once again look at an example. A manager knows that there are three possibilities regarding the future demand for the product he manufactures. Either it will remain the same, or it will increase by 20 per cent, or it will decrease by 20 per cent. But he does not know what the chances are of any of these three alternatives happening. However, he has to choose between the three possibilities: (a) he can maintain production capacity as it is by replacing old machines with new ones; (b) he can decrease production capacity by not buying new machines; (c) he can increase production capacity by replacing old machines with new ones and purchasing additional machines. If the manager is pessimistic by nature he will expect the worst, a 20 per cent reduction in demand, and he will restrict his investment to a minimum. If he is an optimist he will increase his production capacity in order to be able to meet an increased demand should it occur. And if he is moderate in his outlook he will take the middle path. It is important that the criteria for such decisions should be clearly established, since a decision can be justified only with regard to a certain criterion (optimistic, pessimistic, etc.).

The theoretical foundation for this type of decision process was laid in 1944 by von Neumann and Morgenstern with the publication of their book *Theory of games and economic behavior*.[8] Though its application has been restricted to a few simple decision problems, the theory of games has given us a clear insight into the decision process.

The three types of model can be summed up as follows:

— deterministic models – the future is known
— probability models   – future alternatives and their chances of occurrence are known
— game-theory models – future alternatives only are known.

Theoretically there is also a fourth possibility, namely a situation in which no future alternatives are known. Naturally in such a case it would be senseless to construct a model. A case like this would be rare in practice, since it would mean that the environment was entirely unknown.

Finally, a remark about the limitations of quantitative models. In general, it is found that these models describe systems with static structures. This does not deny the existence of dynamic or growth models. However, in a quantitative model the number of variables and parameters rarely changes in time. If a system is subject to structural change, in other words if it is developing, the different structures it acquires will as a rule have to be described by different models.

Good management policy is characterized by the discovery of new forms of organization and of new possibilities and alternatives, and not solely by making optimal decisions in a momentary situation. This is aptly illustrated by a case reported in OR literature. The management of a hotel received complaints about the length of time guests had to spend waiting for lifts. An OR team was called in, and expected to come up with a conventional solution to the problem, e.g. a recommendation for more lifts, faster lifts, larger lifts, or perhaps a reprogramming of the lifts. Instead the team simply advised the management to hang a few mirrors nearby, so that the time would pass 'more quickly' for the guests, who would now be able to look at themselves in the mirrors. The problem was indeed solved by this original method. The psychological aspect had given it a completely new dimension.

This brief description has not dealt in detail with the special techniques and methods of solution used in operational analysis. But in order to give a little more insight into this field, we present in the next section a more detailed analysis of two problems, referred to in the literature as the diet problem and the problem of the travelling salesman. The techniques employed are, respectively, linear programming and the 'branch and bound' method. Those who wish to study these subjects further are referred to the references listed on pp. 257 and 258.

## THE DIET PROBLEM AND THE LINEAR-PROGRAMMING TECHNIQUE

The diet problem is particularly suitable for demonstrating the application of the linear-programming method, because the essential points of this technique, namely the existence of restrictions, non-negative variables, and linear equations, come clearly into view. We have selected the following specific example.

A poultry breeder feeds his hens with a mixture of two products, M and S. The percentage of carbohydrates and proteins in each of these products, and also the price of each, is shown below:

|  | M | S |
|---|---|---|
| carbohydrates | 80% | 50% |
| proteins | 10% | 40% |
| money units | 2 | 5 |

The minimum requirement per time unit is 20 kg of carbohydrates and 4 kg of proteins. The poultry breeder wants a mixture which meets these requirements at minimum cost.

Three variables are involved:

$x_1$ = number of kg of M in the mixture
$x_2$ = number of kg of S in the mixture
$y$ = price of mixture.

It follows from the above that:

$0.8x_1 + 0.5x_2 \geqslant 20$ (carbohydrate restriction)
$0.1x_1 + 0.4x_2 \geqslant 4$ (protein restriction)
$y = 2x_1 + 5x_2$ (price equation).

The decision variables $x_1$ and $x_2$ have to be chosen in such a way that $y$ becomes minimal while at the same time the restrictions are complied with. The graph overleaf illustrates this case.

The first restriction can be depicted by the line AB determined by the equation $0.8x_1 + 0.5x_2 = 20$ and the points to the right of this line. In the same way, the second restriction can be represented by the line CD and the points to the right of it. Since the variables $x_1$ and $x_2$ are not negative, the solution or realization area is represented by the shaded part of the diagram (to the right of the line CHB).

If the poultry breeder wanted to spend 25 money units on hen food, then this could be represented by the line EF which is based on the

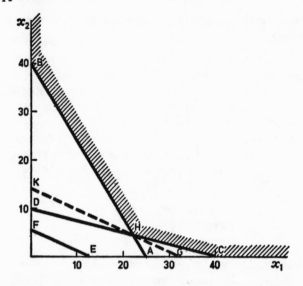

equation $2x_1 + 5x_2 = 25$. Every point on this line represents a mixture which he could buy for 25 money units. If he wants to spend less than 25 units, this can be represented by a cost line shifted to the left, proportionately to the line EF.

The problem calls for a solution in the form of a point on a cost line which lies as far to the left as possible but yet remains within the realization area. Point H on the broken line GHK meets these requirements. Thus H is the optimum point. It is the point of intersection $(x'_1, x'_2)$ of the lines:

$$0.8x_1 + 0.5x_2 = 20$$
$$0.1x_1 + 0.4x_2 = 4$$

From this he can derive the optimal solution:

$$x'_1 = 22^2/_9 \text{kg}, \quad x'_2 = 4^4/_9 \text{kg}, \quad y = 66^2/_3.$$

In words: the optimal mixture consists of approximately 22·22 kg of M and 4·44 kg of S. For this mixture, which satisfies the diet restrictions, the breeder will pay the minimum price of 66·67 money units.

It is clear that the two-dimensional graph method is limited to problems with two decision variables. In practice, however, one frequently has to work with a larger number of variables. The simplex technique developed in 1951 is a method for solving these larger problems rapidly and efficiently. But we shall not discuss this technique here (see, for example, Churchman, Ackoff, and Arnoff[9]).

## THE TRAVELLING-SALESMAN PROBLEM AND THE 'BRANCH AND BOUND' METHOD

As has already been said, the travelling-salesman problem can be solved by enumeration. However, a solution can be found much more quickly by making a careful selection from the available alternatives and rejecting in advance those that do not promise a solution. The 'branch and bound' method is based on this philosophy and is illustrated in the following example.

A salesman is to visit 5 towns, and the expense $c_{ij}$ of travelling from town i to town j is determined by the following matrix of expenses:

|  | to town | | | | |
|---|---|---|---|---|---|
|  | 1 | 2 | 3 | 4 | 5 |
| 1 | $\infty$ | 5 | 8 | 3 | 6 |
| 2 | 9 | $\infty$ | 4 | 1 | 7 |
| 3 | 7 | 3 | $\infty$ | 2 | 2 |
| 4 | 8 | 5 | 7 | $\infty$ | 1 |
| from town 5 | 3 | 4 | 5 | 5 | $\infty$ |

From this table he can see, for instance, that the expense of travelling from town 1 to town 2, denoted briefly as route (1,2), is 5 money units. Route (1,1) is prohibited and its cost has therefore been shown as infinity.

In order to generalize the problem as much as possible, an asymmetrical table of expenses has been chosen for this example, i.e. $c_{ij} \neq c_{ji}$. The distances are thus replaced by expenses, which in many cases depend on the direction in which the salesman travels.

The matrix shows that the minimum cost of all routes going *from* town 1 is 3 money units. From towns 2, 3, 4, and 5 the amounts are, respectively, 1, 2, 1, and 3 money units. We can say, then, that the whole journey will cost $3 + 1 + 2 + 1 + 3 = 10$ money units, plus the costs indicated by the following table:

|  | 1 | 2 | 3 | 4 | 5 |
|---|---|---|---|---|---|
| 1 | $\infty$ | 2 | 5 | 0 | 3 |
| 2 | 8 | $\infty$ | 3 | 0 | 6 |
| 3 | 5 | 1 | $\infty$ | 0 | 0 |
| 4 | 7 | 4 | 6 | $\infty$ | 0 |
| 5 | 0 | 1 | 2 | 2 | $\infty$ |

This table is derived from the previous one by subtracting 3 from the figures in the first row, 1 from the figures in the second row, and so on.

It shows us that it costs at least 1 money unit to travel *to* town 2, and at least 2 money units *to* town 3. By subtracting these amounts from the figures in the appropriate columns we arrive at the *reduced table*:

|   | 1 | 2 | 3 | 4 | 5 |
|---|---|---|---|---|---|
| 1 | ∞ | 1 | 3 | 0 | 3 |
| 2 | 8 | ∞ | 1 | 0 | 6 |
| 3 | 5 | 0 | ∞ | 0 | 0 |
| 4 | 7 | 3 | 4 | ∞ | 0 |
| 5 | 0 | 0 | 0 | 2 | ∞ |

Conclusion: the cost of the journey is $10 + 1 + 2 = 13$ money units, plus the extra costs indicated in the above table. For instance, a journey from town 1 to 4, from 4 to 2, from 2 to 5, from 5 to 3, and from 3 to 1 will cost $13 + 0 + 3 + 6 + 0 + 5 = 27$ money units.

There are no extra costs for routes $(1,4)$, $(2,4)$, $(3,2)$, $(3,4)$, $(3,5)$, $(4,5)$, $(5,1)$, $(5,2)$, and $(5,3)$.

If route $(1,4)$ were to be *omitted* from the itinerary, this being denoted by $(\overline{1,4})$, there would be an extra cost of 1 money unit. In this case the salesman would travel *from* town 1 *to* towns 2, 3, or 5 at a minimum cost of 1 money unit and *from* towns 2, 3, or 5 *to* town 4 at a minimum cost of 0 money units. Therefore the total extra cost would be 1 money unit. Similarly, he would find that for $(\overline{2,4})$, $(\overline{3,2})$, $(\overline{3,4})$, $(\overline{3,5})$, $(\overline{4,5})$, $(\overline{5,1})$, $(\overline{5,2})$, and $(\overline{5,3})$, there would be minimum extra costs of, respectively, 1, 0, 0, 0, 3, 5, 0, and 1 money units. This enumeration shows that it would be a good idea to include route $(5,1)$ in the itinerary, since this would bring about the greatest saving. This result is shown schematically below:

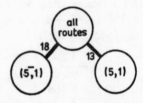

An itinerary including route $(5,1)$ costs a minimum of 13 money units.

An itinerary not including route $(\overline{5,1})$ costs a minimum of 18 money units.

Let us now make a table of costs for an itinerary including route (5,1). The fifth row and the first column of the previous table are omitted because the problem states that all journeys starting from town 5 and ending at town 1 are prohibited. Route (1,5) is also prohibited, since the journey (1,5), (5,1) would be a round trip which did not include all the towns. The result is as follows:

|   | 2 | 3 | 4 | 5 |
|---|---|---|---|---|
| 1 | 1 | 3 | 0 | ∞ |
| 2 | ∞ | 1 | 0 | 6 |
| 3 | 0 | ∞ | 0 | 0 |
| 4 | 3 | 4 | ∞ | 0 |

This table can be further reduced by subtracting 1 money unit from the figures in the second column. This means that the cost of an itinerary including route (5,1) will now be $13 + 1 = 14$ money units, plus the costs shown in the following table:

|   | 2 | 3 | 4 | 5 |
|---|---|---|---|---|
| 1 | 1 | 2 | 0 | ∞ |
| 2 | ∞ | 0 | 0 | 6 |
| 3 | 0 | ∞ | 0 | 0 |
| 4 | 3 | 3 | ∞ | 0 |

The minimum extra costs for itineraries which did *not* include routes (1,4), (2,3), (2,4), (3,1), (3,4), (3,5), and (4,5) would be, respectively, 1, 2, 0, 1, 0, 0, and 3 money units. On this basis, route (4,5) would be included. Thus, itineraries including route (5,1) and route (4,5) will cost a minimum of 14 money units, and an itinerary including route (5,1) but not route (4,5) will cost a minimum of $14 + 3 = 17$ money units. This can be depicted in the diagram below:

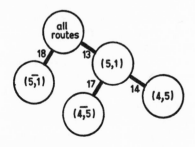

Continuing in the same manner, the salesman chooses a number of routes until all the towns are included in his itinerary. This procedure gives the result shown below:

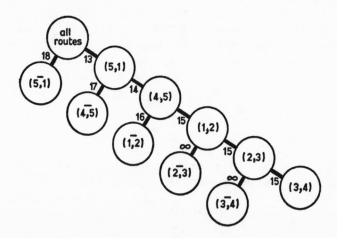

Following the right-hand chain, the salesman will find an itinerary which covers all the towns. Starting with town 1, he will arrive at the itinerary: (1,2), (2,3), (3,4), (4,5), (5,1), for which the total cost is 15 money units. It is immediately obvious that there is no itinerary which costs less. Thus this technique has helped the salesman to find the optimal solution. (For further study see Ackoff and Sasieni.[10])

**REFERENCES**

1 SCHUMACHER, C. C. & SMITH, R. E. A sample survey of industrial operations research activities II. *Operations Research* 13, 1965, pp. 1023-37.
2 WESTBROOK, G. F. Management sciences – the state of the art in the chemical industries. Presented at the national meeting of the Institute of Management Sciences, Dallas, Texas, 16-19 February 1966.
3 FORRESTER, J. W. *Industrial dynamics.* New York, 1961.
4 DANTZIG, G., FULKERSON, R. & JOHNSON, S. Solution of a large-scale travelling salesman problem. *Operations Research* 2, 1954, pp. 393-410.
5 ABRAMS, J. W. Implementation of operational research: a problem in sociology. *CORS Journal* 3(3), 1963, pp. 152-60.
6 ZADEH, L. A. & DESOER, C. A. *Linear system theory.* New York, 1963.

7 CANNON, W. B. Self-regulation of the body. In W. Buckley (ed.), *Modern systems research for the behavioral scientist.* Chicago, 1968.

8 VON NEUMANN, J. & MORGENSTERN, O. *Theory of games and economic behavior.* Princteon, N.J., 1944.

9 CHURCHMAN, C. W., ACKOFF, R. L. & ARNOFF, E. L. *Introduction to operations research.* New York, 1957.

10 ACKOFF, R. L. & SASIENI, M. W. *Fundamentals of operations research.* New York, 1968.

# Recommended Reading

*Appendix*

CHERNOFF, H. & MOSES, L. E. *Elementary decision theory.* New York, 1959.

HALL, A. D. *A methodology for systems engineering.* Princeton, N.J., 1962.

KAUFMANN, A. & FAURE, R. *Invitations à la recherche opérationnelle.* Paris, 1963.

MACHOL, R. E. (ed.) *Systems engineering handbook.* New York, 1965.

MORSE, P. M. & KIMBALL, G. E. *Methods of operations research.* New York, 1951.

STARR, M. K. & MILLER, D. W. *Executive decisions and operations research.* New York, 1960.

# Name Index

259

# Subject Index